FOREWORD BY PULITZER PRIZE WINNER ANTHONY R. DOLAN

ROGUE TOWN

THIS STAMFORD, CT STORY SERVED AS THE CATALYST FOR PRESIDENT RONALD REAGAN'S INITIATIVE AGAINST THE AMERICAN MAFIA AND THE ESTABLISHMENT OF THE PRESIDENT'S COMMISSION ON ORGANIZED CRIME.

VITO COLUCCI, JR.
AND DENNIS N. GRIFFIN

© Vito Colucci, Jr. 2013, 2023

Second Edition

First Edition published by Houdini Publishing, 2013

Published by Byron House Books
Stamford, Connecticut
For more information, contact the author: vito@coluccipi.com, melodye@coluccipi.com

ISBN (paperback): 979-8-9878477-0-1

Cataloging data on file with the Library of Congress

Book Design by Bookery.design

ROGUE TOWN

DEDICATION

I DEDICATE THIS book to all the good and honest police officers who wore a badge in Stamford, Connecticut between 1965 and 1985, the peak years of corruption. They continued to do great work for the citizens of Stamford despite the terrible working conditions and low morale.

Also, to Stamford Advocate reporter Anthony Dolan. I cannot even imagine what Stamford might be like today had it not been for Mr. Dolan's investigative skills and tenacity in digging out and exposing the corruption that existed there. Stamford was forever changed because of his efforts and he has my eternal gratitude. The Pulitzer Prize he received for his reporting was well deserved.

And to my wife, Joanne (Pinky). God brought you into my life forty-nine years ago. We have stayed together through the hard years and now rejoice in the good times we share. Even though you knew that I was an undercover cop, you never really knew the details. Now you do. We have grown so close in our walk with the Lord. I love you.

To our children, Kimmy, Melodye, Valarie, Jodi, and Marc. I am so proud of each one of you. Thank you for all your patience with me during the crazy years. God has truly kept his hand on each one of us. You have all my love forever.

And finally, to my Lord and Savior, Jesus Christ. Where would I be today without Him? He changed my life forever. He put joy into my heart and compassion in my soul. He has watched over me and kept me safe all these years. All honor and glory belong to Him. I will praise His name forever.

Vito Colucci, Jr.

ACKNOWLEDGEMENTS

WANT TO personally acknowledge and thank the following entities and persons—three of whom are deceased—for their assistance in putting this book together. I could not have done it without them.

The many articles in the New York Times and Stamford Advocate helped me to confirm my recollection of events and to tell my story as accurately as possible.

Angela Carella and Erin Walsh of the Stamford Advocate. Your research was invaluable. Thanks so much for pulling all the old stories out for me.

Ellen Sullivan of the Ferguson Library, Stamford CT – Thank you for digging up all of the history on countless cases for me.

Melodye Colucci, thank you for all of your hard work and coordination on this revised version of Rogue Town and all you do behind the scenes for Colucci Investigations.

Joe Cochran, you are an accomplished investigative reporter and provided invaluable research towards portions of this book while becoming a great friend.

Jane Ryder, your writing skills and diligence are superb. You took all of the facts given and finalized the new stories.

Colleen Sheehan, you brought this new edition to life. Thank you!

Arvil Chapman. You were the one who started the ball rolling by supplying Joe Ligi and I with invaluable information on the crooked cops in the Stamford Police Department. You literally took your life in your hands. You fought the good fight, changed your life and died as a man of God.

Chief John Considine. A few days before you died, I was given a message that you wanted to see me at the assisted living home you were in. I will never forget the smile on your face when I walked in. You pointed a finger at me and told me to come closer. You then said, "Vito, you need to understand that we are bound together forever because of the shootout we were in. We were shoulder to shoulder and walked away without a scratch. Don't ever forget it." I looked at you and said, "I promise, I won't forget it, Chief." And I will not. Thanks for always watching out for me!

Joe Ligi. What can I say? You picked me for your partner in Narcotics. That started us on the crazy ride that neither of us knew where it would end. You taught me so much. I'm proud to call you my cousin, my forever partner, and always my great friend. Thank you for your help with some of the details of this book.

Faith Griffin. Thank you for the tedious work of proof-reading the original manuscript.

Dennis Griffin. Thank you for agreeing to write my story. It is an honor for me, that after all the successful books you have written, you chose to write Rouge Town. You brought all the stories to life and have my deepest appreciation. You became a good and trusted friend in the process.

FOREWORD

STORIES OF hero cops are usually about policemen who amidst danger and excitement show resilience and courage in protecting the laws and citizens they are sworn to defend.

Such is Vito Colucci's story.

Though much more is also here.

As in Donnie Brasco, the movie about FBI agent Joe Pistone's secret work in the mafia, Vito Colucci lived the dangerous double life of the undercover cop, facing not only physical danger but the psychological pressure of existing in a clandestine world where a single mistake can quickly become a last mistake. Vito Colucci's story then is about not just his singular acts of courage but his willingness to endure an enervating and sometimes unimaginable day-to-day struggle – and display a quotidian, psychological strength that is itself an extended act of courage.

This story is different in another important, indeed, remarkable way. Because Vito Colucci's adversaries here are not just the usual street hoods, drug dealers, murderers or gangsters but a dark enemy from within – fellow cops who themselves were drug dealers, murderers and gangsters. And not only were these police officers dangerous and ruthless criminals but they enjoyed the protection of a political culture established by powerful, prodigiously selfish city officials.

Still, there is something even more distinctive about Vito Colucci's story.

We never know – we never really know — what will come of a simple decision to do the right thing. So, even if at times our efforts seem hopeless – and, of course, there is never a shortage of people willing to tell us that – we try to do the right thing. We are Americans, after all; as Americans we believe the good guys win. Sometimes perhaps it takes a while, but in the end the right and true must prevail.

In Vito Colucci's story the right does prevail and yet the ultimate consequences, the pervasive effect of that victory are largely unknown. Because I was not only a part of Vito's story but part of that largely unknown aftermath, I saw how this Stamford victory had impact not just on one city and its people but America and —perhaps this is not too much to say—beyond America.

Let me explain.

As a reporter for the Stamford Advocate I had begun working in 1974 on stories about a classic matrix of orga-

nized crime and municipal corruption — serious wrongdoing in eight city departments including a police department
where a rackets commander was taking $1800 a week (real
money in those days) from the Gambino crime family and
a detective sergeant was running the largest drug ring in
southern Connecticut out of police headquarters. Eventually,
15 city and state officials would resign or be fired; so too,
police officers, other officials and organized crime figures
would be indicted and convicted. Stamford's leading political figure — who was also State Senate majority leader
and talked about as the next governor — would lose both
his reelection bid and a lawsuit he brought against me and
The Advocate.

In 1980 I left the Advocate to join the presidential campaign of Ronald Reagan, a man I had long admired. I then
went to the White House as chief speechwriter. During this
time Attorney General William French Smith learned about
Stamford from a Rolling Stone article President Reagan had
sent over to him and about my own concern that our administration take up the fight against organized crime and official corruption from his chief of staff and my friend, Tex
Lezar. Thus, one day in June of 1982 I found myself seated
next to Smith in his small personal office facing a Department of Justice senior staff that had crowded into the room,
among them then unknown people like Rudy Giuliani and
Kenneth Starr and Theodore Olson. At the Attorney General's request, I told the story of Stamford but explained
first that I had made a promise to those I had worked with
in that city that if I ever got the chance to tell people in
power – people like themselves who could make sure what

happened in Stamford no longer happened in America – that I would do just that. And so I told my story –no, their story — and ended by presenting a five point program for a crackdown on organized crime that ranged from more federal agents and prosecutors to a Presidential Commission on Organized Crime.

Out of that meeting came months of bureaucratic struggle carried on competently and sometimes valiantly by Lezar, Giuliani (the head of the criminal division) Presidential Counselor Edwin Meese and Smith himself. Finally, at a cabinet meeting in September of 1982, the Attorney General presented the plan to President Reagan. On the way into the cabinet room I remember FBI Director William Webster –he had done much to focus the FBI and America too on the dangers of organized crime – smiling and shaking my hand and saying something about the "guiding spirit" — by which he meant the meeting in Smith's office and the story of Stamford told that day. As an illustration of the extent of official corruption in America, the Attorney General and Giuliani played a wiretap recording of a federal prosecutor caught negotiating a bribe with a gangster. I watched as President Reagan listened and noticed what the staff always knew was a facial signal that the Gipper was struggling to control his fine Irish temper. I saw the tightening around his mouth and knew Ronald Reagan was angry.

That anger came as no surprise. During that earlier meeting in the Attorney General's office Giuliani had pointed out that the prior year the Justice department had asked for a modest increase in agents and prosecutors and been refused on budgetary grounds. Why, he asked, did I think such an ambitious plan costing so much more could succeed now. I told him President Reagan understood about organized crime and its power; I had heard him talk about it and I knew that he also understood — just as he did about another, more international form of organized crime called communism – its evil. I was certain that if presented with a proposal that was not just one more department's request for a budgetary increase but a comprehensive attempt to destroy the power of organized crime in America that Reagan – whose moral compass was always on true north — would approve and implement it.

About all that I was right. Because after Smith was through his presentation to Reagan the Office of Management and Budget made its fiscally-based objections. These President Reagan heard out politely. But then made it plain – his administration would go ahead with this plan to break the mob.

A few minutes later as I walked back across the driveway in the White House complex that led to my office in the Old Executive Office Building, I was thinking about Reagan and Smith – their simple goodness and that of the good men who worked for them – but especially of the people of Stamford and good cops like Vito Colucci and, most of all, a man whose story Vito tells here — the man who first asked him to go under cover, Police Chief Victor I. Cizanckas. Taking the job in the wake of the former chief's forced resignation Cizanckas had been amazed at the corruption he had found. In those days we grew friendly and talked about not just winning our struggle in Stamford but taking our fight to the national stage. Before that had happened though, and just as the struggle in Stamford was won, Cizanckas died at 42 of a stress heart attack. Thinking now about what had just happened in the cabinet room and about Vic too, I looked up at the sky as I walked across the driveway, raised an arm in celebration and I am not ashamed to admit — corny as it sounds – that I said audibly "We did it Vic. We did it."

That October in the Great Hall of the Justice Department President Reagan announced his mob initiative in a lengthy speech – it is on the web to read. In many other speeches he kept at it as well as in a lengthy article for the New York Times Magazine explaining why he wanted nothing less than victory in the fight against the mafia. In a few years organized crime prosecutions quadrupled, the President's Commission on Organized Crime under Judge Irving Kaufman was holding hearings (Pistone and I spoke at a first private meeting), and US attorneys everywhere made the attack on the mob a priority. In New York Rudy Giuliani became US Attorney and then a legend for his war on the gangsters. Nor did he forget, in a further testimony to his character, about this struggle once he went in politics. Even as Mayor of New York Giuliani picked fights he didn't have to with the mobsters over their control of neighborhood block parties and even broke, mirabile dictu, their iron grip on the Fulton Fish Market, a last redoubt of the American mafia.

In only a few years the head of the FBI's organized crime squad was saying a federal government that had been losing the struggle against the syndicates had suddenly begun holding its own and then for the first time actually winning that struggle. So too The Los Angeles Times, in the person of veteran Justice Department reporter Ron Ostrow, picked up on the role played by the meeting in the Attorney General's office. In running the LA Times syndicate story my old newspaper in Stamford headlined it: "Reporter's Dream Comes True."

Well, yes, it was my dream. But Vito Colucci's dream too, as this book shows, as well as that of Vic Cizanckas and so many others.

And, while we can be grateful to Vito Colucci for carrying on this struggle in a unique way and putting himself in much danger to do it, we should also be grateful to him for this book which in its own way is an act of courage and resilience.

Here then is a book from Vito Colucci, the legacy of a hero cop. A hero cop who also proved that Ronald Reagan was right—as he so often was–in something he once said.

"Evil is powerless if the good are unafraid."

Anthony R. Dolan
November 13, 2012
Alexandria, Virginia

Anthony R. Dolan's work as an investigative reporter at the Stamford Advocate won him seven journalism awards including the 1978 Pulitzer Prize for investigative reporting. He was later chief speechwriter to President Ronald Reagan for eight years and served in the Bush administration as senior advisor in the Office of Secretary of State Colin Powell and special advisor in the Office of Secretary of Defense Donald Rumsfeld.

INTRODUCTION

I N 2007 I wrote my first book, *Inside the Private Eyes of a PI*. In it I told about my career as a private investigator and talked about some of the more famous cases I had worked on. I enjoyed writing that book, but I knew in my heart that the story I really wanted to tell was about my time working as a police officer in Stamford, Connecticut.

I became a cop in Stamford in 1969 at the age of twenty-one. I was filled with a young man's enthusiasm and envisioned myself as being a guy who would make a difference for the citizens of Stamford. I would get the criminals off the streets and help turn Stamford into a place where people could venture around their town with little fear of getting mugged or assaulted. That idea was a good one and I gave it my all. But it turned out that locking up the low-level street punks was the easy part. The crime problem in Stamford ran much deeper.

As I soon came to learn, not all the crooks and killers were lurking in alleyways or hiding in the shadows waiting for a victim. Back then, Stamford was infested with organized crime figures that oversaw the illegal gambling and drug rackets. The higher-ups were very much out in the open. They ran businesses—both legal and illegal. They could be found in bars, restaurants and social clubs. But you could not tell what they were really all about just by looking at them. The criminals that I found to be the most abhorrent, though, were those that carried badges. My fellow police officers.

Another thing I learned was that Stamford was corrupt in other ways. It was a place where getting a job in City government and being awarded City contracts had more to do with who you knew than how qualified you or your company were. Politicians ran amok and nepotism and influence peddling were the order of the day.

As I became aware of the reality of the situation, I was determined to do whatever I could to bring justice to Stamford. In these pages you will read my honest account of those efforts.

I imagine there will be some who will read this book and then tend to dismiss it as a work of fiction. Before you do, let me assure you that everything I relate here actually happened and there are ample newspaper stories and other documents to back up my words. So, as you are reading, if you start to think that certain things couldn't possibly happen, don't kid yourself. They did happen in Stamford; and they have or can happen in any other fairly large city.

It is the responsibility of the people and the media to be vigilant and make sure that government agencies and those who run them are serving the citizens and not merely taking care of themselves.

Vito Colucci, Jr.

A CHAPLAIN'S PERSPECTIVE ON ALL THAT UNFOLDED

To SAY that the continuing saga of Rogue Town has been an adventure would be an understatement. The story itself is as old as the timeless tale of good versus evil - with the exception that I know the participants personally.

Vito is my father-in-law, and I was born and raised in the city he once protected. Vito also worked with several of my relatives who proudly wore the badge of Stamford Police Officer as well. Like so many others, Vito and members of my own family were and are just good, honest, hard-working people who want to make a difference in their communities.

Growing up in a cop's family, a long and proud legacy that began in 1947, I had mixed emotions reading this tale of a town gone rogue. But the world of corruption, greed, power and money will do that to you – mix up your emotions.

Its ultimate message is one of hope and triumph. Good always triumphs over evil. And in a world where hope seems all but lost, one man can and does make a difference by taking the first step out of the darkness and into the light of truth and righteousness.

As you read the stories within, I know that hope will be restored. Whatever rogue circumstances you may be struggling with, please know that darkness must always yield to light, truth will always triumph over deception, but also remember that before the truth can set us free, it will probably make us miserable first.

I want to encourage you to be honest with yourself as you consider your own circumstances. There are things happening right now that are just not ok, and for "such a time as this" you may be the one to lead others out of darkness. Each one of us must decide whether we will accept that challenge or allow things to continue unabated.

Just as sure as every righteous deed will not go un-contested, so too is the ongoing battle of good versus evil in Vito's life. In early Spring of 2022 Vito lay unresponsive in the hospital. With no answers and no hope, we had to begin preparing for the inevitable. The man who once wore a wire for the feds, confronted organized crime, and engaged in a desperate gun battle with escaped felons now lay silent beneath a tangled web of life-support wires and tubes.

As he had done years earlier against the rogue activities of a corrupt few, we took our stand in the darkest blackness of imminent death and despair as we united in prayer and hope for Vito to return to us. And then one day, just as suddenly as he left us, he returned without medical explanation. It's been a long and difficult road, but today Vito has defied the darkness again and is back fighting for truth and righteousness.

Pastor Gary Cortese, Jr.

Police and Fire Department Chaplain
statelinechaplains.com

LETTER OF AFFIRMATION

AFTER ROGUE Town was released, I began receiving e-mails, Instant Messages through Facebook and phone calls reiterating what I depicted within this book and additional corruption others witnessed and lived through. Rogue Town spoke to more people than I could have imagined and I am thankful I was able to share this story. I wanted to include one e-mail I received from former Fire Chief Robert McGrath shortly after the release of Rogue Town:

> "Vito, I just bought your book *Rogue Town* and got it in yesterday's mail. Could not put it down and read it cover to cover. You may not know me because we never met but I was a city employee at the same time period as you. I know the same names, I know about the same

corruption you write about. I was a firefighter and subsequently moved up through the ranks to become chief of the department in 2000. I am aware of the corrupt police officers, and some you don't mention by name, and am aware of the corrupt fire inspections and fire department employees that covered up arson fires and one in particular a bowling alley fire that the inspector noted as an accidental cause, when there in fact multiple points of origin. I also know where the bones are buried.

You may or may not remember my father who was a police officer at the time whom I went to complain about what I heard and suspected about illegal activities in both the police and fire department at the time. He told me "keep your mouth shut if you know what's good for you". I retired after 41 years of service with the SFD and a lot of them were discouraging after knowing how some of the good old boys got promoted and other assignments. I finally got a chance to help clean the house and so forth. I wish to commend you on your fine work on this book and I only wish my father was alive to read it and show him the truth. Thank you and God bless you and your family! You for sure are one of my heroes."

Bob McGrath

PART ONE

A Naïve Rookie Cop
Gets an Education

I

MY NAME is Vito Colucci, Junior. I was a police officer in Stamford, Connecticut, a municipality that from 1965 through 1985 was known as one of the most corrupt cities in the country. That combination nearly cost me my life.

January 11, 1974, was the day I almost died. The only thing between me and a killer with a knife was my four-year-old daughter, Melodye. We were backing out of the driveway of my grandfather's house on Liberty Street in Stamford in my 1971 black Grand Prix. Before pulling out into the street I stopped to check for traffic. It was clear to my right; but when I looked left my heart caught in my throat. Standing next to my window, pressed right against my door, was Stamford police sergeant Albert "Duke" Morris.

Morris was a black man in his late thirties. He stood about five feet ten and was a muscular hundred and seventy-five pounds. He had been a cop for many years. But he was not just a cop, he was a dirty cop. He was heavily involved in drug trafficking and illegal gambling, and had a reputation for using a gun to keep people in line. He was also known for being proficient with a knife.

Morris knew that my partner Joe Ligi and I were onto him and other corrupt officers in the Stamford Police Department. He knew that because of the information we had developed he was in jeopardy of facing serious legal problems. Morris did not like that and he did not like me.

As our eyes locked, I could read his intentions clearly. Morris was going to kill me right there, in front of my grandfather's house and in front of my daughter.

Morris' hands were in the pockets of the black leather jacket he was wearing. This was an era before car seats were required for kids and Melodye was standing on the seat next to me. I knew he would be able to clear his hands from his pockets before I could move her out of the way and get to my gun. I was a dead man.

It was a perfect setup for Morris: middle of the day, a few knife thrusts to my neck or chest, quiet and no witnesses except Melodye. Yes, I was a dead man.

And then a miracle happened. Melodye leaned around in front of me to see what I was looking at. Morris' eyes left me and went to her. I will never know for sure what went through his mind at that moment. I sensed surprise and confusion. Maybe he was thinking that if he killed me, he would have to kill her too, and he hadn't sunk low enough

4

yet to murder a little girl. In my mind that is what happened. Melodye's presence saved my life that day.

Whatever the reason, after a couple of seconds he turned around and walked down the street. Not a word was spoken during the encounter that seemed like an eternity to me, but, lasted only a few seconds.

Those brief moments had been the scariest of my life. As Morris walked away, I sat there with my heart pounding in my chest like a jackhammer. It hit me that Melodye and I could very easily have left that place in the back of the coroner's wagon. I grabbed her and held her close. She had a surprised look on her face. But she did not cry or say anything. She just hugged me back.

As my heart rate returned toward normal, I asked myself a question: How in the hell did I end up in this position?

SGT. ALBERT "DUKE" MORRIS. DUKE REMINDS
ME OF DENZEL WASHINGTON'S CHARACTER
ALONZO IN THE MOVIE TRAINING DAY.

2

WAS BORN in Stamford, Connecticut in 1948 and am a first-generation Italian American. All of my ancestors came from Avigliano, Italy, located in Potenza Province near Naples. We were a working-class family living on the Westside. My father, Vito Senior, was a barber and served as a special officer for the Stamford Police. As a Special Police Officer, he walked in the local parades and worked at the parks and Italian functions throughout Stamford.

My mother, Sadie, was a housewife. She told me for many years that I was a mistake because I was born late in her life. I have a brother Salvatore Colucci who is 15 years older than me; and a sister, Donata Marie, 11 years my senior.

While attending Rippowam High School, one of my friends and classmates was Bobby Valentine. He was a legendary local athlete who later played for the New York Mets, and went on to manage them and the Boston Red Sox. I had known Bobby since we were kids playing baseball and football at Southfield Park. He was a good guy then and still is. I was not a good student. I barely got by each year with a C-minus average. I tell people now that I was in the top ninety-eight percent of my graduating class. You would be surprised at how many people don't get the joke.

My mother did not allow me to play any organized or school sports, so my playing was limited to local ball fields. Other than sports, my social activities included hanging out with my friends and practicing my guitar. I had a lot of friends, but unfortunately, not many of the female persuasion.

Elvis Presley inspired me to learn how to play guitar. In the mid-1950s, Elvis was skyrocketing to fame and all the kids I hung with wanted to be like him. Up to that point the accordion was the musical instrument of choice for many, but it was soon overtaken by the guitar. My accordion-player friends were learning how to do a bellow-shake to Dick Contino's "Lady of Spain." But that was not for me. I wanted to learn how to play "Jailhouse Rock."

The guitar lessons lasted for several years. When I was still a teenager I played in several local bands, usually as the youngest member. We mostly played in clubs and at private parties. Even though I was underage, none of the club owners seemed to care. My mother was always up waiting for me to come home from playing. As I got older, I realized that it was just a mother's thing.

Those gigs were fun and brought me recognition and popularity with my peers. But my dream then was to rip guitar riffs in the mold of the British invasion bands like The Beatles and the Rolling Stones. I figured that after high school I would play music for the rest of my life. Although that did not work out for me, I thank God that I'm still able to play on occasion. Music has been and always will be an integral part of my life.

At the age of twenty I married my first wife, Jill, and our daughter Melodye was born a year later. Shortly afterward we purchased our first home in Darien, Connecticut. I was teaching guitar full time by then and playing in bands several nights a week. The music business can be erratic, though. You could make a lot of money one week and not have anything coming in for the next two. With a young family I had to have a job that would bring more financial stability. The only other profession that I had an interest in was being a police officer. I guess that came from my father's time as a special cop.

With no other realistic options, I began the process of becoming a police officer. My first step was to visit the town hall and pick up a Civil Service application for a Stamford Police Officer. My cousin, Augie Tamburri, was already a veteran police officer in Stamford and gave me a lot of advice on how to prepare for the written exam, which I passed.

And then Augie coached me for the next step, the oral interview. It was a nerve-racking experience since it was done in front of the police chief and the police commissioners. I remember being asked why I wanted to be a police officer. Thanks to cousin Augie, my answer was a prompt, "Because it would be a fine way to serve my community and help out the general public." I left the interview room feeling confident that I had done a good job. The panel agreed and

I moved on to the final stage of the hiring process, the physical exam.

At that time police physicals were performed by an elderly physician named Nemoiton. I was a little worried about the eye exam because even though I was 20/20 with glasses, I had terrible vision without them. But Dr. Nemoiton passed me with flying colors. After that came the really tough part: waiting.

Approximately five months after submitting my application I got the call and letter. I had been accepted to become an officer on the Stamford Police Department.

I'll never forget the swearing-in ceremony for me and the seven other rookies. The mayor walked up and down our line looking at us and made the following statement: "What a fine bunch of looking fellows" We all had to muffle our laughter at the screw up.

As my badge was pinned on I thought to myself, I'm gonna make this city a better place to live."

Little did I know what was in store for me.

3

ITH THE police academy behind me, I became a full-fledged Stamford police officer in November 1969. I and all the other rookies were assigned to the graveyard shift, working from 11:30 at night until 7:30 in the morning. And that would be our assignment until the next batch of rookies arrived on the scene in nine months.

That winter was one of the coldest we had had in a long time and we had to walk a beat all night long. I remember one night it was below zero and the moustaches on my partner and me were frozen stiff. We had heard from the other rookies that sometimes the shift sergeant would make his rounds on the streets around three o'clock and ask the rookies on foot patrol questions about the job. If you answered right, he would have you get in his car and take you back to the station. There you'd be assigned one of the old patrol cars to drive around in for the rest of the shift.

We figured this was our lucky night when the sergeant pulled up. He cracked his window open an inch or so. It was not much, but when we leaned in close, we could feel that beautiful warm air on our faces and the moisture soon began to drip from our thawing moustaches.

The sergeant asked if we had walked our whole post. "Yes, Sergeant," we answered. Had we checked all the doors in the businesses? "Yes, Sergeant. They were all secure." Whatever he asked, we had done. I figured his next words would be, "Okay boys, hop in."

But they were not. Instead, he said, "All right. Have a good night." The window closed and the car pulled away. We stood there in shock as the taillights faded into the darkness. Our moustaches again frozen, we resumed our patrol.

Those were a tough nine months for us rookies, but we learned a lot on foot patrol. For one thing, we gained an intimate knowledge of the city. By the time the next batch of recruits arrived to replace us, we knew the streets and alleys. We knew where criminal activity was likely to take place and where the bad guys might hide. Just as important, we got to know each other better and how we would react to real-life situations rather than training scenarios.

After completing our foot patrol assignment, we were placed in squads. I was thrilled to be assigned to a squad that was made up almost entirely of Italian officers. Some around the department called it the "goomba squad." But that did not bother me. I was 21-years-old and working with wily older veterans who were in their mid-twenties and older. No, that goomba thing did not bother me at all.

The strategy was for us new guys to ride with a seasoned officer whose regular partner was off for a day or two. Over time that allowed us to work and develop a rapport with everybody in the squad. As it happened, my first shift in a patrol car I was partnered with one of the few non-Italians in the squad, a black guy named Al Breece. Al was from the Deep South and had such an accent that it was very tough for me and everyone else to understand him.

At about two in the morning, we were patrolling in an area called Southfield Park. It was near where I grew up and I knew it well. Without explanation, Al turned the car onto a long downhill road that led to the beach. He shut all the lights off, put the car in neutral and we coasted down the hill. It was pitch black and I could not see a thing. Anticipating that we would crash into something at any moment I grabbed the dash and braced myself. But Al seemed to know every twist and turn of the entrance road and managed to get us safely to the end of it.

Al shut the car off and then told me to grab my flashlight and follow him. And to be very quiet. After we walked a short distance, I could make out the shape of a car ahead. As we reached the car Al motioned for me to go to the passenger side of the vehicle while he went on the driver's side. Al turned on his flashlight and directed the beam inside. I did the same. On the floor in the back seat was a pile of clothes and on the seat were a naked young man and woman engaged in an act of oral sex. I did not know what to do and just stood there with my mouth hanging open. But Al had obviously been in this kind of situation many times before. "Chow time is over," he drawled as the couple scrambled to get their clothes on. "It's time to go home."

I was now trained in how to conduct myself during a visit to a lover's lane.

A few days later I was riding with an officer named Sal Ladestro. Sal was a few years older than me, but he was a friend of my parents and I'd known him all my life. We were working the Westside and got a call to respond to a domestic dispute. As we walked up the steps to the house, we could hear a man and woman yelling inside and noises that sounded like pots and pans being thrown around.

We were let in and Sal had me take the man over to one side of the room while he took the woman to the other. After we got them calmed down, Sal brought everyone together in the middle of the kitchen. But in seconds more yelling and screaming broke out. Sal told them to shut up and keep quiet while he asked some questions. The first thing he asked the woman was what her relationship was to the man.

"We're both Baptists," she said. "That's right," the man joined in. "We go to the church right down the street and that's how we got related." Somehow Sal and I managed to keep from laughing. The couple made peace and we got out of there.

Between that call and the earlier lover's lane experience, I knew being a cop was the life for me.

One night a short time later I was again doing a midnight shift with Al Breece. I loved to drive and he let me take the wheel that night. It was around 2:00 a.m. and we were stopped at a traffic light right in the middle of town. I glanced over at Al. His chin was down on his chest and he was snoring away.

As we were waiting for the light to change, the sergeant's car pulled up next to us on Al's side. I kicked Al and when he raised his head, he saw the sergeant looking at him. The sergeant motioned for Al to lower his window and asked, "Were you sleeping, Breece?"

For a guy who had just been awakened to find his boss watching him, Al was as cool as a cucumber. He said smoothly, "No Sarge. I was watchin' my shoes. I was just watchin' my shoes."

The sergeant glared at him for a few seconds, and then drove away without saying another word.

Another time I was working with Joe "Spike" Coviello. It was a beautiful afternoon and we were patrolling in an upscale neighborhood inhabited by mostly wealthy people.

An older lady on the sidewalk motioned us to pull over to the curb. She came up to my window and said hello. After a little small talk, she looked at my name tag. She said, "You're Colucci, huh?" I proudly admitted that I was. She then leaned forward and looked at Spike's name tag. "And you're Coviello?" Spike said yes. "You're both Italian," she concluded.

I waited for the compliment I was sure was coming. Instead, she said, "I have no use for Italians." Then she turned and walked away. Spike and I looked at each other briefly and then he drove away. Sometimes things are better left unsaid.

As the weeks passed by my education continued. I worked with several experienced officers. I always tried to retain what I thought were their good habits and disregard the bad. The job was both exciting and rewarding for me and I looked forward to going to work.

But the passing of time also brought on some other things. There was negative talk about the department and how it was run. According to some people, deserving officers were sometimes held back from promotion to sergeant and lieutenant because they did not have the right contacts. They said it was not what you knew, it was who you knew. That was a primary complaint, but there were others, too.

I was happy though and was not going to let the moaners and groaners influence me. I let those stories go in one ear and out the other.

And then one day I noticed a posting on the bulletin board for people interested in joining the Narcotics Squad. That was a very prestigious unit and offered assignments in Stamford and all areas of Fairfield County. There were six openings and a lot of people had already signed up. I'd only been on the job about a year and a half and probably didn't stand much chance of being selected. But I figured it would not hurt to try, so I added my name to the list.

A couple of guys who were a little bit senior to me passed by and started making fun of me for submitting my name. One of them told me there was no way a rookie like me would land a slot in Narcotics. Who in the hell did I think I was?

When I got home after work I thought about the Narcotics Squad and what that other cop had said. At that time my cousin, who I will call Carmine, was serving on several City government boards. His mother and my mother were sisters. I called Carmine that night and told him what I was

A PHOTO OF VITO WITH HIS DAUGHTERS
MELODYE LYNN & JODI LEE

trying to do. He said he would mention me to some people he knew who might be able to push for me.

A couple of days later Carmine called me back. He said he had talked to a couple of guys who owed him favors and asked what were the chances of me getting one of the Narcotics openings. They told him there was a good chance they could make it happen.

Carmine called again a day or two after that. This time he was stressed. His mother and his aunt Sadie, who was my mother, were yelling at him. He explained that my mother had called his mother and said she did not want me to get that job in Narcotics. It was much too dangerous for me. Carmine did not know what to do.

I pleaded with him to disregard what my mother had said. I wanted that assignment more than anything else and I needed his help. I did not envy the position he was in, but I hoped he would see it my way. The days of waiting seemed like they would never end. And then Carmine finally called and said I would be given the slot in Narcotics. The people in power thought with my young age and appearance I would be able to fit right in with the people I would be dealing with. He asked that I act surprised when the chief called me in to give me the news.

That was the only time in my career that I used outside influence to help me get what I wanted. And little did I know then that the strings my cousin pulled would end up changing my whole life forever. My assignment to Narcotics catapulted me into a series of events that I never would have thought possible. And once they started there was no turning back.

4

BOUT 4:30 on a Monday afternoon, I and the other new
Narcotics officers met in the office of Chief Joseph Kinsella. He was a political appointee in his mid-fifties and
had been heading the department for about fifteen years.
Prior to that he had been a postmaster and had no law
enforcement experience of any kind. Kinsella wasn't particularly popular with the rank and file; he was not a cop's cop.

Chief Kinsella congratulated us on our promotions to the
Special Services Squad, calling it "The most elite squad in
all of Fairfield County." He went on and on about the great
responsibility we all would have in keeping the crime rate
down and putting the bad guys away. After his spiel, Kinsella escorted us to the Narcotics office. As we walked, he

continued to sing the praises of the Squad and especially its boss, Lieutenant Larry Hogan.

Upon arriving at the office door, I glanced around to see what the home of this elite operation looked like. It was disappointingly tiny. There was one old desk facing the door, a couple of chairs randomly situated, an old file cabinet that had seen better days, and a lot of Narcotics Identification Kits were scattered around. That was pretty much it. Although the office fell short of my expectations, I did not let it dampen my enthusiasm.

In addition to the furnishings, Lieutenant Hogan was inside the office. I had not met Hogan before. But I knew who he was, having seen him around the station and on the road driving his new black Pontiac Grand Prix, a hot car for that time. He was a big, robust man in his forties. Like Kinsella, he had been with the department about fifteen years. Hogan was known as a gruff and rather miserable character who did not seem to be liked by anybody. On that day it appeared he had not shaved for a while and had a growth of whiskers.

Also in the office was Joe Ligi, someone I knew well. Joe was a distant cousin of mine. His mother was a sister to my uncle's wife. I had seen Joe many times at family functions over the years.

Before Chief Kinsella headed back to his own office, he made a comment that I never forgot. He advised us that we would probably hear stuff from the people on the street. They would tell us things about Hogan and Sergeant Duke Morris. They would say those men were corrupt. But he warned those stories would be lies and not to pay any attention to them.

I snuck a peek at Hogan as Kinsella talked. He had a smirk on his face. It turned out that the smirk was an almost permanent fixture, and as time passed it was something I grew to hate. I came to learn that it was there because Hogan was confident that no one would ever get to him or Morris. They were too smart and too well insulated. In his mind they were untouchable.

But I did not know any of that then. On that day I was a naïve rookie starting a new assignment. It would be some time before I developed the urge to wipe that smirk off Hogan's face.

Joe Ligi picked me as his partner and we hit the street. He had an even cooler car than Hogan. It was a new coral-colored Mustang GT. And the squad had two unmarked cars of its own, a new red Mercury Cougar and a gold Plymouth Fury. We alternated using those cars and our personal vehicles. Joe taught me a lot about how the Squad operated, the names of the known drug dealers and where they lived and did business.

I learned quickly that in addition to all the serious stuff Joe told me, he also had a sense of humor. One time we were parked in front of Buzzeo's Market on Stillwater Avenue when Joe spotted a young guy walking toward us. Joe said, "I think he's got drugs on him." Then in his most serious tone, he said, "Jump out of the car, identify yourself, and ask him if he has any drugs on him."

I leaped from the car with one hand holding my floppy hat on my head and the other holding my badge. I asked the guy if he had any drugs on him, just like Joe told me to do. I could not believe it when he answered, "Yeah, some pot."

I told him to put his hands on the car and spread 'em. In his back pocket was a baggie with the marijuana in it. I told him he was under arrest, handcuffed him and placed him in the back seat of the car.

Joe, who had gotten out of the car and was standing on the sidewalk, was laughing like a madman. Figuring I had screwed up, I asked him what was so funny. Between guffaws he explained, "I was just kidding you. I didn't know he had any drugs on him. I cannot believe what I just saw."

My first narcotics arrest may have been kind of a fluke, but the many that followed were not. Joe and I developed a reputation as effective officers who got the job done. And the other Squad members, Steve DeVito, Sergeant Dante Fedeli, Mike Moon and John Ruggles were tearing it up on a regular basis too. In our minds, we thought we were cleaning up the whole town. We did not realize then that we were only netting the small fish. The big boys would prove to be much tougher to catch.

Ignorant of what was ahead, I relished seeing Joe's and my name in the paper on a regular basis announcing our latest collars. And those arrests meant court appearances and more money, because we were guaranteed a minimum of four hours pay when we had to go to court.

One afternoon we responded to a call of a disorderly person on Peveril Road. We rang the bell and when the subject opened the door, we were looking down the barrels of two loaded .45s. Joe and I grabbed his arms, took him to the ground and disarmed him. The headline in the next day's paper was, "Police Disarm Local Gunman." Thankfully, my mother never saw the piece. If she had she would have called my cousin Carmine and cursed him out for helping me get that job. But I was loving it and thanked Carmine every chance I got. He would just stare at me and shake his head.

The bad guys and girls on the street always wanted Joe and me to know they knew a lot about us, too. They knew our private vehicles, where we lived and the names of our children. When they mentioned that stuff it was in a non-threatening manner, but it still got their point across. I learned later that they got our personal information from dirty cops.

Because I had grown up in and around most of the high crime areas we worked, I already knew the ins and outs of those neighborhoods. I knew the alleys, the short cuts, the backyards, and which fences could be jumped. I also knew many of the people.

When you are a Narc you have to play a game with the drug dealers. You must be able to con them while they are trying to con you. Joe always told the street people how tough and crazy I was. He would tell them that on a dare in headquarters I pinned my badge onto my bare chest and walked around with blood dripping all over the place. Those kinds of stories were silly, but some people actually believed them.

A guy I now know told me that he quit drugs back then because he heard about this crazy narcotics cop named Carlucci [a common mispronunciation of Vito's last name].

He decided to clean up his act rather than take a chance of having to deal with that Carlucci guy.

Here I was, a hundred-and-fifty-pound kid intimidating guys based on a reputation that was created by Joe's storytelling.

Police Disarm Local Gunman

Two members of the Police Special Service Squad disarmed a man -who pointed two 45- cal. automatic pistols and threatened to kill them if police did not "leave him alone" in a Peveril Rd. apartment Monday-night.

PD Joseph Ligi and Vito Carlucci responded to a phone call that a man had kicked open a door in an apartment at Peveril Rd at 6:13 p.m., police said.

Entering the apartment through the forced door, the two policemen confronted Joseph L. Coviello, 27, pointing the two loaded handguns at them. Police later learned: that the apartment door Coviello had kicked was his own.

Police said Coviello told the two policemen that he would shoot them if they did not leave immediately. The two .patrolmen continued to talk with Coviello and managed' to disarm him

The truth is, I was not a tough guy then or now. I must thank God that in all the situations I was in as a cop, the fights, shootouts, and working undercover, I was never injured. Jesus Christ has protected me all my life.

One of the funniest arrests I was ever involved in was what we came to call the fried chicken caper. The Squad had gotten a phone tip that several well-known local drug dealers were on their way back from New York City on a train. The tipster said they would be "heavy," which meant they would be loaded up with drugs. He also said that the heroin would be concealed inside containers of fried chicken.

Six of us responded to the Stamford railroad station. The suspects were two men and two women who we knew by sight, so spotting them would not be a problem. We set up in three positions and waited for the train to pull in. It arrived filled with commuters, mostly businessmen and women. The men, in their three-piece suits, carried brief-cases with newspapers tucked under their arms. The women were also wearing business attire, but the newspaper seemed to be a guy thing.

The four dealers exited from different train cars and approached our positions from different directions. They each carried five or six boxes of fried chicken, just as the tipster had said. We had to squeeze through the several hundred other passengers to get to the suspects.

We knew the dealers, but they also knew us. They recognized us before we could reach them and things quickly went downhill. The suspects began to run in all directions, throwing the chicken boxes as they fled. There were yells of surprise as some of the commuters were struck by pieces of flying fowl and tried to flee the scene.

We scooped up one of the boxes and saw glassine bags of heroin tied to every chicken leg, wing and breast, with rubber bands. One by one we caught each dealer and placed them under arrest. And then we started the difficult task of recovering all the pieces of chicken.

Suddenly, I noticed one of our better-known town drunks sitting on some steps nearby. He was about to put a chicken leg and the attached bag of heroin in his mouth. I yelled at him to stop and grabbed the leg and heroin from him, saving the evidence and possibly his life.

As I stood there holding that piece of chicken, filthy from being touched by the dealers, being on the station floor and covered with the drunk's drool, I could not help but wonder what Colonel Sanders would have thought if he knew how his product had been used.

When Joe Ligi and I transported one of the suspects to the station for booking we kept singing a line from a then current KFC commercial. "If you can visit the Colonel, why cook?" Our prisoner did not appreciate our humor and kept hollering for us to shut up.

Yeah, back then I felt I was serving the community and was having a good time doing it. But as I soon began to learn, things are not always what they seem. And nothing lasts forever.

Fried Chicken Leads To Arrest Of 4

Four persons were arrested by members of the Police Narcotics Squad at the Stamford Railroad Station Thursday night.

5

As 1972 rolled around Joe Ligi and I were certainly making names for ourselves. We were pretty much able to work any hours we wanted, as long as we continued to make arrests on a regular basis and got the arrest reports on the captain's desk before we went home. We were making a difference. The department loved it and so did the news media.

But not having set work hours had a downside. It gave you a lot more time and opportunity to get into trouble if you were so inclined. It did not take long for most of the married men in our squad, including me, to find ourselves having serious marital problems. We were either cheating on our wives, separated from them, or getting a divorce.

My situation was this: I was still married, but had a steady girlfriend, whom I'll call Donna, on the side. Jill had given birth to our second daughter, Jodi, on July 27, 1971. With two young kids I wanted to keep my family together, only I did not want to give up my private social life to do it. I tried to have it both ways, but it turned out I could not. I was forced to part company with Donna in early 1972. It was an incident that could have cost me my job. And my marriage ended a little over a year after that.

The thing with Donna was unexpected because I thought everything was going good between us. What I did not know was that she had told her mother about her cop boyfriend. Her mother knew of me because of all the publicity I had been getting on the job. Unfortunately, she also remembered seeing Jodi's birth announcement in the newspaper. Apparently, the lady did not think much of a new father and married man taking up with her daughter.

One day while I was at work, I got a call from Chief Kinsella. He said he wanted to see me in his office. It's seldom a good thing when the chief calls you into his office and says he wants you there right away. That was true then and I am sure it is still true today. When I got into the office Captain Lester McDonald, Kinsella's chief confidant, was standing in the corner; kind of like a cigar store Indian, stone-faced and mute. I suspected right then it was not going to be a time for party hats and balloons.

My suspicions were quickly confirmed when I noticed a brown paper bag on the chief's desk. It had a clock radio on top of it. I recognized it as the radio I had given Donna a few months earlier. Now I knew why I had been called in. The only question was how bad it was going to be.

Kinsella began to read me the riot act. He said he had just had a meeting with my girlfriend's mother. She informed him that I was having an affair with her daughter and she wanted it to stop. He assured her it would stop and told me in no uncertain terms that it had damn well better. He said to me, "You're getting accolades for doing good work. At the same time, you're a married man out having affairs with other women. This has to stop and it will stop, or else."

Today, situations like that are handled differently. The higher-ups will tell the complainant, "We are not the marriage police. There is nothing we can do about it." But in that era Kinsella might have terminated me on the spot if not for my good track record. I took his threat seriously and broke off my relationship with Donna that same day.

My home life may not have been good, but at work I was on top of the world. I had almost no accountability on the job. My partner and I roamed the streets at will, making arrests and getting our names in the paper. Vito the cop could not have had it any better. And then something happened that very few cops ever have to deal with. I was involved in a shooting in which a man died.

It began innocently on Friday, May 5, 1972, when Lieutenant John Considine called Joe Ligi and me into his office when we arrived for work that afternoon. He told us about a pair of 26-year-olds that had escaped from the Arizona State Prison in 1971. After their escape, Thomas Murphy and Charles Blevins engaged in a spree of auto thefts, robberies, kidnappings, rapes and other assorted crimes, as they traveled across the country. They were armed and dangerous and the FBI was on their trail.

Lieutenant Considine said he had received information that these two individuals were going to be at a place called the Showboat Hotel in Greenwich, the next town over from Stamford. He asked Joe and me to go over to that area to try to locate the red Pontiac rental car Murphy and Blevins were believed to be driving. If we were successful, we'd sit on the Pontiac until the FBI arrived on the scene to take over. It sounded easy enough. Locate the vehicle from a distance, call it in and wait for the feds to relieve us.

Wearing civilian clothing and driving our unmarked car, Joe and I arrived at the Showboat around 6:30 and pulled into the huge parking lot to check for the rental car. We spotted it almost immediately. The only trouble was that before we could even call it in, the two subjects left the hotel, got into the Pontiac and drove away. We notified headquarters of the situation and said we would tail the car while the FBI mobilized and caught up with us.

Murphy was originally from Stamford and his familiarity with the area was obvious as he drove the back roads out of Greenwich and crossed over into New York State. Joe was driving our car and I kept in constant contact with headquarters. Lieutenant Considine advised he was leaving the station and would join us in the surveillance shortly.

We stayed as far behind the Pontiac as we could and still keep the car in sight. But I continued to worry that we would be spotted and kept telling Joe, "They're gonna make us. They're gonna make us." They apparently did not though. At least not then.

It seemed like we followed those guys for hours. But it had actually been only twenty minutes or so when we entered the Playland Parkway in Rye, New York. I had been on that road many times as a kid when I went to the Playland Amusement Park. It was right down a dead-end road from the Parkway. I notified headquarters that we were on the Parkway and that the road ended at the amusement park. I had no idea why Murphy and Blevins were heading that way, but I did not like it. The amusement park would be crowded at this time on a Friday evening. If things went bad there would be a good chance that civilians would be injured or possibly taken as hostages. Unexpectedly, just before getting to Playland the Pontiac turned onto a side road. That was a welcome move on one hand. But it could also mean they had finally noticed us.

We were now in a residential area and there was a neighborhood bar called the Cove East Tavern. They pulled into the bar's parking lot and we were right behind them. I notified headquarters and told them we were going to attempt to apprehend the subjects.

The Pontiac came to a stop and we did likewise about ten or twelve yards away. Murphy and Blevins got out of their car, .38 caliber revolvers in their hands. Joe and I were exiting our vehicle at the same time with our .357 magnums drawn. The big difference was that our car doors were in front of us while theirs were behind them.

Before we had a chance to announce that we were the police and order the bad guys to drop their weapons, they started shooting at us. Joe and I crouched behind our open car doors and returned fire while Murphy and Blevins were without cover. Seconds after the shooting began Lieutenant

Considine materialized. Armed with a shotgun, he joined the fight. Blevins went down first, fatally wounded. Murphy then dropped to the pavement on his stomach after suffering a minor wound to his left shoulder.

I remember noticing as I ran over to Murphy, that the FBI and units from the Greenwich Police Department were on the scene and had joined the fight. I sat down on Murphy, pulled his arms behind his back, and handcuffed him. FBI agents had their shotguns pointed right at Murphy the whole time. Other agents were covering Blevins, not realizing at that point that he was already dead.

The shootout had lasted only a half-minute or so. Newspaper reports said that during that brief period over thirty rounds had been fired.

Joe and I put Murphy in our vehicle. The feds told us to take him to the police department in Rye, New York, and stay there with him until they arrived. Up to that point I had not felt nervous or frightened. But as I sat in the back seat with Murphy and looked out the window, I could see literally dozens and dozens of people lining the sidewalks, pointing and talking. That is when what had happened began to hit home. Anxiety and nervousness set in at the realization that I had just been in a shootout where someone had been killed. It was not a good feeling.

After the FBI relieved us, we left Rye and returned to Stamford. I think Joe and I were in a daze during the ride. I do not remember any conversation between us. I guess we were both lost in our own thoughts.

When we arrived back at headquarters we were greeted by our superiors and many other officers that had listened to the whole episode on their car radios. From the time Joe and I began tailing Murphy and Blevins from the Showboat until the shootout, all non-emergency radio traffic had been suspended. For all the cops on duty that night, the Murphy and Blevins incident had been the only game in town.

Joe and I became local heroes for a while. There were headlines splashed all over the papers about us. But it was a different time back then. There were no psychologists to talk with you after a shooting. We were told to take a day off and then get back to work. Today you would be given time off and must attend counseling.

On June 26, 1972, Joe Ligi, John Considine and I, were awarded the Citation for Valor by the Connecticut Detective's Conference. The inscription said: For outstanding valor and unswerving devotion to duty in the face of grave danger and imminent death in the apprehension of two felons who had escaped from the Arizona State Prison.

In 1975 we each received The Combat Cross for that same incident. It read: In recognition of his performance in an act of extreme heroism while engaged in personal combat with an armed adversary at imminent personal hazard of life in the performance of duty.

Up until that night in 1972 I never really liked going to the police range to qualify with my weapon. I just was not a gun enthusiast. I always got passing grades, but was never a Marksman or Sharpshooter. After the shootout I developed a deep appreciation for the training involved in being a cop, though. Two untrained criminals went up against well trained police officers. And the guys that were better prepared—the good guys—won.

Many years later, after I had left the police department and opened my private detective agency in Stamford, I got

ADVOCATE

Sun And Tide
Tomorrow
Daylight Saving Time
Sun Rises 5:45 — Sun Sets 7:37
High Water .... 6:38 a.m.
Low Water .... 1:00 p.m.

D 7829

SATURDAY, MAY 6, 1972.   26 PAGES   FIFTEEN CENTS

Man Killed, Companion Wounded In Gun Battle
— Escaped Felons Cornered In Rye

By NICK SEMINOFF
Advocate Staff Reporter

One man was killed and his companion, who police said is a Stamford native, was wounded during a shootout with police in Rye, N.Y., early Friday night.

Police said more than 40 shots were fired in the exchange that left Charles B. Blevins, 26, dead, and convicted murderer Robert Thomas Murphy, 24, formerly of Stamford, superficially wounded.

34

information from someone at the courthouse that Lieutenant Considine, who went on to become Chief of Police of the Stamford Police Department, wanted to see me. He was then in an assisted living facility suffering from terminal cancer.

When I saw him, it was a shock. He did not look anything like I remembered. He was very frail and his hands were paper thin. But he was happy to see me. A nurse was in the room with him and he bragged to her about me. He was proud of how well I had done as a private detective and that he saw me on the television news shows all the time.

After the nurse left, we talked for a while. He lifted his head and pointed a finger at me. In an excited voice he said, "Vito, you need to understand we're bound together by that shootout. We are locked shoulder to shoulder, just like we were that day. We will always be bound by that."

I told him, "I know, Chief. I know." We would always be linked together because of that day in 1972. It was a very emotional session, but I am glad I got to see and talk with him before he passed.

GETTING OUR CITATIONS FOR VALOR AT THE
DETECTIVE CONFERENCE. L TO R- JOE LIGI,
VITO COLUCCI, JR., LT. JOHN CONSIDINE.

UNITED STATES DEPARTMENT OF JUSTICE

FEDERAL BUREAU OF INVESTIGATION
770 Chapel Street
Post Office Box 1890
May 16, 1972
New Haven, Connecticut, 06508

In Reply, Please
Refer to File No.

Joseph Kinsella
Chief of Police
Police Department
Stanford, Connecticut 06901

Dear Joe,

Now that the dust has settled somewhat, I want to take this opportunity to extend our sincere thanks and appreciation to you and the members of your fine Department for the outstanding- assistance and cooperation given us which resulted is the apprehension of Robert Thomas Murphy and Charles Benjamin Blevins extremely dangerous fugitive escapees from Arizona.

The performance of Lieutenant John Considine, Detective Joseph Lege and Detective Vito Colucci certainly is worthy of the highest commendation due to the complete disregard these men exhibited for their personal safety in participating in the final confrontation and shoot-out with these fugitives which resulted in the death of Blevins and the surrender of Murphy.

The overall cooperation extended by your Department as well as the outstanding personal efforts of Lieutenant Considine and Detectives Lege and Colucci exemplify the great spirit of cooperation which has always existed between our Departments. I hope to have the opportunity to extend my congratulations to you and your fine men personally on my next visit to Stamford.

Sincerely,

Charles E. Weeks
Special Agent in Charge

cc -   Lieutenant John Considine
        Detective Joseph Lege
        Detective Vito Colucci

FAIRFIELD COUNTY DETECTIVE CONFERENCE

Citation for Valor

OFFICER VITO COLUCCI
STAMFORD POLICE DEPARTMENT

For outstanding valor and unswerving devotion to duty in the face of grave danger and imminent death in the apprehension of two felons who had escaped from the Arizona State Prison in December of 1971 and wanted in the Arizona area for several armed robberies, grand theft auto, and kidnapping. Subjects armed and dangerous, identified as one Robert Thomas Murphy, age 26 and one Charles Blevins, age 26.

On this date, May 5th, 1972, special agents of the F.B.I. and members of the Greenwich and Stamford Police Departments located the two subjects in question at a motel in Greenwich. A surveillance was established. Subjects were observed leaving the Greenwich motel and followed to Rye, New York to a parking lot of the Cove East Tavern. At this point, the apprehension of the two wanted subjects was attempted, the two subjects Robert Thomas Murphy and Charles Blevins observed the police officers, exited from their vehicle and began firing at the officers, who returned the gunfire. As a result, Charles Blevins was killed and Robert Thomas Murphy was taken into custody.

Officer Vito Colucci displayed remarkable fearlessness and persistence in a situation fraught with grave personal danger.

We hereby commend him, Officer Vito Colucci, for valor in the performance of duty and award him this Citation for Valor.

Board Of Awards   FAIRFIELD COUNTY DETECTIVE CONFERENCE

President

DATED AT WESTPORT, June 26th, 1972

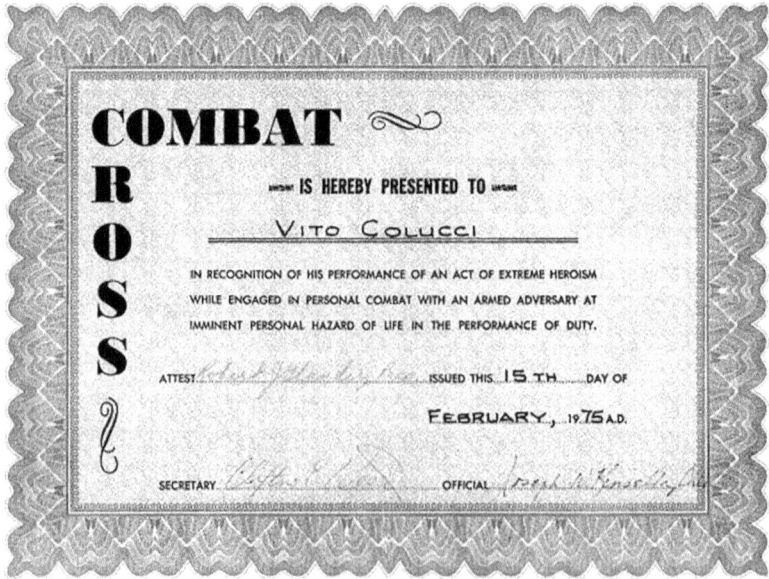

COMBAT CROSS

IS HEREBY PRESENTED TO

VITO COLUCCI

IN RECOGNITION OF HIS PERFORMANCE OF AN ACT OF EXTREME HEROISM WHILE ENGAGED IN PERSONAL COMBAT WITH AN ARMED ADVERSARY AT IMMINENT PERSONAL HAZARD OF LIFE IN THE PERFORMANCE OF DUTY.

ATTEST   ISSUED THIS 15 TH DAY OF

FEBRUARY, 19 75 A.D.

SECRETARY   OFFICIAL

6

I N MAY 1973, I gave up on my efforts to hold my family together and I left Jill. Looking back now I realize that I did not have a valid reason for it. She had been a good wife to me for the almost five years we had been together. It was probably a marriage that never should have happened. I was only twenty when we took our vows and that was much too young to take on the responsibility of a wife and family. And the lifestyle I was leading was a road map to a failed marriage. Being a police officer with almost no accountability and playing in a band on weekends provided too many opportunities for me to go wrong.

I was caught up in my own world and did not want to be married any longer. I was a hero cop and a weekend rock star. I had a number of women available whenever I wanted and there were plenty more where they came from. I was not going to let anything restrain me from doing what I wanted to do and getting where I wanted to go. One day I told Jill, "That's it, I'm gettin' out of here." I was one screwed up guy!

Jill and the girls stayed in the home that we had bought in Darien and I moved into a bachelor apartment at 50 Glenbrook Road in Stamford. It was a spacious two-bedroom luxury apartment. It was brand new and had a doorman, a beautiful pool and a rooftop suite for parties; all the bells and whistles. I shared the pad with Ellis Crawford, a good friend of mine who was also on the force. Ellis was going through a divorce himself, so we were a good match.

Money was not a big problem for me at the time. My weekly take home pay from the department was only about a hundred and sixty bucks. But I was making good money playing weddings and dinner dances on the weekends. I was able to pay child support to my ex-wife—although I fell behind frequently and had to catch up—keep up my end of the apartment and still have some fun money in my pocket. Whatever spare time I had was spent doing a couple of other things I liked. Dating and playing poker.

Poker had always been an attraction to me. My parents played poker regularly and I watched the games as a kid. Sometimes the stakes were pretty high for everyday people and looking at all that money in the pots night after night hooked me. I knew that when I was old enough, I'd be at a table myself. It just goes to show how kids grow up wanting to do what they have seen their parents do. Both good and bad.

The poker games I played in usually had two- and four-dollar betting limits. That meant I would not get in a game unless I had at least a hundred bucks in my pocket. The other players in those games were amateurs like me— not the pros I had run into later in my career.

———

Living with Ellis was a lot of fun. He was a good friend then and remains so today. Because we were both newly single, there was a steady stream of women coming in and out of that apartment at all hours. We thought it was the cool way to live. I was still working Narcotics and setting my own hours. I saw my love interests and played in bands whenever I wanted.

To Ellis and me, we were living the good life. We were in a new bachelor pad and we tipped Vinnie the doorman good money to help us out with our many women visitors. When one showed up that we did not want to see he lied for us, saying we were out of town due to the illness, the death of a relative, or some such story.

A girl once asked me how many grandparents Ellis had. Apparently, Vinnie had told her that Ellis attended the funerals of four grandmothers over a couple of months period. I said he had real ones, step ones and foster ones. Incredibly, she believed it.

For a while I thought the single life was great fun and would last forever. But I was soon to learn otherwise.

The change began for me on what should have been a very upbeat night. I had won some money earlier in the day playing poker with some fellow cops. That evening, one of the bands I was with at the time played with the group Sha

Na Na at a concert at Fairfield University. It was a packed house and the audience raised their cigarette lighters to us in tribute. For a musician, that is about as good as it gets.

After the concert one of my girlfriends came over to the apartment to top off the evening. After she left, I went out onto the terrace. As I was standing there, I suddenly became very depressed. I cannot remember having ever felt so lonely or sad. How could I feel so unhappy and lost with my life after the great day and night I had? As I tried to rationalize my feelings, I realized I missed my daughters Melodye and Jodi a lot. Seeing them once or twice a week instead of every day was starting to affect me.

Looking back now as a Christian, I know what really went down that night. My soul was crying out to God. I had been trying to fill my life with the things of the world. But they do not give you peace in your life. Only Jesus Christ can give you that peace.

Although my communication with God had begun, I did not realize it at the time. It would be several more years before I totally surrendered my life to my Lord and Savior.

No God — No Peace.
Know God — Know peace.

TWO OF THE GOOD ONES! A PHOTO OF MY
PARTNERS JOE LIGI & ELLIS CRAWFORD

7

ON THE job, Joe Ligi and I continued to work the streets. We made the arrests and did whatever we could to make the city a safe place to live. But it was an uphill battle. There was virtually a drug epidemic. Large amounts of heroin, cocaine and marijuana flowed into Stamford on a daily basis.

This was the era of the Super Fly movies and many of the songs that came out advocated the use of illegal drugs. Drug dealers drove around town in their fancy cars. Caddys with big white wall tires and a diamond in the back were a common sight.

One night we happened to see a guy walking on the street who we knew had outstanding warrants on him. His name was Arvil Chapman. We placed him under arrest without incident. It was strictly routine, or so it seemed at the time.

In reality, though, it was far from routine. That encounter with Arvil Chapman has affected every day of my life, right up to the writing of this book.

Joe knew Arvil from the streets, but that night was the first time I had met him. As we drove Arvil to headquarters for booking, he said, "What if I give you guys some great information, some really juicy stuff? Would you go talk to the prosecutor for me and get these charges dropped?"

I looked at him and said, "Arvil, we're all ears. But you gotta give us something good because there are a lot of charges here."

And then he blurted out those life-changing words. "Your boss, Hogan, is running the whole drug and gambling racket all throughout Fairfield County."

I immediately pulled the car over to digest what Arvil had said. I glanced at Joe. The look in his eyes told me he wanted to hear more. So, did I. Even though we were making a lot of arrests, the really big fish seemed to always get away somehow. We ended up with just the minnows in our net. When we got search warrants that should have implicated the main players in the drug and gambling operations, we always came away empty. Some of us had begun to doubt that all these misfires were simply bad luck. Maybe the targets knew we were coming. Maybe someone was protecting them. Arvil's statement offered an explanation that fit. But the word of a handcuffed suspect looking for a free pass out of jail was a long way from proof.

I drove to the parking lot of the Pitney Bowes factory where we could talk some more with little risk of being observed. That is when Arvil told his extraordinary story.

Arvil said he had gone to work for Stamford police sergeant Duke Morris as a drug runner. His job was to go to New York City, pick up supplies of drugs and deliver them to Morris' apartment located on the eighth floor of St. John's Towers in Stamford. Arvil related that he would sit at a table in that apartment while Morris and Lieutenant Larry Hogan cut up and bagged the heroin and other drugs. And these were big shipments that supplied illegal drugs throughout Fairfield County.

We asked Arvil if he ever saw anybody else at the apartment during those transactions. He said that sometimes a police detective named Freddy [not his real name] was there. Freddy, who was a very good friend of Duke Morris, would sit in the living room while the cutting and packaging went on. But he never participated directly. This enhanced Arvil's credibility because Joe and I knew that Morris was indeed friends with a detective named Freddy.

Joe and I were amazed, almost in a daze, as we listened to Arvil provide great detail as to where he made his buys, what he bought and how much it cost, and the depth of the involvement of Morris and Hogan in planning and running the operation.

He told us that Duke Morris would stab or shoot rival drug couriers that refused to work for him. These were not life-threatening injuries. They were intended to gain the victim's cooperation and send a message to others.

We had heard stories on the street of minor dealers being dragged into an alleyway and shot in the kneecap or leg, or beaten up by Morris. We had also heard that he was responsible for several drug-related murders throughout Connecticut. The word was, "Duke's the Man." I tell people nowadays that the Alonzo Harris character played by Denzel Washington in Training Day, had nothing on Morris when it came to pure meanness.

Arvil further confirmed those stories and brought Hogan into the picture as well. And listening to Arvil it made sense. Morris was the mover and shaker, the enforcer. And with Hogan overseeing the whole regional squad, he could do whatever would benefit him. If he wanted someone arrested, he could arrange it. If he wanted someone left alone, he could arrange that as well. It was all up to him. The bottom line was power and money. It appeared that Morris and Hogan had the power and were making plenty of money because of it.

We next brought Arvil to headquarters. Because this was a warrant arrest, we couldn't just let him go. Joe went to talk to the prosecutor and told him that Arvil was working with us on some big narcotics cases and we would appreciate it if he could drop the charges against him in order to continue the flow of information. The prosecutor agreed and the charges were dropped.

Joe and I continued to talk with Arvil. He was able to additionally enhance his credibility with his knowledge of the surveillances we conducted and the search warrants we served that produced absolutely nothing. He recounted how Morris and Hogan would sit at the table handling their drugs and laugh about the various raids we had made that went nowhere. Arvil said that Hogan was always one step ahead of us.

A couple of days after Arvil's arrest, one of the big drug dealers in the area, James "Pepper Red" Whitfield, pulled up alongside of us. He asked that we pull over so he could talk with Joe privately. Joe got out of the car, but stayed in range so I could see everything that went on.

Joe came back to the car and told me that Pepper Red just offered him and me a bribe. Pepper wanted to know if Joe and I would take five grand a month to leave him alone and let him do his business.

We had arrested Pepper a couple of times previously. And even when we did not arrest him, we were still able to disrupt his operation. We were a thorn in his side and his desire to buy us off was understandable. But the amount of the bribe offer was stunning. What kind of profits must he have been making to be willing and able to pay us that kind of money?

Joe told him no deal. We were never interested in lining our pockets with money from the likes of Pepper at any time in our careers. We tossed around the idea of charging Pepper for the bribe attempt. But with no other witnesses and nothing on tape, it would have come down to Joe's word against Pepper's. And with all the animosity between us and the drug dealers it would have been a tough sell. We decided not to press it. But we continued to arrest or at least harass Pepper at every opportunity.

———

Joe and I knew we had to be very careful in how we handled our new informant. Arvil Chapman was in a position to provide information that could take the suspicions about Duke Morris and Larry Hogan from just being street rumors to landing them in a courtroom. If what Arvil had told us was true and word got out that he was cooperating with us, he would be in serious danger. We decided that for security purposes we would not tell anybody what we had going just yet and do our own investigation. We worked our regular shift every day and then did what we called our Arvil Chapman shift on our own time. Nobody knew what we were doing with Arvil.

On the Chapman shift we monitored his every move. We were especially interested in any of his activities with our supervisors. Arvil was constantly at Morris' apartment with Morris and Hogan while the drugs were being cut and bagged. He was also involved in distributing them.

But Arvil's role was not limited to handling drugs. He was also active in the illegal gambling and bookmaking part of the operation. There was a lot of activity going on and Arvil Chapman was turning out to be a gold mine.

We came to find out that Lieutenant Hogan had a close connection to the Mob families in the area. He was not only working with them on the narcotics end, where he protected his own people and arrested those who were not in his organization, he was doing the same thing with gambling operations. Hogan looked out for all the top bookmakers and their gambling partners. When he heard about rogue bookies trying to set up shop, he put a quick stop to it. Interlopers were arrested immediately and either put out of business or told to get out of town.

Joe and I were gathering huge amounts of information. I kept asking Joe what we were gonna do with it. He was not sure. Joe put out feelers to connections he had in state agencies. But it was hard to know for sure who to go to. Who was on the payroll and who was not? Who could be trusted and who could not? We did not know. One thing was certain, though. If we told the wrong person, Arvil Chapman could very well end up dead and Joe's and my police careers would be over at the very minimum.

Joe said that until he could decide where we needed to go with the information we had, we would continue doing what we were doing. We knew we needed to document everything we did for evidentiary purposes and to back ourselves up if we ran into problems within the department. Joe diligently kept the necessary records.

We were working a killer schedule and so was Arvil. He was gone virtually every day from morning to night, making his trips to New York City and back to the apartment, handling and distributing the drugs, and then reporting back to us.

We continued to meet with Arvil in the Pitney Bowes parking lot at night when it was always pretty deserted. We parked in the rear of the lot with our car facing forward to detect any approaching vehicles or pedestrians.

Arvil would park around the corner and then walk to our vehicle. We always patted him down to check for a wire or weapons before he got in the car. Even though we felt we could trust him, we needed to be sure. We could not take the chance that he might be recording us for some agenda of his own. After the pat down he would get in the car and we'd talk.

Joe and I had stumbled onto something with the potential to stand the police department on its ear. But how was it going to end? The uncertainty of the situation began to take a toll on me. I never felt at ease anymore.

Even though it was exhausting and unnerving, we believed we were doing the right thing for the right reasons. Our hope was to help clean up the city, to make it a better place to live and work. Perhaps we were being naïve, but we felt we had to keep going.

The problems in Stamford were not limited to the activities of Morris, Hogan and their merry men, though. Corruption was not only happening in the police department, but in most City agencies. If you wanted a promotion in any of the city departments it was not a matter of a candidate's qualifications. It all came down to the candidate's connections. Who he knew and how much influence they had. The clout you needed for advancement could come in a couple of ways. One was through nepotism. If you were part of a family with political power, your future in local government was pretty well assured. If you lacked that kind of connection and wanted a certain position badly enough, influence could be bought for the right price.

If you felt you were denied a position or advancement unfairly, who could you complain to? There was a strong chance that the person you asked to fix the problem was actually a part of the problem.

In addition to putting in the extra time on the Arvil Chapman shift, I continued to play in a band every weekend. I had to bring in enough money to pay child support, which at that time was a hundred bucks a week, and pay my share of the apartment rent, plus food and utilities. There was also the cost of gas and maintenance for my car, and I needed poker and spending money. There was no way I could give up the band and stay afloat financially.

Every man's way seems right in his own eyes, but the Lord weighs the heart.

PROVERBS 21:2

ARVIL CHAPMAN, EARLY DAYS   LATER YEARS

8

URING THIS high stress time in my life there was one thing that provided some relief and was also a positive thing for the Stamford Police Department. We formed a band called Cops on the Beat. It was comprised of about a dozen police officers that had different musical talents. Sergeant Ken Lowman was good at doing impersonations and working an audience so he became the emcee. Some of the members did country music, while others could play and sing rock and roll and play various instruments.

The band got started by accident when Ken Lowman got a call from a local middle school that wanted to know if the department had any cops who were also musicians and would do a performance for them. Ken asked around and found there were several of us with some musical talent that were willing to participate in an all-cop band. And that was the beginning of Cops on the Beat.

We did our first performance at that middle school. The auditorium was packed with students, teachers and parents. It was standing room only. The music we played ranged from the old rock tune Duke of Earl, to county and western, and pop songs. The audience thought we were good and gave us standing ovations after almost every song. After the performance the school principal wrote a nice letter to the Stamford Advocate saying how much they enjoyed and appreciated us. He said, "The students were enthralled with Cops on the Beat."

As the word of our successful debut got out, we began getting requests from other schools. The kids were clamoring for us and we had to arrange our schedules to fit these weekly concerts. This was probably the best form of community policing I have ever seen and the media played it up big. The students came up to us after the shows and asked for our autographs.

We even played for the Mayor's Inaugural Ball where we were a big hit. It was a great opportunity to make contact with the public. That band really opened doors of communication for us. It gave us a chance to make a favorable impression on both the kids and the adults. We became so much in demand that ABC Eye Witness News out of New York City came and did a feature on us while we were performing at one of the schools.

And then, right at the height of our popularity, Ken Lowman was called into Chief Kinsella's office. Without explanation Kinsella told him to put an end to Cops on the Beat. I could not believe it and went to see Chief Kinsella myself to find out why he wanted the band to fold. His answer was curt. "Do you want to be a cop or do you want to be a musician? Take your choice because you are not gonna be both."

I was sad because the community policing aspect had really been taking off. We were building a rapport with the public, both young and old. Unfortunately, Chief Kinsella did not have the foresight to see that and he threw away a highly effective public relations tool.

I believe this was a concept that could have been used by the police force right up to the present day. As long as the talent was there and the musicians were willing to play, why not do it? The order to disband the band was one of Kinsella's poorer decisions.

———

It was decision time. After weeks of conducting our private Arvil Chapman investigation, Joe and I were ready to let other people in on the information we had amassed. We had received word from a source we trusted that private meetings could be set up with two of the police commissioners. Our source said these guys were honest and would be stunned by the amount of corruption we had uncovered. We could trust them to have our backs as things moved forward.

Commissioners were political appointments made by the mayor. Although the positions were part time and unpaid, the commissioners wielded great power. They controlled all appointments to, and promotions within, the police department. And they obviously had influence with the mayor and other City bigwigs.

Our source arranged for us to meet with commissioners Mitch Hightower and Gerry Fisher [not their real names]. We would see Hightower at midnight and Fisher ninety minutes later. Both meetings were to be held in the home of the commissioner.

We arrived at Hightower's residence a few minutes before midnight. He was fifty-something, tall and distinguished looking, and gave the impression that he was anxious to talk with us.

Joe and I told him a lot of what we knew; the nature and depth of the corruption and some of the players, including Morris and Hogan. But we held some stuff back, such as Arvil's identity. It seemed wise to not tell it all until after we saw what he did with what we told him that night. As Joe and I sat on the couch and told our story, Hightower seemed to get agitated. He paced back and forth in front of us. As he walked, he proclaimed that he would not tolerate corruption in any form and vowed to go through proper channels to make sure the problems got resolved the right way. And he promised to protect us throughout. As the meeting closed, he said he would get back to us soon.

From there we headed to Fisher's house. He was around the same age as Hightower and gave the outward appearance of being interested in what we had to say. Other than the pacing, this session was almost an instant replay of our meeting with Hightower. There was a lot of bluster and promises of action.

As a precaution in case the commissioners were not being honest with us, Joe and I used a trick that was very effective; one that I still use sometimes in my private investigator business. We gave each commissioner a different piece of information that was a lie. If the lie got back to us, we would know which commissioner had done the talking.

When we left Fisher's, Joe and I sat in the car and talked things over. We both saw it the same way. According to the commissioners, the corruption would be weeded out and those responsible held to account. When it was all over, the city would be better off and Joe and I would come out as heroes in the end.

We agreed on something else, too. Despite the assurances from our source, their words hadn't rung true. We hoped he was right and we were just being paranoid. But it turned out that was wishful thinking.

———

Ever since Arvil had first told us his story, Joe and I tried to avoid contact with Larry Hogan as much as possible. Because we could set our own work hours and to some degree knew Hogan's schedule, we were usually successful. But when we came into work two days after our meetings with the commissioners, we found a note from Hogan to Joe. It read, "Joe, I want to know what this secret investigation you and Colucci are working on is all about."

So much for our trustworthy commissioner friends. One or both had spilled the beans to somebody and the word got back to Hogan. The cat was out of the bag and our cover was blown. We had to figure out what to do and we had to do it fast.

We decided to ignore Hogan for as long as possible in order to buy some time to come up with another plan. There were more notes from Hogan that we also disregarded. As the days passed Hogan's notes got nastier and more threatening. He wanted an explanation damn soon or there would be serious consequences. We did not respond to those notes either.

After about two weeks Hogan's patience ran out. When Joe and I arrived for work around six o'clock one evening there was yet another note. But this one was not from Hogan. It was from Chief Kinsella and he did not sugar coat his message. "Officers Joseph Ligi and Vito Colucci, Jr. are directed back to uniform immediately," it read. We were disappointed, but not surprised. Hogan had warned that something was going to happen if we did not talk to him, and now it had.

Joe and I were not only back in uniform; we were assigned to different squads and had different days off. The Arvil Chapman shift we'd been running was history. Arvil himself heard about what had happened. Fearing that his own safety may have been compromised, he was making himself scarce. At that time cell phones and email were things of the future. We had a tough time keeping in contact with Arvil and figuring out a way to protect him.

We were confident that a large percentage of our fellow cops were honest and supported us. We were just as sure there were some who did not; but who and how many were unknown to us. That made it crucial that we not tell anybody that despite all the obstacles in front of us, we intended to find a way to keep the investigation going.

Joe and I had suffered a setback, but we were not beaten. We were determined that somehow, some way, we would be able to get the information out and there would be a day of reckoning.

———

Although I did not know it at the time, a very important future ally had arrived in town. In 1974 the Stamford Advocate hired a young reporter named Anthony R. Dolan. He was born in Norwalk, Connecticut in 1948 and received a BA from Yale University in 1970. The Advocate was his first job as a reporter.

Unbeknown to Hogan, Morris and others, their days of seemingly unlimited power were in jeopardy. But they would not be exposed quickly; there was a lot of work yet to be done.

Looking back, I cannot help but think of the quote from a speech by former British Prime Minister Winston Churchill. On November 10, 1942, following the British victory in Egypt he said, "Now this is not the end. It is not even the beginning of the end. But it is, perhaps, the end of the beginning."

"COPS ON THE BEAT"

BACK ROW, LEFT TO RIGHT
Tony Northern, Bruce Rosa, Vito Colucci Jr, Eugene Bell,
Ellis Crawford, John Forlivio, John Geter

FRONT ROW, LEFT TO RIGHT
Art Morrison, Ken Lowman, Ted Georgoulis, Frank Little.
A lot of fun during a bad part of my life.

9

ACK IN uniform, my sergeant assigned me to patrol the Westside, home to many of Stamford's Italian and Black citizens. It was where I grew up and he wanted to take advantage of my intimate knowledge of the territory and the people, both the good and the bad. The Westside was also home to many of the drug dealers. And organized crime figures spent a lot of time there as well. Clubs and poker rooms flourished.

On the Arvil Chapman front, we are getting good information that he was hiding from Joe and me because he was upset with Joe. He had known Joe much longer than he knew me, and he started thinking that maybe Joe had something to do with why Duke Morris and Larry Hogan were looking for him. He figured that maybe Joe did not do enough to protect him.

But Arvil did not realize that he was part of the reason Morris and Hogan were suspicious of him. When we were working the Arvil Chapman shift we told Arvil to never come around the station. That we did not want anyone to connect him with us or think he had any business at the department. But he had shown up at the station one night anyway, pounding on the back door and looking for Joe and me. He was spotted by a group of police officers and word got back to Larry Hogan. So, Arvil was partly responsible for his own problems.

Now Joe and I had to work our regular assigned shifts and afterward try to locate Arvil. And we were not having any luck. Separately we spoke with all our sources on the street to get a location on him. But no one was saying anything.

At the same time, I was becoming obsessed with all of the corruption in the city and the difficulty in finding the right person or persons to do something about it. Even after being put back in uniform for doing what I thought was right, I was not going to let it go. The poker games I played in were no longer just for pleasure and to make a few bucks. I began to use them to gather information about what was going on in the city, learning who was doing what and who with. And I started to spend more time hanging out in areas where there were more informants and people with information.

Meanwhile, organized crime was operating virtually unrestricted. It was becoming more and more open. Even some of the cops were getting more brazen in their soliciting junkets to Las Vegas arranged by top organized crime figures.

When an employee is not accountable to anyone, they have very little to worry about in the way of being disciplined. That is how the Stamford Police Department was operating at that time. The few bad cops never worried about what the rest of us knew about them. They were totally protected and had nothing to fear.

———

My friend and apartment mate Ellis Crawford transferred into the Narcotics Squad. One day Larry Hogan told Ellis to arrest a small-time bookmaker nicknamed "Ed the Head." Ed was an independent and was not connected to anybody of importance. He was the type of crook Hogan went after to show Kinsella that arrests were being made, but not hurting any of his friends in the process. Hogan told Ellis to take a uniformed officer with him. Ellis picked me.

As soon as my boss agreed to let me go, Ellis told me to change into civilian clothes. I laughed to myself because I knew that when Hogan found out I was out on the street in plain clothes making an arrest he would be furious.

We went to the areas Ed would likely be at taking numbers action, but could not locate him. I figured that since it was still early in the shift we might as well see if we could shake things up at one of the organized crime-backed bookie operations. I suggested to Ellis that we go to Sam's Corner Store, a place run by a guy named Joe "Cigar" Nelson [not his real name]. He was the connection to the mob bosses. Nelson was seldom at the store, stopping in a few times a day for a couple of minutes to handle the money. The store was in a predominantly Black area of town. The doors to the store were always locked. It could be opened by a buzzer located under the counter by the cash register. The clerk would eye you up and if you looked okay, he'd buzz you in.

I told Ellis to try to get inside the store and place a numbers bet. I would be watching through the window and if he were successful, he would rub his fingers through his hair. I had come to the door and Ellis would open it and let me inside.

Ellis got buzzed in with no problem. I watched as he talked with the clerk. After a few seconds he took some money out of his pocket, gave it to the clerk and then ran his fingers through his hair. Bingo! I was at the door in a heartbeat and Ellis opened it for me. We identified ourselves as police officers and placed the clerk under arrest. While we were confiscating his notes and logbook, he kept yelling that we must be from the Connecticut State Police. No, we were from Stamford we said. The clerk was in a state of disbelief. He said, "You can't be! You can't be from Stamford!"

At that point Ellis did not understand why the clerk was so upset about us being locals. But I knew why. Sam's Corner Store was protected, he thought. This had to be some kind of mistake.

We took the clerk and the evidence back to the station for processing. While I was doing the paperwork, the clerk was allowed to make a phone call to arrange bond. A short time later the door to the squad room opened and Larry Hogan came in. He took a look around and saw the clerk under arrest. The look on his face was a combination of shock and anger. And then our eyes met. I nodded at him and I am sure there was a smirk on my face. Hogan's face flushed in apparent rage. He yelled at the top of his lungs, "What are you trying to do, get me killed?"

Hogan's hollering quickly drew a crowd around the door to the office. Realizing what he had done, he tried to regain his composure. He lowered his voice and stammered out a couple of sentences nobody could understand. He then turned around and left the building via the back door.

After Hogan was gone, I tried to put myself inside his head. I was pretty sure he was trying to figure out how he was going to explain to his business associates that one of their outlets got taken down while it was under his protection. I felt a smile cross my face knowing that I'd helped put Hogan in an embarrassing position.

But this was just the start as far as I was concerned. I was dedicating myself to making the lives of Larry Hogan and Duke Morris as miserable as I could.

━━━━━━

Following the Sam's Corner Store bust I was even more determined to learn everything I could about Hogan and Morris, who they were connected with, who they were protecting and for how much. It became an obsession.

Working the Westside, I was already in the thick of things. I started arresting more people who thought they were immune from action by the Stamford cops. I was a law enforcement officer, after all, and there was nothing that said you had to be working in Hogan's squad in order to bust bookies or drug dealers

As I launched my one-man crusade some of the cops that were my friends started looking at me like I had lost my mind. "You're acting crazy. Just let it go," they would say.

I would smile and tell them I was not crazy. There was a method to my madness.

———

Joe and I met every few days between shifts to talk things over. We would compare notes and talk about any progress that had taken place. We both realized we were making enemies of very dangerous men. Our lives might already be in danger or could become so at any time.

And there were other non-lethal ways Hogan and Morris could get us. They could set us up at work and frame us for some misconduct that would cost us our jobs. We had to be careful not to walk into a trap of any kind. We were in a war in which carelessness could cost you dearly.

———

Also, in 1974 I experienced another life-changing event that had nothing to do with Hogan or Morris. I fell in love. It was totally unexpected and came about as a result of my attraction to poker.

I was playing lots of poker then. The games were usually held at a player's home and you could find a game almost every night of the week. The host might be a relative, a friend, a police officer; or maybe a businessman in town.

One night I was at my mother's house for a game and in walked a young lady that I was not familiar with. But I knew right away I wanted to get to know her better. She had long dark hair, a really nice body, and was very pretty. To me, she was the most beautiful girl I had ever seen. Her name was Joanne.

As the game went on, I learned that Joanne was recently divorced and that her nickname was "Pinky." She got that handle at birth when her aunt commented that Joanne was pinker than the rest of the babies in the nursery and the name stuck.

We played cards a lot after that, I made sure of it. As I saw more and more of Joanne, I decided to ask her out. She turned me down flat and I guess that made me want her even more. One of her closest friends owned a convenience store on the Westside and Pinky was a frequent visitor. Every time I saw her blue Ford Pinto parked outside the store I had to stop. I even pointed her out to my cop buddies and said, "I'm gonna marry that woman some day."

But in spite of my best efforts Pinky kept turning me down for a date. So, I came up with a plan to force the issue. If my buddies on patrol spotted her, they would pull her over and then call me on the radio. They would say they had the subject I wanted to speak with stopped at such and such a location. I would show up and say, "Are you going to go out with me or not?" After her usual no, I would threaten to keep her pulled over until she changed her mind.

I do not know if she really did not want to date me or was just playing hard to get. She finally gave in, though. And after she said yes, I do not think my feet touched the ground for a while.

I want to be clear about something. This was not a time when cops would pull women over and try to work out a deal for sex if they dropped a speeding ticket. It was a more innocent time in that regard. After all, she was already a good friend of mine and we played poker together several times a week. We live in a different time now and I would never dare try that kind of thing if I were on the job today.

On our first date we went up to Ridgefield, Connecticut to the Red Lion Restaurant. I gave her a beautiful diamond heart that night and she wears it to this day. That is how nuts I was about her.

Our whirlwind courtship lasted about three months and then we were married in August. Joanne had two girls from her previous marriage, Kimmy and Valarie Bergman, who were eight and four years old. It happened so fast that Joanne and I barely knew each other, much less each other's kids.

In fact, the only thing Joanne and I really had in common was that we were both poker players. And today when we see all those poker tournaments being played on television, we laugh because we realize we were way ahead of our time.

I really started to question what we had done when Pinky's daughters and mine met each other for the first time. We were all in the car and Joanne and I were trying to explain to them that they were now sisters. Those poor girls were totally confused and it made for an interesting conversation to say the least.

In addition to trying to get our kids to accept the situation, our living arrangements were a little awkward at the start. Joanne and the girls moved in with me and Ellis in the bachelor pad while we were looking for our own place. Her girls really did not want to be living there. They did not know me very well and did not know Ellis at all. And my girls were very shy when they came over because they did not know Joanne. While at the same time Joanne and I were trying to adjust to each other and each other's children. What a show.

In reality, we probably had no business getting married at that time. There were a lot of strikes against us. But by the grace of God, we overcame them all. We are still together after forty-nine years and still very much in love.

━━━━━━

My new marriage did not affect my work schedule, I continued to do my regular shift at the police department and play in the band on weekends. And my obsession with Hogan and Morris had not waned. If anything, it was getting stronger. I wanted to arrest anyone even remotely involved with either of them. I would conduct my surveillances and wait for the right opportunity. It did not matter to me if it was a simple motor vehicle infraction that I could turn into an arrest or something larger.

The point was that I was arresting people who were not supposed to be arrested. I was disrupting the operations of those that supposedly could not be disrupted, at least by a local cop. In my mind I was sending a message to Hogan, Morris and the rest.

Although that made me feel good, I was not delivering any knockout blows. I was only an annoyance to them. I had to do more than make nuisance arrests every so often. There had to be a way to bring the hammer down.

VITO & JOANNE, THE EARLY YEARS. NOT
MANY SMILES DURING THOSE YEARS.

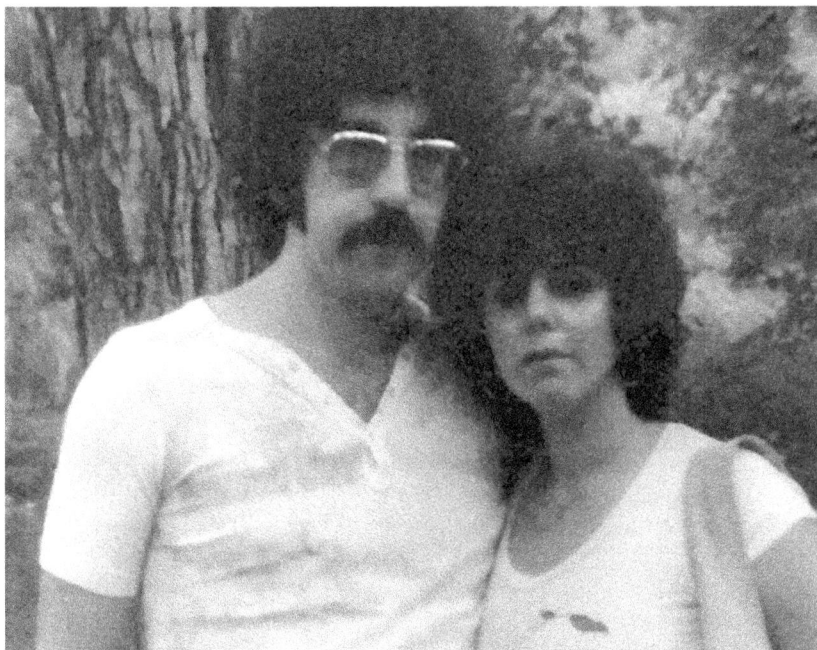

AM I CHEECH OR CHONG, KOTTER OR FREDDY FENDER

10

Ime was going by and we still did not know where Arvil
Chapman was hiding out. Joe and I were worried about
him. Our sources told us he was around, just not interested in socializing with anybody. We figured the fact that
he was alive meant Hogan and Morris did not suspect that
Arvil was our snitch. Or at least they were not sure enough
about it to silence him permanently. But they had their own
informants and the situation could change at any time. We
needed to catch up with Arvil for his own good and for
our investigation. Without him and his cooperation the
chances of us being able to deal the bad guys a fatal blow
was slim to none.

Joe eventually received a message from Arvil through one
of our street sources. He said he wanted to be left alone

until he could figure out who he could trust and what he should do. He'd reach out to us when he was ready. We sent a message back that we had not compromised him and wanted to help him.

And then we learned the rest of the story from a friend of Arvil's. Hogan and Morris indeed suspected Arvil was the rat. Duke Morris had approached him and told him he knew he was working with Joe and me. Arvil fled as Morris appeared to be reaching for his gun and had been in hiding since.

It was no wonder the guy was scared. He believed Morris wanted to kill him and had to wonder if Joe or I had sold him out. Arvil needed time to sort things out. It would be several more weeks before he decided we were on his side.

———

One day when I was talking with Joe Ligi he asked if he had ever told me the story of Cleveland Spencer. I knew who Cleveland was because Joe and I had tried to arrest him on a few occasions, but were unsuccessful.

Joe went on to tell me about an incident that took place before he and I were partners and when he was unaware that Larry Hogan was dirty. One night, Cleveland, who was a mid-level drug dealer, approached Joe and said he wanted to talk with him. They pulled onto a side road to talk. Cleveland offered to pay Joe fifteen hundred bucks a week to protect him from arrest and from the other dealers working the streets. Joe turned him down flat.

I know this seems like a lot of money. And it was, especially for the time. But the drug dealers were making huge profits. For example, we served a search warrant on two brothers that were dealing in the housing projects. During our search we found the floor plans, complete with artist renditions, for a mansion they were planning to have built in a southern state for themselves and their mother. We are talking some serious money here.

After rejecting Cleveland's offer, Joe went to Hogan and told him about the bribe attempt. Hogan told Joe he had done the right thing and that he would personally take care of it. Joe was comfortable with that, figuring he had left the matter in good hands.

Hogan was happy too. He met with Cleveland and told the drug dealer that if he wanted to stay in business and continue to enjoy good health, he would have to pay a street tax. Hogan's levy was at least the fifteen hundred a week Cleveland had offered Joe, and probably a little more. So now Cleveland was happy as well. He had purchased the protection he was looking for.

That was why our subsequent attempts to arrest Cleveland never went anywhere. Our search warrants never produced anything because Cleveland always knew we were coming and was clean by the time we got to him. Arvil Chapman later confirmed Joe's story that Cleveland was one of Hogan's flock.

It was a wild time. You could not tell the good guys from the bad guys without a score card. The whole damn town was running amok. But an agent of change was coming. And he was coming soon.

For what shall it profit a man,
if he shall gain the whole world,
and lose his own soul?

MARK 8:36

II

I T WAS a beautiful, chilly Wednesday night in the late fall of 1974. I was patrolling the Westside and thinking about the news that my wife Joanne had that day. She was pregnant and the baby was due at the end of next summer. I was excited over the good news. But I also had some reservations. We were already having financial problems. Money was tight with a new family. I was paying child support for my previous children and a new baby would just add to that burden. It was gonna be tough.

As I drove around the streets, I saw many of the regulars. There was Pepper Red and others with street names such as Cooter Red, Willie the Box, Dootsie, Blood, Shoulders, Piggy, June Bug, and The Head, Big Snake and his son Little Snake, Two-brush, Geek, Spoon, The Wig, and Skank, just to name a few.

Everyone had a nickname. I knew them all, where they lived, what their game was and who they hung with. Yeah, I knew them all and there was always someone I could go to when I was looking for information.

West Main Street was one of the more popular streets in the Westside for criminal activity. It was always hopping with music. People hung out and drug dealers did their thing. The liquor store and the pool hall were hives of activity. Many of our drug arrests took place at the pool hall.

As I drove by the pool hall that night, I spotted several guys hanging out. Among them was one of the bigger drug dealers, Harry "Ham Bone" Johnson [not his real name]. He started taunting me by mispronouncing my name as he yelled out, "Look at Carlucci, he's back in a police car." I turned the car around and pulled up to the front of the pool hall. Back in my Narcotics days, when I pulled up the dealers or drug addicts would walk away. It usually meant they were "heavy," that they were carrying drugs. What happened that night was unusual. No one took off. They all stood their ground. They figured there was no reason to be afraid of me now that I was back in uniform driving a squad car.

Ham Bone went on a rant. "Hey what happened to Carlucci? He got his ass put back in uniform. You can't do nothin' no more, Carlucci. They fixed you good. You're a nobody now." His words were riling everyone up. They pointed fingers at me and Ham Bone kept going. "I bet you wish you could just jump out of that car and grab us. But you don't know what's goin' on anymore. You got no probable cause. You got nothin.' You're washed up."

I could feel my face turning red. I was fuming. I wanted to jump out of that car so bad I could taste it. But I knew

I had to keep my cool until I could figure out a way to pop this guy.

Just as things were heating up, a black woman I knew as Sister Sarah came sauntering by. I had helped her out one time when her teenage son was causing her some problems. Before I left her home that day she said, "I just want to tell you that Jesus Christ loves you and He has a plan for your life." But at that time in my life, I was not interested in hearing anything about God. I had stopped going to church when I was thirteen or fourteen because I thought I had had enough of that God stuff. I just nodded my head at her and walked out the door.

And now here was Sister Sarah, Bible in hand, amid this group of thugs. She saw me and said, "Officer, Jesus loves you." She then looked at Ham Bone and his friends and told them God loved them too. Each and every one of them.

Ham Bone mocked Sister Sarah by looking up at the street light and saying he could see the light. He asked his buddies if they saw it too. She never said a word back to him. She just smiled and slowly walked away.

After she left Ham Bone got back to me. "Carlucci, don't you wish you knew what was in our pockets?"

I just said, "Someday, Ham Bone, some day. Mark my words." As I pulled away, I wondered if my words were just an empty threat uttered in frustration. I hoped not.

I had not gone very far when headquarters advised the Westside and Waterside units of an anonymous female reporting a man with a gun in his coat pocket. The description of the suspect was a man in a long black leather jacket, striped pants, and wearing a black "Super Fly" hat. It was Ham Bone!

I turned my car around and radioed in my location. I could hear the approaching sirens of the other cars that were on their way. But I got there first. And this time I had probable cause.

I pulled up and jumped out of my vehicle like a madman. I grabbed Ham Bone and threw him against the car. He yelled for his buddies to help him. But none of them wanted any part of the action. I went through his pockets and found a whole stash of Heroin in glassine bags with an elastic band around them. There was no gun, but it did not matter. I responded to a man with a gun call and had every right to frisk the suspect and make the arrest for the narcotics violations.

As I was cuffing Ham Bone the Waterside car arrived and handled crowd control. I put a very unhappy Ham Bone in the back seat of my car. He was kicking and screaming that it was an illegal arrest. He said he would be released right way. I told him about the report that he had a gun. He said, "But I don't have a gun."

I smiled at him and said, "Yeah. But I had to go through your pockets to see if you did."

After booking Ham Bone I went back out on the street. I was again driving up West Main when I noticed Sister Sarah walking up the street. She saw me and motioned for me to pull over. She said she had been able to see from way down the hill that something had gone down with Ham Bone after she had walked away and wanted to know what had happened.

I explained to her about the anonymous woman who had reported a man with a gun. That I had not found a gun, but I did find the Heroin. A little smirk appeared on her face. I said, "Sister Sarah, did you make that call?"

She smiled and said, "I just got out of Bible study and the Lord don't want me to lie. So don't ask any questions and I'll tell you no lies."

She then proceeded to walk away into the night, still clutching her Bible. I'll never know for sure, but I believe Sister Sarah paid me back that night for what I'd done to help her with her son's problems.

When she saw what I was in the middle of she decided to give me a hand. In my mind the anonymous caller was no longer anonymous. Thank you Sister Sarah!

———

What I began to do with any of the guys I knew were under Hogan's protection was to find a way, any way, to arrest them and bring them into the station. It was usual procedure to bring arrestees in through the back door and go straight to the booking desk to complete the paperwork and processing.

But when I busted one of Hogan's people I did it a little different. I would park my vehicle next to the detective bureau door, right near the Narcotics Squad office. I would then march my prisoner in. When we passed by the office door, I would slow down and try to catch Hogan's eye. I wanted to make sure he knew who I had arrested. On those occasions he would get pretty mad at me. Sometimes he had come to the door and say, "I'm going to get you Vito. Someday I'm going to get you." I would just smile at him and walk my prisoner to the booking area.

It probably was not very smart to antagonize a man like Hogan. But my own cockiness and my anger toward him made me exempt from the fear of retaliation. I relished in embarrassing him and tarnishing his reputation for being the "go to" guy. I had come to hate several people for their roles in the corruption that was rampant in my home town and Larry Hogan was at the top of my hit parade. Duke Morris was a close second.

As I continued my investigation, I came to realize that while Hogan and Morris may have been the worst of the bunch, they had a lot of company when it came to corruption in Stamford. Appointments to almost any City department and other prominent positions could be purchased or were given as favors to friends and relatives. Lucrative service contracts were awarded the same way. Merit meant very little. It was all about how much you were willing to pay or who you knew. If you were an average Joe without the money to grease a few palms and did not have any names to drop, you were screwed.

I went on with my private war against Hogan and Morris, arresting their protected people at every opportunity. I had a list of who I wanted to get and crossed the names off as I made the arrest. As I look back now, I was kind of like the Beatrix character played by Uma Thurman in the *Kill Bill* movies.

While all this craziness was going on I noticed an older guy sitting on a stoop opposite my grandfather's house on Liberty Street. The guy stared at me every time I stopped to see my grandfather. He would watch me as I drove down the block until I entered the house. It was the same when I left. His eyes were on me from when I backed out of the driveway until I turned off the street. This happened a half dozen times over a couple of week period. There was no doubt that he wanted to make sure I was aware of him.

One day I noticed a car in front of the house this guy was at and he was standing near its trunk. I jotted down the New York plate number. Because this was a personal thing, I didn't want to run the plate through my own department and let anyone there know what I was doing. Instead, I contacted a friend of mine in the New York City Police Department and asked him to get the data for me. My NYPD friend said the vehicle was registered to a high-ranking member of the Gambino crime family, who I'll call Salvatore Laratonda.

The next time I went to my grandfather's my daughter Melodye was with me. I saw Laratonda watching me as I pulled into the driveway. My eighty-five-year-old uncle was there and seemed to know about the crusade I was on against Hogan and Morris. I was surprised and asked him where he was getting his information. His source was none other than Salvatore Laratonda. My uncle said Laratonda was a nice guy and could not understand why I was causing so many problems. I shot back, "He's a gangster. Stay away from him, he's no good!"

I left the house and as I was backing out of the driveway, through my rear-view mirror I could see Laratonda sitting on the stoop. He always watched me drive away, but this time he got up and went into the house before I got out to the street. That is odd, I thought.

I stopped at the end of the driveway to check for traffic and the next thing I knew, Duke Morris was standing next to my door. As previously described, that was the day I thought I was going to die. I know in my heart that Melodye's presence saved my life. Morris would had to have killed both of us and he did not want the blood of a child on his hands.

As I drove home with Melodye, I realized that Laratonda got up and walked into the house to signal Morris that I was on my way out. That gave Morris time to come out from wherever he was hiding and move in for the kill.

A few days later, as I was coming out of headquarters, I found a typed note under one of my wiper blades. It read, "You are lucky that you had that little girl with you the other day."

I was furious! I drove directly over to see Laratonda. He was in his usual spot on the stoop. I leapt out of the car and yelled, "Are you looking for me, Laratonda? I'm here now without my daughter. If you want to do something to me this is your chance. Or do you need your buddy with you?"

The bastard stayed as cool as a cucumber. He just smiled at me and said, "In due time. In due time"

That should have scared me, but it only made me angrier.

The Lord is my light and my salvation; whom shall I fear? The Lord is the strength of my life; of whom shall I be afraid?

PSALM 27:1

12

I HAD SOME problems. The Mob was after me and my second marriage was in danger of failing for several reasons. There were the long hours away from home, financial struggles, and Joanne and I and our four daughters were still trying to get used to each other.

On top of that, I could not even find any peace at work. Larry Hogan, Duke Morris, and who knew how many others in the department, would have loved to have me out of the way. How many people go to work and find written threats left on their car's windshield? I did. And right in the police department parking lot, of all places.

Off the job, I would book the band for dinner dances and parties a year or two in advance and wonder if I would be around to play them. I walked the dog late at night with my gun tucked in my pants pocket and watched every car that drove by, wondering which one might have someone inside that wanted to kill me. Where could I turn? What could I do? Everything was starting to get to me.

I was sitting in my squad car contemplating all of this when I remembered a case that Joe Ligi and I worked on together in 1973. Joseph Pellicci was a partner in a popular Stamford restaurant whose clientele included such celebrities as Joe Dimaggio, Tony Bennett, Howard Cosell, Nancy Sinatra, Danny Glover and Walter Cronkite. Pellicci disappeared from Stamford on February 4, 1973.

On that morning Pellicci telephoned his children from his mother's Stamford home to tell them he was on his way to pick them up to go bowling. He left his mother's at around eleven o'clock and then got into the red Pontiac he had borrowed from his sister and drove away. The car was later discovered a block from the house, with no evidence inside the vehicle to indicate there had been foul play.

There was no further sign of Joe Pellicci until March 2, when his body was found across the state line in North Salem, New York. It was wrapped in a blanket and the hands were tied with a cord. He had been shot twice in the head and once in the torso.

Police from New York launched an investigation and so did my department. The whole Special Services Squad was assigned to the case. Joe Ligi and I jumped right in with both feet. We not only knew Pellicci from the restaurant, but Joe had grown up with him right from grammar school.

Progress was quick. A witness came forward with information on a possible suspect vehicle. A partial identification was made based on the initials on the license plate of the car. And an examination of the blanket and cord linked them to that same individual. We were confident that an arrest warrant was imminent.

Unaware at that time of who Hogan really was, Joe and I told him that we needed to go out of state for a few days to obtain the final information that would put the case over the top. Hogan looked at Joe and said, "I'm taking over the case now, you guys go back to working narcotics cases."

We were stunned, to say the least. We were almost at the end of the investigation and felt we were so close, but were not allowed to see it to completion. I remember Joe and me going to lunch totally confused about what had just taken place. After talking it over we concluded that Hogan wanted the collar for himself. He wanted the glory of solving a major murder case, and he would get it from this one.

As I thought about the Pellicci case it hit me. Hogan had been presented with a case that was relatively easy to solve, yet there still had not been an arrest. Joe and I had been wrong. Hogan had not taken over the investigation for the glory it could bring him. He took the case over because he wanted to make it go away.

My God, I thought. Not only was Hogan running the drug and gambling activities, but he was compromising a murder investigation.

The Pellicci case was lost in that era of corruption and incompetence. Under Hogan's control the investigation was botched beyond repair. Evidence was lost, leads were not pursued and witnesses were threatened. In one glaring example, dog hairs were found on the victim, the blanket that covered him, and in the suspect's car. Incredibly, they were not retrieved.

A search warrant was never executed on the suspect's vehicle. He washed it at home not long after the murder; and the following day drove it through a car wash with the windows down.

Now, nearly forty years later, the Pellicci family still does not have closure or justice for the death of their family member. The main suspect is still walking the streets of Stamford to this day. And the police have never publicly identified him.

He lies in wait near the villages; from ambush he murders the innocent, watching in secret for his victims.

PSALM 10: 8 NIV

13

As I was riding in the squad car one day, I got a message to report to headquarters to meet with Lieutenant Considine. When I got to his office we exchanged pleasantries, and then he brought up the shootout. Whenever we got together the shootout always got at least a brief mention. Considine was very firm in his belief that the incident had formed a strong bond between us. He was right and neither of us ever forgot it.

But Considine did not want to see me just to talk about the past. He told me there was a transfer in the works for me. It involved me being assigned to the Stamford train station, which at that time was pretty run down and in need of work. He told me there were a lot of car break-ins going on and things were being stolen, particularly CB radios. At that time everyone wanted to talk on a CB and if you had one in your vehicle you were a target. In addition, several assaults and muggings had taken place in the area and Considine said we needed to get things under control.

He outlined the hours for me. One week I would work nine to five; the next would be four to midnight. I would mostly be working plain clothes, but would be in uniform on occasion. He explained that seeing a cop in uniform would be a deterrent to the criminals and make the commuters feel safer.

Considine also said he was assigning his son Mike to work with me. Mike was working as a Special Police Officer at the time and was trying to get hired by the Darien Police Department. His father thought it would be a good idea for Mike to get some solid experience under his belt. And he trusted me to teach Mike what I had learned about working the streets. Special Police had full arrest powers and I had no problem teaming up with Mike. I was honored that the Lieutenant had enough confidence in me to place his son in my hands.

I started my new assignment on the day shift the following week. Mike met me at the station and I showed him the ins and outs of the railroad station and where the crimes were being committed. We decided that sometimes we would work together and other times we would go solo. But even then, we would always be just a walkie-talkie call away.

I was excited about this new assignment because it allowed me to work on a regular shift. I would always know exactly what time I would be finished so I could then work on my personal Larry Hogan investigation. It gave me so much more flexibility and allowed me to be in plain clothes most of the time. I had always hated being in a uniform. Right from the beginning I hated putting on a uniform. I much preferred plain clothes detective-style work. So, I felt this was a great opportunity for me.

Very quickly Mike and I started making plenty of arrests and curtailing the number of crimes that were taking place around the station. We watched the cars that came and went, got their plate numbers, and monitored their activities. Many times, they would pull right up to a parked car with a CB antenna, smash in the window and pull out the CB radio. We arrested a lot of them right in the act. Once Mike and I got in gear there were very few incidents that got past us. Lieutenant Considine was very pleased. The chief was happy. And so were the city fathers and the citizens.

In addition to assaults and thefts, there was also the problem of gay men having sex in the stalls in the rest rooms. As this was the 1970s, the gay movement was still very much undercover so to speak. There was not the openness that there is now. Everyone was afraid of someone finding out that they were gay. At that time, they knew such a disclosure would seriously hurt their reputation. Somehow, the railroad station had become the place to meet someone for a quickie. It had reached the point that people started complaining that they did not want to use the men's room.

We noticed a City of Stamford vehicle being driven by a city official pull in on a regular basis. He was an older fellow—probably in his late fifties—who I will call Vinny Antonelli. We started paying attention to what he was doing. He always went into the men's room and would be in there quite a while. We began to wonder why Antonelli was such a frequent visitor to the station and spent so much time in the rest room. We decided to find out.

One day when Antonelli stopped in we waited a few minutes and then pushed open the bathroom door. This was an old heavy metal door that squeaked violently when it was opened. Once inside you were facing the end of the stalls and up around the corner were the urinals. Antonelli and another man were each standing in front of their own urinals. I went into a stall for a few minutes and then left.

Although Antonelli had not been doing anything wrong that time, Mike and I were convinced his frequent visits to the station and the men's room were for gay sex. Nothing else made sense. We tried to catch him a few more times and it was the same thing—Antonelli and another man standing in front of their respective urinals. His conduct was suspicious, but not criminal. Mike and I were determined to nab Antonelli, though. But how were we going to catch him?

One day when Antonelli was there, we were outside the station and noticed a very small window about twenty feet off the ground. We figured it might look into the men's room. The window was cracked open a bit, so Mike agreed to climb up and peek inside. Stacking up trash cans to make a ladder, Mike got up to the window. Bingo! Antonelli was on his knees performing oral sex on a young man who looked to be in his twenties. We now had the probable cause to make an arrest.

Mike climbed down and we went inside. Alerted by the sound of the door being opened, by the time we got fully into the men's room Antonelli and his companion were in the usual positions in front of the urinals. To a casual observer they were just taking a leak. But now we knew better.

I told Antonelli that we had been watching him come and go on several occasions, and that he had been observed performing oral sex on the other man. I pointed out the window through which Mike had observed the sex act. We placed both men under arrest, cuffed them and took them to headquarters. One of the captains told us we had done good work and they would handle the paperwork so Mike and I could get back on the street.

I went home that night feeling good about the arrests. But when I got into work the next day, I found out that Antonelli and the other guy had been cut loose! I was really upset and started asking questions. In addition to Antonelli being a powerful guy in the city, the younger man was a Stamford middle school teacher and he was scared that he could lose his job.

The captain told me that he had to let them go because people in City government were afraid that if Antonelli's conduct became public it might look bad for all the officials. Reputations and careers would be damaged. Parents of students at the school where the younger man taught might be concerned about having him mentor their children. The powers that be had decided this was not the time to have such potentially explosive allegations get out to the public. He assured me both men had been read the riot act before they were let go. He was confident they would go forward and not sin again.

What the hell was going on here? I could not believe these guys were not charged with anything. They just let them walk.

Although I was furious, I still had to continue to train Mike. I did not want him to be too discouraged before he got into the police department, so I did not tell him how angry I was. But I did tell him about some of the corruption that was going on. I did not tell him the extent or just how big it was getting, though.

A few days later Mike and I are standing in the station when one of the big commuter trains was pulling in. I was in uniform that day and wanted to be visible to the commuters. All of a sudden, a man in a Botany 500 suit, carrying a briefcase and a New York Times, ran out of the men's room and up to me. He was completely flustered, sweating and shaking all over.

Excitedly he said, "Officer, Officer, I just walked in the bathroom and a man asked me how I was doing today. I said I could be better, and then went into a stall and began to read my newspaper. Within a minute a penis came through a hole in the partition of the neighboring stall [gays made holes in the partitions so that oral sex could be performed or just to peek at someone in the next stall].

Holding back my laughter, I asked him, "Well, what did you do about it?"

He caught his breath, held up his tightly rolled newspaper and said, "I kept hitting it with my New York Times!"

I do not know to this day how Mike and I kept our cool and did not burst out laughing in the guy's face. I told him that we would take care of it and he hurriedly walked away. I did not tell him that in those days the code words to show that you were interested in gay sex were "I could be better." By the time we got to the men's room there was no one in the stalls.

It was times like this that brought some levity into my life. Over all these years, whenever I remember this story, I cannot help but laugh or smile.

———

Working the railroad station with Mike continued to be fun. It gave me someone to talk with about sports and the daily goings on. And we caught a lot of crooks, which was always a plus. I taught Mike everything I could about being a good cop and anything else I thought would help him when he got on the force. I liked his father very much. Lieutenant Considine was always a straight shooter as far as I am concerned and I wanted to do right by him.

Another area of police work began popping up around the station. It was prostitution. Girls of the night were hanging out and soliciting men whenever they could. I decided that Mike might be good bait for some of these girls. I had him get into his Volkswagen Karmann Ghia and drive by them. I told him what to say, how to act and what to do if one of them waved him down. I watched from a distance because many of the girls knew me.

When a girl got in the car, I gave her a few minutes to proposition Mike. If she did, Mike would give me a sign out his car window for me to move in. When I saw the signal, I'd pull up to Mike's car and place the girl under arrest. We did this routine for quite a while with good results.

One night Lieutenant Considine showed up at the railroad station. He got out of his car and Mike and I walked over to meet him. I could tell from his demeanor that he was upset. He said," Vito, what are you doing with Mike. You're all over town and your post is here in this railroad station."

I answered, "Lieutenant, we are here ninety percent of the time. We leave during lunch time to see if we can make a prostitution arrest. We are still doing good work here, and during lunch I try to give Mike more experience that will make him a better street cop."

The Lieutenant stared at me for a while and then shook his head. Mike broke in and said, "Dad, this is working out great for me. Vito is teaching me an awful lot about police work and I'm getting so much on the job training under my belt for when I start as a cop in Darien."

Considine thought things over for a few seconds and then said, "Fine. But from now on make sure you spend ninety-nine percent of your time here inside the station."

We made a lot of good arrests at the railroad station, many of them for vehicle break-ins. Word got around town that the cops assigned there were serious about doing their jobs. There was a large drop in the number of auto break-ins and other crimes. I was thankful for the twenty-six months I had that post.

And although they did not happen right in the station, the prostitution arrests worked out especially well for me because several of the girls were friends of Duke Morris. He supplied them with drugs in return for sexual favors. Once they found out I was willing to do things for them like calling lawyers or bondsmen, and they thought I could help them out, they were ready to give up what they knew about Morris. I was filling up pad after pad of information on him.

VITO & MIKE CONSIDINE, PLAIN CLOTHES
DETAIL AT STAMFORD RAILROAD STATION.

MIKE WENT ON TO BE A LIEUTENANT WITH
THE DARIEN, CT. POLICE DEPARTMENT.

When the girls were cooperative, I always let them go on a Promise to Appear, where they didn't have to put up any bond money. And after they gave me the information, they knew I would not hit them again. If another officer picked them up, that was out of my hands

All the arrests helped me in another way as well. I was getting lots of extra days off from my sergeants and lieutenants as perks for my performance. That gave me more opportunities to pursue my Morris and Hogan investigations. I had page after page of notes that I still was not sure what I was going to do with. But they knew I was still building up evidence against them. And they had to think it did not bode well for them.

———

One evening when I was working at the railroad station alone, I was in one corner of the building and happened to glance across to the opposite corner. The hair on the back of my neck rose as I saw Duke Morris standing there watching me. As our eyes locked it reminded me of an old-fashioned gun fight that you would see in a Western movie. The two potential combatants glaring at each other and looking for a sign of what their opponent planned to do next.

I was not about to let him get the drop on me again, as he almost did that January day outside my grandfather's house. I put my hand inside my coat and onto the clip where I carried my .357. I kept my hand on the butt of the gun, ready to draw if I felt threatened. Morris had his hands in his pockets.

As Morris started walking toward me, I scanned the area to make sure he had not brought any of his friends with him. He had not. It was just him and me. As he got closer, he took his hands out of his pocket and waved them at me to show me he was not holding a weapon. He said, "Hey Carlucci, can we talk?" I told him we could if I could see both of his hands at all times. He agreed and put his hands to his sides.

He said he wanted me to know there were no hard feelings from the past. I found that laughable and could not help but chuckle. He then said he wanted to tell me a little about his life. I could not figure out where he was going with this. I told him, "I'm not interested in hearing about your life. You were out to kill me, remember? And that's all I need to know."

He ignored my comment and continued talking. "A lot of things have been happening. I want you to know that I personally do not have any hard feelings against you. Let me tell you what the department has done to me right from the time I started the job until now."

He went on about how there were very few colored officers when he started. The ranking officers used his race and knowledge of the neighborhoods and the streets by sending him into areas other cops could not penetrate. There were many times he was assigned to watch and arrest people that were his personal friends or even relatives. And when he told them the guy was an uncle, a cousin or a friend, they didn't care. Morris felt he was being used and resented being forced to do things he did not want to do. He wanted me to know this so that maybe I'd understand why he started doing the things he was doing. I did not accept his story as a reason to become the very thing he had taken an oath to fight, though.

When Morris finished talking, he said he was boarding a train and leaving. I did not know what he was trying to say. I asked him, "What do you mean, are you gonna go cop something?" At the time that was a street term for buying drugs.

He said, "No. I just want you to know that I am here to take a train and not here to bother you."

I said, "Let me ask you something. What was supposed to happen that day on Liberty Street?"

He said, "You were as close as you probably could come to buying the farm. You gotta realize that I had to do what I had to do. The streets are bad, the department is bad, so you get bad with them. You don't have to worry about me anymore because I'm not gonna be around. But you still better be lookin' over your shoulder because it ain't over yet."

I watched him until he got on the train and it pulled out of the station. It was headed for Grand Central Station in New York City. I never saw Duke Morris again after that night. But I know he spent some time in New York and did a stretch in prison there on a drug conviction. A few years later I heard he was killed in a shootout with rival drug dealers somewhere down South.

There was no official word about why Morris unexpectedly left Stamford. But the gossip around the department was that he felt the walls were closing in and decided it was time to look for greener pastures elsewhere. If true, then maybe I had something to do with his decision. The main thing was that Morris was gone, and that was a victory for me and Stamford.

But his final words to me were true. It was not over yet. There was still Larry Hogan and his people as well as all the corruption going on in other City departments. No, it was far from over. I needed an ally I could trust to help me expose all the dirty secrets. Little did I know that I would soon be dropping dimes into a payphone to give Anthony Dolan, the new reporter at the Stamford Advocate, information on the cesspool Stamford had become. And once he got going, his aggressive reporting would result in his receiving a Pulitzer Prize.

14

THE RAILROAD station job ended and I was back in uniform, back to driving a squad car. I know it is a part of every police officer's job during their career, but I hated it. After having full reign at the railroad station for over two years, wearing plain clothes with mutton chops on my face and side burns that met my mustache, I now found myself literally ducking in hallways to avoid Chief Kinsella, who frowned on any type of facial hair while wearing a uniform.

My life was like a spinning wheel at that moment. I was obsessed with continuing my investigation of Hogan and all the other corruption that was running rife in Stamford. My still fairly new marriage was rocky, which left me vulnerable if I ran into my ex-girlfriend Donna again. And sure enough, one day when I was in a convenience store, I ran into her. I had not seen or been in touch with her since the whole thing with Chief Kinsella and Donna's mother. She let me know she was available and gave me her phone number. Just like that I was back in the middle of the same affair that I walked away from years earlier.

I had not had much contact with other cops while I was assigned to the railroad station. During that time, I only went to headquarters when we made an arrest. We would just bring the subject in the room, do the paper work, book him and leave. I never had to see the brass, which was fine with me.

Now that I was back on the street, I started interacting with my colleagues again. Talking with them made it obvious to me how much the morale in the department had deteriorated. There was a lot of complaining and talk about a series of news articles written by the new reporter at the Advocate, Anthony Dolan. He was taking on the issue of corruption in various City departments, but so far none had focused on the police.

With a few exceptions, the cops were excited about what they were reading. But they were also skeptical that the stories would result in anything being done. Comments like, "Nothing is ever going to change here, things are too entrenched for that. Nothing will come of this," were common. And there was disappointment that the many problems within our department had not even been mentioned.

I had different thoughts, though. With all the mounds of hand written notes I had accumulated, I had hopes that Dolan's stories would eventually get around to the police department. I decided to find out who this Dolan guy was and what made him tick. I picked up back editions of the paper to read his articles and did other research as well.

I learned that Anthony Dolan had been a "right wing" protest singer at Yale University in Connecticut. He played the banjo and guitar, and was a song writer. He was quite the right-wing activist of that era. When he completed Yale, he spent some time as a lounge singer in New York City. After that he spent a couple of years as a press secretary and campaign consultant for right wing politicians such as Jesse Helms and James Buckley. And he began to hang around the press rooms of Trenton, New Jersey, where he realized that deep in his heart, he wanted to be a reporter.

He began his career in the newspaper business as a cub reporter for a small paper in Westchester County, New York. After a short stint there, he was hired by the Stamford Advocate. So Dolan moved back to Connecticut, a move that would have a profound impact on his life and on Stamford itself.

At that time Stamford had a population of approximately a hundred and ten thousand people. The Advocate's circulation was about thirty thousand copies, which was considered a small-time local newspaper. But Stamford was trying to become a major commuter city. It was growing quickly, not only in its size, but also in its tax base and importance as a business center. Two large companies, Olin and Xerox had moved their corporate headquarters there. Throughout the seventies, the Stamford area became home to many Fortune 500 corporations.

I was excited about what Dolan was doing and what he was saying about Stamford. Would this reporter who was the same age as me, and had ridden into town on his white horse, be able to change the political landscape of this City?

I decided to take a chance that he could and that I would help him. I blew the dust off my notes and got ready to reach out to Anthony Dolan. Little did I know that this would be the beginning of something so big that it is still talked about today as a turning point in the history of Stamford.

━━━━━

When I had researched Anthony Dolan, I put all his articles in order by the date they appeared in the paper. The first story he had written made it right to the front page. It was a farewell tribute to a fellow by the name of Ed Connell. Connell had just retired as the Superintendent of Parks after 22 years. He alleged that the appointment of his replacement had been fixed. The replacement, Eugene Berube, a high school dropout with powerful political connections, was far less qualified than other candidates, according to Connell.

In his interview with Dolan, Connell said that the fix was in with the Park's Commission. The selection of the incoming superintendent had been rigged. The former super-intendent was upset that with such an impressive list of applicants from all over the county to choose from, some of whom had graduate degrees, Berube had been selected without considering any of the other candidates. Based on his writing, it was obvious to me that Dolan took these alle-gations seriously.

As I read the Connell story, I knew the powers to be in Stamford could not have been jumping for joy when they saw it. The Watergate scandal involving President Nixon was raging in Washington at the time. That type of investigative journalism was okay there, but it was unheard of in Stamford. Rather than just reading about local sports and seeing ads about the price of oranges, the City's residents were now being exposed to truths that might be hard to take. Dolan's type of reporting was bound to arouse the citizens and ruffle feathers in the halls of power.

But that did not deter Anthony Dolan. For almost a year he wrote numerous stories on the Berube controversy. He was able to show that Berube racked up thousands of dollars in questionable bills that the city paid for vehicle maintenance. And Connell continued his claims of corruption, stating that the Personnel Commission acted illegally and unethically in permitting Berube to take the examination for Superintendent of Parks. He pointed out that the job requirements clearly specified that a college degree was necessary in order to take the exam.

An investigation by the Advocate determined that the examination qualifications as issued by the Personnel Director, listed under education: "Graduation from college with a major course of study in horticulture, forestry, civil engineering, landscape architecture, or park planning and management."

Connell said that there were several local people that were otherwise qualified that did not apply for the exam because of the supposed college degree requirement. Yet Berube, lacking even a high school diploma, was allowed to take the test, and be appointed to the position.

Dolan followed the Berube affair and exposed a corrupt civil service system in which people got City jobs based on friendships and political ties. That way, if you wanted to put your hand in the till, your friends would not tell. Eventually, Berube was ousted, as was the Personnel Director and the Chairman of the Personnel and Parks Commissions.

It seemed to me that Anthony Dolan was just the guy I had been looking for. He was tenacious and had guts. The next thing was to contact him and see if he was interested in what I had to say.

———

My initial reaching out to Anthony Dolan did not go so well. I obtained the phone number for the news room at the *Advocate*. I prepped for what seemed like twenty-four hours before I made the actual call to him. *What was I going to say if he answered? What would I say if another reporter answered?*

I made notes on a piece of scrap paper: "corruption in the Stamford Police Dept. Lt. Larry Hogan, Sgt. Duke Morris, and possibly other officers." I also wrote down ties to organized crime. When I felt I was good to go I found a pay telephone booth to use, and then prepped myself yet again before I reached for the phone. Although I had been involved in a major shoot-out, the thought of making that call scared me to death. Here I was, a young guy about to give big time information to a reporter that I did not even know.

I was nervous and sweating as I dialed Dolan's number and had to leave the phone booth's door open to get some air. After a couple of rings, a man's voice said, "Dolan."

My words just started tumbling out. I remember saying something like, "You gotta look into the police department. When are you gonna look into the police department? Bad stuff is goin' on in the police department."

I heard Dolan ask, "Who is this? What bad stuff? What's your name?"

I hung up the phone abruptly without answering. As I thought things over, I realized I had not said anything about what I had put in my notes. I had given Dolan nothing— no names, no organized crime link, nothing. *Great going, Vito. You really busted this thing wide open, didn't you?*

———

Even though my first attempt to speak with Dolan had failed, I could sense the tide was starting to turn. After being exposed to his stories for a few months, the police officers were beginning to have respect for him and his work. The term heard around headquarters when talking about investigative reporters was Woodward, Bernstein and Dolan. I thought that was a pretty high honor for Dolan to be mentioned in the same breath as the Watergate reporters.

The many honest and hardworking cops in the department were guys who just wanted a fair shake. Many of them began to suggest that I should go to Dolan and give him any information I had gathered while on the Narcotics Squad. They did not even really have any idea of how much I knew. They just figured I knew something. On the other hand, there were a few of my colleagues that did not like me. And they would do anything they could to keep me from rocking the boat.

Some of the cops who suggested I contact Dolan had information of their own about the unethical and illegal activities going on in the police department. Several of them asked if they could give me the information to pass along to Dolan for them. A few even mistakenly thought I had already given Dolan information. I did not tell them that my one attempt to reach out to him had ended in failure and that I still couldn't quite bring myself to give my own information to him. And I sure did not want to be the liaison between the police officers and the Advocate. I did not need to take on that burden.

Instead, my answer to all of them was, "Call him yourself. Pick up the phone and call him anonymously. Or if you feel comfortable with it, use your own name, and give him the information that you have."

Not everyone was happy with Dolan, though. One night as he was leaving work, he found a large chunk of concrete had been thrown through his car window. Someone let him know that they knew who he was, what he drove and where he parked. The message was that if they knew where to find his car, they could find him, too.

Despite that, Dolan kept writing and the people of Stamford took notice. Many became angry about what was going on in their town and gradually began to take a stand. Ed Connell, who had triggered the whole civil service scandal with his allegations, spoke of the city being dominated by an out-of-control political machine.

Others joined Connell in speaking out. A Board of Representatives meeting turned contentious when a representative by the name of Leonard Hoffman said the Civil Service scandal was only the tip of the iceberg. That was the first time that phrase was uttered. But as more corruption was exposed it would be repeated again and again.

At long last, the good guys were beginning to rise up. Municipal workers and other citizens with important information now had someone that would listen to them. They started calling Anthony Dolan. The calls were only a trickle at first, but they caused cracks in the dam. The trickle would eventually become a torrent that would bring the whole dam down.

Even though most of the cops liked what Dolan was doing, they remained skeptical, fearing that the public's upset would prove to be only a tempest that would run its course and fade away with no long-term effects. And who could blame them for thinking that way? According to Ed Connell, Dolan and those who supported him were fighting an uphill battle against a powerful machine. That power made them dangerous and they would not go down without a fight. I remember a comment one cop made about Dolan, "This dude's gonna wind up dead."

One night as I was in the locker room getting ready for a midnight shift, an officer named Eddie "Hickey" Miller was at his locker opposite mine. Miller had the reputation of being a drug user. One of the other cops walked up to Miller and said, "Hey Eddie, get the crap off of your mustache."

I turned around to see white powder on top of Miller's black mustache. Miller got nervous and vigorously wiped the hair above his lip. I thought, *Here's a cop reporting for work totally stoned, and he's going out on the road to protect the people and enforce the law.*

At line-up I was assigned to patrol the Westside. I paid particular attention to where Miller would be working. He drew the Waterside area, which meant that I would be his backup car and he would be mine. On this particular night we were both one-man units.

As fate would have it, I got a call to go to a housing project where a father was having an altercation with his teenage son. Miller was told to back me up. When I got to the fifth-floor apartment, the father was trying to hit the teen with his belt. The boy was fending off the blows and screaming obscenities at his father. A group of tenants had formed outside the apartment door, attracted by the commotion.

Miller arrived shortly afterward. He had apparently been at the building before because some of the crowd seemed to know him and spoke to him. Miller and I separated the combatants and it looked as though things were calming down. But suddenly, the father lunged at his son again, swinging the belt. The buckle struck the boy in the head. I grabbed the father and in the struggle we both ended up on the floor. The man's wife was standing there screaming, "Arrest him! Arrest the son-of-a-bitch!"

I was getting the better of the father, but I could not quite get the cuffs on him. I looked up at Miller for help. He just stood there watching. He said nothing and did nothing to assist me. He just stood there like a statue.

I was finally able to subdue the father and get him cuffed. I was furious with Miller, but did not want to get into it with him right then. I took the father downstairs to my car and drove to the station to book him. Miller went back to his patrol zone.

When I pulled into headquarters, I saw my sergeant at the booking desk. I told him, "Don't ever put that son-of-a-bitch with me again. He did nothing but stand there while I was wrestling with the suspect. *He's worthless and he's gonna get somebody hurt.*"

Not long afterward I found out that the higher-ups knew about Miller and his drug habit. On one occasion prior to the incident with me he had been found in a semi-conscious state in his patrol car. The department failed to take any action at that time. Despite lab tests that showed illegal drugs in his urine, he remained on active duty. They wanted to take care of the Miller situation in-house and did not even let the police commissioners know about the problem. It was kept quiet until Dolan caught wind of it and wrote about it in the *Advocate*.

A few months later, my old partner Joe Ligi was sent on a call to Eddie Miller's address. Ligi was met there by Lieutenant Considine, our former boss. When they arrived, they found Eddie Miller lying dead on the floor from a drug overdose. Maybe if the police department had done what they should have done with Miller and not tried to cover it up, he would still be alive. Had they gotten him the help he needed, it may not have ended like it did. Even though I did not like him, no cop really wants to see another cop die.

While I was on patrol one day, I heard headquarters order another officer to pick up some people and drop them off at Chief Kinsella's house. That made me think back to the spring of 1971, when I was told by my lieutenant to go to Rowayton, a town about fifteen minutes from Stamford, to pick up an individual by the name of Horace McMahon. I knew an actor by that name had appeared in the Naked City television series that aired on ABC from 1958 to 1963. I asked if this was the same guy. It was. I was to transport him to a function he was attending in Stamford.

I asked the lieutenant if we were running a taxi service. He said the assignment was a direct order from Kinsella. He told me to shut up and do as I was told. That meant that my entire post on the Westside of Stamford would be unprotected while I chauffeured the star to his event.

When I got to McMahon's house, I noticed several really nice-looking cars in the driveway. I asked if they were all his vehicles. They were. I found it incredible that the citizens and taxpayers of Stamford's Westside were left without police service because I had to provide transportation for a guy with a whole fleet of cars sitting in his driveway.

A similar thing took place on a Sunday morning. I was told by my sergeant to pick up the Sunday editions of several different newspapers and bring them to Kinsella's house. Again, I was being ordered to leave my patrol area unprotected while I went to the store and then travelled all the way across town to bring Kinsella something to read while he had his morning coffee. When I questioned the order, the sergeant said, "The Chief wants his newspapers as soon as possible. Stop arguing and get moving."

That is what happens when your Chief of Police is a former post office employee with no clue of what police work is really all about. That lack of understanding was evident during Kinsella's entire tenure. But even with all his political connections, Kinsella would not be able to survive the coming tide of reform that would wash over the city.

15

WHILE THE world was getting caught up in Disco Fever
and Saturday Night Fever, Stamford was getting a case
of Anthony Dolan fever. Dolan was playing an increasingly important role in what was happening in Stamford.
The city was now immersed in the Gene Berube case. Every
place you went people were talking about Dolan and his
articles. They either loved him for what he was exposing,
or hated him because he was shining the light on the activities of them and their cronies. There was no middle ground.

And I had finally become a contributor to Dolan. On
my second attempt to reach out to him I did not panic and
hang up and I gave him a tip that he could follow up on.
The conversation was brief and I did not identify myself.
In fact, during all the calls that followed I remained anon-

ymous. Although my information played a key role in his investigative reporting, Anthony Dolan did not find out who I was until much later.

When I went into a diner for breakfast or lunch, I could always hear the other patrons, waitresses or counter help chatting about the latest outrage to come to light. The vast majority of the comments I heard about Dolan's stories were positive. And unlike me and the other cops or municipal employees, these were mostly people with no personal experience or knowledge about what went on in City government. They were just common folks that were shocked and sometimes outraged by what they were reading.

And Dolan's pieces were all on the front page above the fold. When Linda Blair, the noted actress from The Exorcist with connections to Stamford, was arrested on major drug charges, the initial and subsequent stories were relegated to the bottom of page one or an inside page. Dolan's stuff had top billing.

Anthony Dolan had another side that I came to love: he was doing a Vito Colucci. What I mean is that like me at the police department, he was doing more mundane things at the Advocate as well as conducting his corruption investigations on his own time. He covered such things as Rotary Club meetings and concerts, and then worked on his investigations, sometimes into the wee hours of the morning.

That is how he handled the Berube story. In the beginning, his bosses at the newspaper were not overly thrilled about getting into the corruption stuff. They did not know how their readers would respond and they were also concerned that there could be libel suits filed against them. To slow Dolan down, they tried to fill his time with less controversial assignments that posed little or no risk to the newspaper. But as reader interest in Dolan's investigative reporting intensified and circulation grew, that attitude changed. The decision makers came to realize that these were the stories that were selling papers and they needed to embrace them. Dolan's skill and aggressiveness paid off and earned him front page status.

———

The Berube story was one that had legs, as they say. Applicants that had not been allowed to take the exam for the Superintendent of Parks position, or were skipped over even though they were better qualified than Berube, hired lawyers to see if they had grounds for legal action against the City. And Connell voiced his opinion that eliminating the written test for the job and relying only on an oral interview was highly unusual.

During his investigation, Dolan learned the names of the three out-of-town men who had conducted the oral examinations of the candidates. He placed calls to them, not really expecting they would actually talk to him or agree to answer his questions. To his surprise, they each opted to speak to him on the record. All three said they had not ranked Berube among the top three candidates. Accordingly, he should not have been appointed to the position. When the Advocate ran that story it sent shock waves throughout City government. The citizens of Stamford were learning that City jobs were being given to political cronies or to friends and relatives of those with connections.

As the story continued to unfold, the buzz grew and the number of people passing information to Dolan increased daily. He must have wondered whether working two shifts a day would be enough.

Even though the Berube story did not involve the police department, it was still an exciting time for me. I didn't know then if it was all there would be or if Dolan would continue and act on some of the tips I'd given him. It turned out that Berube was only the beginning. As time went by, that initial scandal that had seemed like a blockbuster at the time, would be small potatoes compared to what was yet to come.

———

When Anthony Dolan first started work at the Advocate, the Watergate scandal was just breaking. The young reporter was not a believer in the Watergate or other corruption stories then. He thought they were mostly media hype— more smoke than fire. At the outset he believed President Nixon was innocent.

But as he did his own investigating into what was going on in Stamford, that attitude began to fade. He learned "first-hand" that not all public officials were honest. Some were hungry for power or money. Their influence or favor could be traded for or bought. His naiveté quickly disappeared as he learned that corruption in government did in fact exist, and that it was alive and well in Stamford.

As Dolan matured as a reporter, he became obsessed with getting to the truth. His reputation as a tireless worker grew, as did his stature at the newspaper. The new kid on the block was leaving his older and more seasoned colleagues in the dust.

When the corruption and eventually the organized crime stories began to take root in the community, some of the politicians began their posturing. City officials that had formerly turned a blind eye to the problems were suddenly screaming from the roof tops that if wrongdoing could be proved, the guilty had to be brought to justice. Many of them really did want to clean up the city. But there were others just trying to put up a good front and save their own butts.

The mayor at the time, Frederick Lenz, declared that he was going to conduct a special probe of the city civil service system because of the Berube situation and other allegations of improper or illegal actions. Although none of those in power would admit any knowledge of the alleged irregularities, they jumped onboard the mayor's train, calling for real probes that would leave no stone unturned.

Feeding off each other, Mayor Lenz promised to get to the bottom of the charges and make things right. He indicated that the investigation would be broad and examine appointments to major positions that had been made over the past five or six years. Lenz cited the reason for going back that far was because of an allegation that the man appointed as Deputy Corporation Counsel, had lacked the five years of experience required for appointment at the time of his selection. The applicant had honestly listed his legal experience on his application, clearly showing his lack of qualification. But the Personnel Commission decided he was their guy and appointed him anyway.

In addition to the Lenz initiative, the Personnel Committee of the Board of Representatives announced their own investigations into civil service appointments. But committee members expressed concern that its inquiry could degenerate into a McCarthy-type witch hunt. Therefore, they decided to limit the scope of their investigation to the specific questions that had been raised about the Deputy Corporation Counsel appointment. Can you imagine that? They were going to straighten out the civil service issues, but were only going to look at that one appointment. Nobody would be able to accuse them of going too far.

As public pressure for action mounted, officials had to do a delicate balancing act. They had to show interest in what was being exposed. And some exhibited disgust and outrage, and demanded deeper investigations. In some cases, those feelings were real. In others they were a false display of emotions to impress the public. Those who had no role in the civil service process could beat the war drums about Berube and others like him, but they also had to think that if the investigations expanded, they could lead to their own doorsteps. They had to talk the talk in front of their constituents, but they knew their own careers could be on the line down the road. The best thing for them was to have enough heads roll to satisfy the public, and then shut the investigations down and move on.

That strategy may have worked except for one thing: the Dolan factor. Anthony Dolan was the joker in the deck for the politicians and officials with skeletons in their closets. So far he had come on like a bull dog. He was tireless and appeared to be utterly fearless. They knew that if Dolan lost interest in the corruption stories, those who were feeding him information would have no one to tell their stories to and things would gradually return to normal. Anthony Dolan was the key. Was there a way to stop him?

To at least slow Dolan down, Mayor Lenz publicly stated that the reporter had a one- track mind. Lenz suggested that Dolan be removed from the City Hall beat because there were other important issues such as housing, urban development, traffic, and taxes, that Dolan was ignoring in favor of the more controversial stories on alleged wrongdoing.

It was a good try by Lenz, but it did not get the job done. The Advocate had several other reporters to cover the topics Lenz had cited. Anthony Dolan had started the train and the people who controlled Stamford were in for a very uncomfortable ride.

16

URING MY career with the police department, I had experienced both good and bad times. Fortunately, on the down side things had leveled off and not too much was happening. And on the plus side, things were going well for me. I was making a lot of arrests and earning many extra days off. But as I found out, sometimes things can change quickly for the worse

One night while I was working 3:00 p.m. to 11:00 p.m. shift, I was asked by one of the men working midnights to fill in for him. Even though I was tired, I figured it would be best to work it. It was a Sunday night and I did not have a gig with the band. So doing the extra shift would fatten my pay check and make up for having the night off from the band.

On the graveyard shift I was riding alone. It was a slow night with few calls for service. I just drove around, patrolling downtown and the surrounding areas. When it got to be about three in the morning I was really dragging. At one point as I was driving down Summer Street, I did not realize that I had started to nod off. I woke up abruptly as the tires of the police car jumped the curb. When my eyes opened, I saw I was heading directly for the plate glass window of a department store. I slammed on the brakes, stopping about ten feet from the window.

I was now completely awake. I quickly backed out onto the street before any other vehicle came by and saw a police car up on the curb. I pulled over, heart still pounding, and sat thinking about what had almost happened. *Suppose I had gone through that window? What if I had hit a parked car or a pedestrian walking on the sidewalk?*

When I had calmed down, I resumed patrol. And I had absolutely no problem staying awake the rest of the shift.

Reflecting, I believe it was just another example of God's hand reaching out to help me. He truly gave me a wake-up call that night and made me realize that I was walking a tightrope. There was just too much that I was trying to keep together financially and emotionally, both on and off the job.

———

One night while my partner Bob Lopiano and I were patrolling the Westside we went by the Dairy Queen on West Main Street. This was a combination burger and ice cream shop. I had eaten there on many occasions while on duty. It was about 9:30 and the store was about to close.

As we neared the restaurant, we had a good view of the inside. There were two black males, one at the counter and the other pacing back and forth looking out the window. That raised our suspicions. We also noticed that one of them had his hand in his pocket and felt that he may have had a gun concealed. We shut off our lights, pulled into the back of the building and took up a position that allowed us to observe what was going on inside.

From this vantage point we were able to identify the two men as members of a religious sect called the Rastafarians. Founded in Jamaica in the 1930s, they were an up-and-coming group in Stamford. Members of the local bunch had previously been involved in police shootings, drug deals, and other acts of violence. They were known for their long dreadlocks and the multi-colored berets they wore.

We radioed headquarters, explained the situation and that there was a possible robbery in progress. Several of the other marked patrol cars responded and stopped out of sight a short distance away.

Bob and I exited our vehicle just as a Dairy Queen employee came out the back door to empty the garbage. We asked him what was going on. He said the two men were acting like they were up to something and he feared they were going to pull a robbery. They had been in about a week earlier and asked about the alarm system. This information gave us probable cause for further investigation.

Due to the possibility that at least one of the suspects was armed, we decided not to go inside to confront them and place the store employees in danger. Instead, we held our position and continued our surveillance.

In a matter of minutes, the suspects came out the front door and got into a gray Thunderbird. We did not know if they had somehow spotted one of the squad cars or just sensed that something was not right. Whatever the reason, they pulled away fast. Bob and I and the other units took up pursuit. The Thunderbird was going very fast and at one point drove down the wrong side of the road against traffic. Eventually it spun out of control and came to a stop. This allowed the officers to approach the vehicle and remove the suspects. An illegal handgun was retrieved from one of them and handed over to me. It was fully loaded with one round in the chamber. The suspects were arrested for Possession of a Deadly Weapon, Carrying a Pistol Without a Permit, and Reckless Operation of a Motor Vehicle. One of them was additionally charged with Threatening, for stating he was going to kill the officers involved in his arrest.

Officer Lopiano, myself and the other officers involved, were commended for outstanding police work in the prevention of a possible robbery and the protection of property and persons. The award said that our demonstration of teamwork in calling in and giving complete information before we took action embodied the true spirit of police service. I was glad to have been a part of the kind of teamwork that got those bad guys off the street. It was great work on the part of all the officers who participated.

———

On another day in that same week, an alarm came into headquarters from a branch of the Hartford National Bank. Several cars were dispatched, both uniform and detectives. A call to the bank established that an armed robbery had taken place. Although I was off duty, I heard the call over my police scanner and took off for the location in my own vehicle.

When I arrived at the scene there were several officers already there, uniformed, plain clothes and off- duty guys like me. The two suspects had fled the scene on foot and we formed into teams to locate and apprehend them.

We found one of the robbers running through the back-yards of an upscale residential neighborhood about a half mile from the bank. We surrounded him and ordered him to the ground. I sat on his rear end and cuffed him. I did not know that one of the other officers had shot the guy in the butt. After I cuffed him, I felt something wet on the inside of my thighs and crotch area. I got up and looked down at my pants. They were saturated with blood, especially under my crotch.

Another team caught the second suspect hiding in a building around the corner from where we captured his partner. They entered the building, disarmed the guy, and took him into custody.

This was another example of great teamwork. The teams involved received commendations for distinguishing themselves by rapidly getting to the scene, entering into the initial chase and apprehending the suspects.

The commendations said we deserved special acknowledgment for alertness, perseverance, bravery and devotion to duty without regard to our personal safety while confronting two armed adversaries. They cited the teamwork displayed in the apprehension of the armed felons, and the recovery of over twelve thousand dollars in cash and a motor vehicle that had been stolen from another jurisdiction, along with two weapons. As it happened, the commendation was signed by my former partner, Joe Ligi, who had been promoted to lieutenant.

I can remember to this day the positive feeling that came over me as I looked around headquarters and saw the team members being congratulated by their peers. Some of the officers being recognized had been passed over for promotions and were disillusioned by the favoritism and allegations of corruption within the department. But despite the low morale that existed at the time, on that day they were all proud cops. And I felt honored to be one of them.

━━━━━

On another day I was patrolling in my own car on a plain clothes assignment when Joe Ligi, who was off duty at the time, came to meet me on a street near the railroad station. As we were sitting there talking about Larry Hogan, Joe asked me what I thought about Anthony Dolan and what he was doing. I said I thought Dolan was the real deal and that one day his stories would focus on the police department. When that day came, the still cocky Hogan would lose his smirk and swagger.

As we talked, we noticed an individual acting suspiciously, peeking in the windows and trying to open the doors of parked cars not too far from us. He was small in stature and appeared to be Hispanic. The guy had a screwdriver in his right hand that he was using to try to pry the car doors open. We got out of our cars and placed him under arrest for tampering with a motor vehicle.

After we checked his vehicle and his personal belongings, we found numerous tools used for break-ins; glass cutters, lock picks, wire cutters and assorted screw drivers. An NCIC check revealed he was wanted in New York City on several warrants for sexual offenses and was a fugitive from justice. What started out as simple tampering with a motor vehicle and possession of burglary tools charges had segued into a major arrest.

After we booked the prisoner Joe and I continued our conversation outside of headquarters. As we were talking, Larry Hogan pulled in and sat in his car glaring at us. When he got out of the car and headed into headquarters, I gave him a friendly wave as he walked past. He did not wave back, but if looks could kill, I'd have been a goner. Hogan's expression left little doubt what he thought of Joe and me or what was on his mind when he saw the two of us together talking.

That day I realized how much I missed not working with Joe. I missed our camaraderie and exchanging notes and thoughts on Larry Hogan. As we split up, I told him that one day all the police department horror stories would come out. And that would be a day of satisfaction for him, me, and all the good guys. As Joe walked away, I could not get a read on whether or not he really believed that.

Not long after my talk with Joe, I was on patrol when I got a call from the dispatcher that Lieutenant Considine wanted to see me. When I arrived at his office, he told me that the master keys for all the public housing units in Stamford had been stolen from a Housing Authority maintenance truck. The theft had taken place a week earlier and the keys still had not been recovered. The crime had been kept hush-hush to avoid causing fear among the residents of the public housing complexes.

Considine told me to get out of uniform and spend the rest of that day and the next couple of days, if necessary, to find those keys. He said, "You're the man that can do it. You have more connections on the street than anyone in this building. If you need money to pay someone to get them back, do what you have to do. Just get it done."

As Considine talked I already had someone in mind that could probably steer me in the right direction. This guy knew everything that was going on in the projects. If the keys were missing, the odds were he knew who took them. I told the Lieutenant rather smugly that I would be back shortly with the keys in hand.

He looked at me and said if I got the keys back in the next few days, he'd be happy. And there would be some additional days off in it for me. He added with a laugh, "With all the extra days off you've been earning everyone around here thinks you only work a four-day week anyway. So, you might as well keep that thought going."

I left headquarters and went to see my source, a man named Phil, who lived in Southfield Village, a low-income housing project with both bungalow and high-rise apartments. Phil had given me information in the past about what went on in the projects that had led to many arrests and convictions. I told him the story and that I needed to find those keys. I could tell by the way he was grinning at me that he knew where the keys were. He said he knew who had them. But it would take a little money for the person who had them, and Phil wanted to be taken care of, too. I told him to just bring me back the keys and we could work out the financial arrangements.

Phil told me to stay in the area and he would be back within the hour. I found a parking place nearby and waited. About forty minutes later I saw him walking down the street carrying a large ring of keys. I was so ecstatic that I almost wet my pants. I gave Phil whatever money I had in my pocket, a little over a hundred bucks I think, and told him to split it up however he wanted.

I was back in Considine's office about an hour and a half after he gave me the assignment. I had a cocky smile on my face as I held up the key ring and said, "Are these what you've been looking for, Lieutenant?"

He just shook his head in disbelief. The next day Considine reimbursed me for my out-of-pocket expenses along with slips for another two days off. My four-day work week reputation would remain intact.

Public housing keys returned; investigation on

Master keys to all public housing units which were reported stolen from a Housing Authority maintenance truck over a week ago have been recovered, Police Lt. John Considine said today.

Lt. Considine said the keys were obtained <u>through investigation by Ptl. Vito</u> Carlucci

OUR OWN LITTLE BRADY BRUNCH

CLOCKWISE FROM BOTTOM CENTER:
MARC, VALARIE, KIMMY, MELODYE & JODI

VITO GETTING READY FOR A GIG IN THE 1970'S

17

O N THE surface, the various governmental committees formed in response to Dolan's stories seemed like a good idea. But the committee members were having a hard time figuring out where to start and what direction to go.

One of the reasons for the indecision was that there were two types of members. There were those that were honest and wanted to do the right thing. Although they meant well, most of them had never been involved in an investigative role and were in over their heads. And then there were the good old boys. They either did not want the allegations looked into at all, or wanted the scope of the inquiries limited to avoid exposing the wrongdoing by themselves or their cronies. These opposing agendas resulted in a lack of progress and mixed messages being sent to the public.

Dolan aggressively pursued the truth about what the committees were up to. He asked members tough questions and received a variety of responses. Some were steadfast that their particular group was not being vindictive and its investigative work was not politically motivated. Others felt they should not move forward unless rules were in place that would protect the integrity of both the committee members and those who came under investigation. Several thought guidelines needed to be established that addressed what could and could not be shared with the public. Still others boasted that their work would be open and transparent.

The public could not be blamed if they were confused. How could they be kept fully informed of a committee's progress while that body was operating in strict confidence to protect the integrity of all involved?

The expected length of the investigations was vague as well. The most common answer to that question was that the time required would depend on the amount of information developed that would have to be followed up on. However, there was one common area of agreement: the main focus of all committees would be on appointments made by Mayor Lenz.

Not to be left out, Mayor Lenz stated that his administration's ongoing probe into the civil service system had revealed several irregularities. He said that everyone was now claiming to have been concerned about the problems for some time. If that was true, he questioned why nothing had been done until his investigation was launched and the press got involved.

While this was going on, Dolan turned his focus to the Terry Conners Ice Rink, a beautiful new facility built in the

Cove area of Stamford. Dolan's reports disclosed alleged irregularities in the appointment of the rink's coordinator. After several articles ran, the coordinator resigned the post.

I was getting more and more excited as I read all these articles because Dolan was highlighting one department after another as he churned out the stories. I was thinking to myself that pretty soon he'd get to the police department and report on some of the information I'd been giving him anonymously. I believed my department was by far the most corrupt and when the influence of organized crime was disclosed it would rock Stamford like an earthquake.

———

But I was not the only one calling Dolan with information. People were beginning to trust him. They could tell he was getting to the truth and they became more than willing to pick up the phone and talk freely.

The reporter next wrote a series of articles about alleged irregularities involving traffic light contracts. Hawley Oefinger, Superintendent of Communications, admitted that expenses for his 1973 winter trip to Sunnyvale, California for a conference were paid for by a New Haven, Connecticut firm that had been accused of failing to perform work on city contracts that were supervised by his office. Oefinger acknowledged that the firm, which had performed the bulk of the City's traffic light installations in recent years, paid for his plane fare and hotel room for the California trip. When asked by Dolan if he could remember who attended the conferences and other details, Mr. Oefinger replied, "To

be honest with you, I'm a little hazy on the entire subject."
When asked again if he could please provide more specifics, Oefinger said he could not and that his records weren't
as good as he had thought.

Dolan's investigation also found that Oefinger's office
made an overpayment of $4,600 dollars to another company
that failed to install signal light mast arms as contracted.
When confronted by Dolan, Oefinger admitted the error
and the company involved refunded the money. Superintendent Oefinger cited a lack of staff as the reason for the
many errors in his department's paperwork.

As Dolan continued to investigate and pound away on his
keyboard, Stamford was developing a well-deserved reputation for incompetence and corruption. The exposure of that
seamy side of City government was long overdue.

But when would Dolan get around to the police department?

As the weeks passed Dolan's investigation led him to the
Public Works Department. He pored over hundreds of City
invoices that showed the operations officer was sending lots
of work to two contractors with whom he had business ties.
In one instance, documents showed that the city rented two
pieces of equipment from one of those contractors at eight
times what it would have cost to purchase the items outright. Dolan found that not only did the operations officer's practices violate bidding procedures, but that he also

had City crews work on property owned by his own family and political friends.

After the operations officer's transgressions were brought to light, two different mayors tried to fire him. But their efforts failed when the Commissioner of Public Works, members of the Board of Finance, other city officials and a state senator came to the man's defense. He was finally fired after being arrested for taking flying lessons while on City time and filling his personal vehicle with city gasoline.

It was subsequently revealed to the public that the operations officer was a former commissioner of the department and that he had private real estate dealings with the two contractors. The questionable contracts involved over a half million dollars of taxpayer money. The operations officer was later arrested again along with the contractors and charged with larceny.

It seemed that almost every week a new scandal was exposed. An arson ring with ties to organized crime that was apparently being protected by a high-ranking fire official; failure of the City Engineering Department to strictly enforce contract provisions on sewer projects; and bidding irregularities in more than $200,000 worth of work awarded by the Board of Education, just to name a few.

Dolan reported that many of those involved in these activities were part of a loosely-knit group of municipal officials and politicians who had dominated City politics in recent years. The major instrument of this domination, of course, was the civil service system, which was used to place the politically connected in sensitive municipal positions.

As Dolan's stories began to expose organized crime's influence over the city, he said that many of the officials didn't only work for the City. They also worked for themselves and the Mob. He stated that organized crime, "wanted to control the personnel department, so they could put people in key jobs, and they wanted to control the police department so they couldn't be stopped."

Anthony Dolan had come to grips with the reality that the Mafia was not just a figment of the media's imagination. It was very real and his adopted city was in its clutches. In addition, the public's attitude was changing from "This can't be going on," to "How long has this been going on and how are we going to stop it?"

And the more wrongdoing Dolan exposed, the more unpopular he became in some quarters. The derogatory comments and death threats against him increased in volume and visciousness. Notes were being left on his car windshield and pictures of dead bodies were placed in his mailbox. On top of that, he came under attack from some City leaders and business owners for sensationalizing his stories and giving Stamford a bad name.

———

I had trouble controlling my excitement when I read Dolan's story that mentioned organized crime for the first time. There was no doubt that the police department would not be far behind. If he had taken my anonymous information seriously, big things would soon start happening.

And it would be none too soon, either. The police department was getting worse by the day. The officers all knew that favoritism is what brought promotions, day shift assignments and special privileges. Uniformed patrol officers in squad cars were being used to deliver documents to the homes of members of the Board of Representatives. And routinely being used as messengers was not an appropriate role for trained police officers. It was a waste of taxpayer money and demoralized the officers. As I think about these things now, I cannot believe the ineptness of the department's leadership.

But Anthony Dolan, the scourge of the corrupt, had the department on his to-do list. He was checking it twice and finding out who was naughty and who was nice.

18

MAYOR FRED Lenz was up for re-election in 1975 and there was a lot of speculation that Louis Clapes, a former Town Clerk who was well-known and liked in the community, would challenge him and likely win. Seeing the handwriting on the wall, Lenz decided to do something for his brother Ed, a sergeant in the Stamford Police Department, before he again faced the voters. He wanted Ed promoted to the rank of Major.

What you need to understand is that we had no rank of Major in the department. Not at all. So, what the mayor wanted to do was create a brand-new rank for his brother and leapfrog him over the existing lieutenants and captains that should have been given first consideration for the newly-created slot. When word got out of what was in the works it hit the already demoralized department like an exploding bomb. The Stamford Police Association convened a meeting at the German American Club to discuss the perceived injustice. The room was jammed with both current and retired officers, most of whom were angry.

There were a few exceptions, though, and they made a compelling case against opposing Lenz' initiative. They argued that the proposal would probably go through whether or not the Association objected. And with the Association amid tough contract negotiations with the City, not picking a fight over the promotion issue might cause Mayor Lenz to soften his position on some of the salary and benefit items that he had so far refused to budge on. With dollar signs dancing in their heads, the majority swallowed their anger and decided not to object.

Chief Kinsella knew that Lenz would want his support as well as that of the rank and file. You must remember that Stamford was a city that had been used to making back alley deals since the 1950s. So, it was only natural that Kinsella's support came with a price. He had a captain he wanted to take care of, but nowhere to promote him to. To secure Kinsella's backing, Lenz had to authorize the creation of two positions with the rank of Major. One to be filled by Sergeant Ed Lenz and the other by Captain Lester McDonald. It was a done deal.

After the promotions took place, the Police Association realized they got absolutely nothing from Lenz in return for their cooperation. It goes without saying that morale sank to new depths as officers grasped the reality that they had been had.

One day at line-up an announcement was made that was so ridiculous it was infuriating. We were told that starting on that day, all police officers, no matter their rank, had to salute Police Commissioners whenever we came into their presence. I can remember the uproar when the announcement was read. Guys were saying, "You're kidding me, right? You want us to salute the civilian Police Commissioners?" But they were not kidding. The department brass and the commissioners were totally serious.

I remember going out that first day with my partner in the squad car. We were stopped at a traffic light and facing us across the intersection was a car with one of the commissioners in it. My partner was driving, so he would be the one closest to the commissioner when our cars passed. As the vehicles neared, the commissioner gave us a sharp salute. My partner responded by flipping him off. I did not salute, but I did not give him the finger either.

As my partner guffawed, I wondered how much trouble we were going to be in. I agreed with him, though. Here are these guys in this totally corrupt town that do not give a damn about the rank-and-file cops, demanding that we show them respect by saluting them. Give me a break!

The reaction to the salute order was so negative it was rescinded after only a couple of days. The powers that be realized that no one was going to adhere to this new rule and figured it would be best to just let it go. It was a good thing they backed off or they could have had a revolt on their hands.

There were a lot of things going on at work over the summer and the excitement over the upcoming mayoral election began to build. And on a personal note, Joanne gave birth to our son Marc on August 7, 1975. Joanne and I were of course delighted; and the girls welcomed his arrival.

———

The Eugene Berube story got more headlines during the mayoral race between Frederick Lenz and Louis Clapes. The new round of coverage cited 28 possible irregularities in the Park Superintendent exam and Berube's appointment. Louis Clapes made the civil service problems an issue in his campaign and promised to get the mess cleaned up if elected. Clapes defeated Lenz and there was a lot of excitement when the new mayor took over. I had always liked the guy personally and was anxious to see what he was going to do. And it did not take long.

Per his promise to reform the system, Mayor Clapes appointed a special committee to investigate the City's hiring procedures and practices. One of the City representatives commented that many irregularities had already been uncovered by the personnel committee of the Board of Representatives. This was a seven-member blue ribbon panel, totally unrelated to Pabst Blue Ribbon, comprised of personnel experts from the private sector. They agreed that the mayor's committee needed to begin its inquiry by determining how civil service regulations were being avoided or deviated from.

I could have given them an ear full on that without any meetings; and so could the other three hundred cops on the department.

Members of the personnel committee noted that they were still learning about the system. One of them opined that it was a political system in many respects, a fact which opened it up to abuses. Another said the committee found it difficult to believe that in the political process, personal relationships would not affect how appointments were decided.

However, the confusing statements regarding the openness of the mayor's committee continued. Mayor Clapes said that all meetings would be open to the press and public. Meanwhile, another high-ranking person said, "We cannot investigate without looking into specific areas that should not be disclosed publicly." Here we go again.

Even with that, I still had a lot of faith in Mayor Clapes. I really believed he might start changing Stamford for the better.

19

N MID-1976, I received word from two sources I considered reliable that got my heart pumping. They both said the Advocate had one or more Anthony Dolan stories ready to run that would address the problems in the Stamford Police Department. Finally!

I pressed my sources for more information about the articles. How many were there and when would they run? They did not know. But the articles had been ready for several weeks and someone at the paper was holding them up. My emotions quickly turned from euphoria to depression. Somebody with clout must have gotten to one of the higher-ups at the paper and applied pressure not to run the stories.

I thought about little else for the next several days. I had to assume that whoever had found out about Dolan's articles knew their content and did not want them to see the light of day. And even though the information I had given to Dolan had been done anonymously, I was bound to be suspected as one of the reporter's sources. In my mind things could not have been much worse. The corruption within the department was not going to be exposed; and at some point, I'd have to pay a price for what the bad guys thought I'd done. I started carrying a gun every time I left my house, even if it was only to walk the dog.

I did not have many options, but there was one that seemed to offer me the best hope. Maybe if I met with Dolan in person and told him who I was and what information I had provided to him, we could lay our cards on the table and come up with a plan. I was sure I was on somebody's S-list; and Dolan's name was certainly there with mine. We both knew stuff and had tried in our own way to make it public. Dolan and I were both in danger and it seemed logical to me that we should work together for our own benefit and protection.

I rehearsed what I would say to Dolan if we met. I would tell him that I loved my job, but there was one big problem: some of my superiors were drug dealers and killers. I would make sure he knew that during much of the 1970s it was often difficult to tell the good guys from the bad. Dolan needed to know that money was flowing from organized crime to some of the officers in the Stamford Police Department.

I would make the reporter understand that many of the cops assigned to patrol the streets had been school classmates with what were now the local hoods. They had known each other for years and in some cases, they were friends. If an officer could supplement his income by looking the other way when a drug deal was going down, why not?

And the higher-ranking officers were open to making some extra cash as well. They were in positions to be more beneficial to the criminals. Not just the street-level guys either. They could open doors for organized crime ventures and influence how aggressively personnel working under them did their jobs. And even if some of their men were a bit too zealous in the performance of their duties, their reports and findings could end up collecting dust on a shelf—or perhaps disappear—with no action being taken. Because of the assistance and protection these ranking officers could provide, their services came with a higher price tag.

I would tell Dolan that the good cops saw their crooked colleagues enjoying the benefits of their relationships with the criminals, such as taking free trips to Las Vegas with the gangsters. They also knew that some investigations, including murder investigations, were dropped for no valid reason. And sometimes arrestees were released after being booked and the charges were mysteriously dropped. I had let the reporter know that some of the men in blue were suffering from corruption flu as they tried to come to grips with the fact that the Gambino and Genovese crime families influenced how their department was run.

On a personal level I would tell him about working for Larry Hogan and Duke Morris in the Narcotics Squad and how frustrated Joe Ligi and I were about the number of drug raids we conducted that came up empty because Hogan and Morris told our targets that we were coming. And I had let him know that a drug dealer Joe and I arrested named Arvil Chapman told us that Hogan and Morris were dirty;

that Hogan was in fact running a major drug operation. And when Hogan learned that Joe and I were onto him, we were both bounced out of the Narcotics Squad and put back in uniform.

I would close my conversation with Dolan by telling him—pleading with him—that somehow this information had to get out to the public. My life had already been threatened and things would only get worse if nothing was done. I was ready to do whatever it took. Was he?

I spent days going over my pitch to Dolan in my mind. I thought about it lying in bed at night, in the shower, while driving to work and when alone in my squad car. Anthony Dolan was the key for me and I had my spiel all prepared. But as happened to me before, I was not able to bring myself to contact Dolan overtly. The phone call was not made and the meeting was never held. To Dolan, I remained Mr. Anonymous.

On a night in October 1976, I reported for duty on the midnight shift. My senior sergeant was on vacation and the junior sergeant—I will call him Bill Rankin—was taking his place. During the pre-shift line-up Rankin assigned me to the Westside, and then told me he wanted to talk with me in private at the conclusion of the briefing.

When we had our chat Rankin said something that was stunning to me. He said, "Colucci, I have a very busy day after work tomorrow. I want to get some rest tonight and get out of here on time in the morning. I know you like to make a lot of arrests and you're always calling in over the radio. But tonight, I don't want to hear your voice unless you're dispatched to a call. Do you understand?"

I told Rankin he must be kidding. He was telling me to just drive around all night and do nothing unless I received a call from dispatch. I asked him if that was what he was saying.

"I'm not kidding," Rankin said. "I don't want to hear or see anything of you for the entire shift. I hope I've made myself clear."

I hit the street and around three o'clock or so I stopped in an all-night diner called the Coney Island Grill to grab a bite to eat. As luck would have it, I spotted a guy sitting at the counter who I knew had several outstanding warrants. I called in on my portable radio to confirm the warrants and then placed the subject under arrest and took him to headquarters.

As I was completing the arrest paperwork a supervisor had to be summoned to set bond. Sergeant Rankin walked into the room looking disheveled, with his hair all mussed up and his shirt untucked. It was obvious to me that he had been getting some of the much-needed rest he'd mentioned earlier. Rankin did not speak a word to me or another officer that was in the room. He just glared at me like I was something that had crawled out from under a rock, picked up the paperwork and walked out.

I was sure that it was not over between me and Rankin, though. He was going to be my direct supervisor for a few more days and would no doubt want to get back at me for disobeying his orders and disturbing his sleep.

Two days later we rotated to the day shift. At the pre-shift line-up Rankin gave me his payback. He said, "Colucci, I want you to do traffic control at Washington Boulevard and Broad Street." He said I was to put the traffic light on flash and stand in the middle of the intersection and direct traffic.

I was confused. And looking around the room I saw puzzled expressions on the faces of my fellow officers. I knew that the intersection I was being assigned to was the location of Bloomingdale's Department Store. To my knowledge it had never been considered a traffic corner.

As I stood outside in the rain that day, I could imagine Rankin sitting around headquarters with a smile on his face. Whenever a patrol car passed me, the officer would stop and express his sympathy. They reminded me that Rankin was friends with some of the dirty cops I had vowed to go after.

Was there any wonder why morale in the department was nearing rock bottom?

PART TWO

My Fight Against
Corruption Takes a Turn

20

FRIDAY, OCTOBER 22, 1976, marked a turning point in the investigation into the corruption in the Stamford Police Department, and in my life. I was off duty and picked up a copy of the Advocate. Two front page headlines jumped out at me and I could feel my heart pounding against my rib cage. The first was about Chief Kinsella. The second was Anthony Dolan's first article focusing directly on the police department.

According to the Kinsella article, during a news conference at the mayor's office that morning, Joseph Kinsella announced he was retiring after a twenty-two-year career so that he could spend more time with his wife. He would leave active duty on February 1, 1977, but would remain on the payroll until that July to collect his salary for 220 unused vacation

Low morale, racket ties plague Stamford police

days. Kinsella denied the timing of his retire-

(Editor's Note: This is the first article in an Advocate series on the Stamford Police Department. The series was prepared several weeks ago and held for extensive rechecking of all facts to assure the accuracy of the details. The Advocate's information on these matters has been turned over to the Connecticut State Police and the Federal Bureau of Investigation along with the names of those sources who would agree to it.)

by ANTHONY R. DOLAN
Advocate Staff Reporter

Declining morale, cover-ups of suspected police crimes including drug pushing, and strong ties between policemen and a racketeer who is close-

ment had anything to do with allegations of corruption in the police department.

Although Kinsella claimed he had made his intentions known during the 1975 municipal elections, Police Commissioner Canio Santoro expressed surprise at Kinsella's announcement. He said that when he and Commissioner Anthony Walsh were invited to the press conference by Mayor Clapes, they were not told the reason behind it. Even though Kinsella's letter of resignation was dated ten days earlier, Mayor Clapes himself said he was surprised. As could be expected, the politicians who had supported and controlled Kinsella all heaped praise on him, which I found laughable.

After reading the story I was delighted. I had always thought Kinsella was a do-nothing guy and a poor police chief. His ineffectiveness left cops such as Joe Ligi and me hanging out to dry. I felt that depending on who replaced Kinsella, his resignation could be a great thing for the department.

If that first article made me happy, the second Dolan piece absolutely put me on cloud nine. It explained that it was the first of a series of articles that had been prepared weeks earlier, and why they had not been run until that day. The story began with this Editor's Note:

"This is the first article in an Advocate series on the Stamford Police Department. The series was prepared several weeks ago and held for extensive rechecking of all facts to assure the accuracy of the details. The Advocate's information on these matters has been turned over to the Connecticut State Police and the Federal Bureau of Investigation along with the names of those sources who would agree to it."

Wow! Even though I was not a particularly religious guy back then, I remember thanking God that Dolan and the newspaper had not been gotten to after all. They were committed to the investigation and were even sharing their information with the CSP and the FBI. Before reading the actual article, I could not help but reflect on Kinsella's denial that his resignation had nothing to do with corruption allegations. Yeah, right!

Dolan titled his article, "Low morale, racket ties plague Stamford police." He cited his 10-month investigation of the police department and listed the most serious problems uncovered: declining morale and a lack of discipline; turning a blind eye to corrupt or illegal activities by department personnel, including a lieutenant suspected of being one of the area's major drug pushers; and close ties between seven Stamford police officers, two of whom were sergeants and one a lieutenant, and one of the City's most important racketeers who was a reputed operative of the Gambino crime family.

Dolan admitted that many of his sources refused to be identified. He explained that those working for other government agencies—both state and federal—frequently worked closely with the police department. They wanted to remain anonymous to avoid jeopardizing their working relationship with Stamford or facing disciplinary action for violating the internal regulations of their own agencies. And police department personnel declined to provide their identity due to a department rule that prohibited talking to a reporter without approval. But Dolan said that in most cases, allegations were verified by a minimum of three sources before appearing in the series.

The reporter stated that these internal sources provided him with information that Chief Kinsella had attempted to hush up the involvement of two officers in a North Stamford burglary. The department failed to act when Patrolman Edward Miller was found semi-conscious in his patrol car and traces of illegal drugs were found in his urine. And that there were irregularities in the awarding of traffic light contracts. Dolan's confidential sources also told him of cases of police brutality that were not properly handled by the department.

The story went on to say that when problems did get reported to the Police Commission nothing was done. Even state and federal law enforcement agencies expressed little or no interest in getting involved with what was going on in Stamford.

Dolan concluded by saying his next piece would address the impact of political interference and a lack of departmental discipline on police work.

When I finished reading, I was impressed by the accuracy of the story. The content was exactly what I and many other officers had complained about for years. Favoritism, lax supervision and discipline, and inadequate leadership at the top. They were all there.

But more than that, I found it amazing that Dolan had been able to do his other corruption stories while simultaneously putting together an army of sources from a variety of agencies for his police department series. And he had done it all without tipping his hand. When I called him with information, I had no idea that I was only one of many. Obviously, we had all corroborated each other to the satisfaction of Dolan and his bosses. To investigate for that long and involving that many people without the cat getting out of the bag was truly incredible to me.

Friday was payday and as I drove to headquarters to get my check, I was anxious to see what kind of reaction the two stories had generated. When I arrived, there were a lot of both on and off duty officers milling around, and the talk was almost exclusively about the two articles. Most of the cops were ecstatic, but there were a few that were not. Their expressions were of anger, and in some cases, fear. One lieutenant, a guy I will call Todd Carney, who ignored the organized crime bookies while arresting the independents, said aloud, "Someday this Dolan is going to get what's coming to him."

That comment brought me back to reality. Although it may simply have been bluster, how would the officers that were in danger of being exposed react? Would they lash out at their accusers, either verbally or physically, if they could learn their identities? Was I now in more danger? And what about Dolan? He was stepping on some well-connected and dangerous toes. Would the bad guys have the nerve to go after a member of the press?

There were other questions as well. What would be the reaction of the public? Outrage or indifference? And who would replace Kinsella? My opinion was that it had to be someone with a strong law enforcement background from outside the department and preferably outside of Stamford. The incoming chief would face a monumental task in restoring the department's image and morale. It would have to be somebody who was not indebted to anyone. And he'd have to be a hardliner who could come in and clean house. That was my hope, but time would tell.

Dolan's second article ran on October 23, under the headline "Politics in the Police Department?" It was another impressive piece. Dolan hit the nail on the head when he said that "Politics," was the word most often used by his police sources to describe the root cause of the police department's problems. I had used that word myself during my conversations with him.

Dolan said his sources thought the most serious impact of politics on the police department was the practice of ignoring, or excusing with minor punishment, criminal activity by police officers. Blame was placed at the feet of commanders that lacked the courage to confront the issue head on, fearing political repercussions or public backlash. It was easier and less risky for them to look the other way or just give an offender a slap on the wrist. Right on.

Using the position of police chief as a political plum rather than seeking to appoint a highly qualified law enforcement professional, resulted in the deterioration of the department, the article said. It cited that Chief Kinsella had been a political figure with no police experience when he was appointed in 1954; and he got the position as a "political payoff." It

Politics in the Police Dept.?

(Editor's Note: This is the second in a series of articles of problems within the Stamford Police Department. The series was prepared several weeks ago and held for extensive rechecking of all facts to assure the accuracy of the details noted that Kinsella's nomination was rejected twice by the Board of Representatives and was approved by one vote the third time it was submitted.

Dolan said that some veteran cops pointed out that under the previous chief, John Brennan, who had come up through the ranks, there were virtually none of the current incidents and allegations that plagued the Kinsella administration.

Dolan's sources said that several high-ranking officers became involved in local political activities in order to further their own careers. They also joined certain social-ethnic clubs that exerted influence in the appointment of City officials.

The political makeup and powers of the Stamford Police Commission came under scrutiny in the story as well. Appointments to that body were allegedly sought by politicians as a vehicle to dispense political favors and influence police procedures.

Sources also criticized the Commission for its handling of complaints against policemen. The Commission was accused of "passing the buck" rather than instituting an effective internal affairs division that would take responsibility for departmental discipline. The Commission's attitude when it received a referral alleging criminal activity by a police officer seemed to be, "do the guy a favor," or "let it go this time."

And while criminal activity was ignored or whitewashed by the Commission, violations of minor rules, such as dress or grooming, were strictly enforced. These practices bordered on harassment and lowered morale; critics charged. Dolan quoted one police source as describing the Commission's order that police officers must salute the commissioners as "Unbelievable." He could very well have been quoting me.

Another of my pet peeves that the story addressed was the use of police officers as deliverymen and gofers for Kinsella and the politicians.

I was sure that after reading this story the politicians would have no choice but to adopt my line of thinking about Kinsella's replacement. That it would have to be a police professional from outside the department, preferably from out of state, with the guts to tackle the problems facing the agency.

I was sure of it. But I was wrong.

———

In the days following Dolan's first two stories I attended a large dinner dance and several meetings at Italian American clubs. Many of the movers and shakers in City government were at those events as well. They were people who had known my family for years and were not the least bit hesitant about talking business with me there. It was amazing to me that they showed no indication that they had read Dolan's articles. It was as though they had never been printed. The very people that Dolan and his sources had pointed the finger at for using their positions and clout to feather their own nests and take care of their friends and relatives, sat around the tables discussing how the next police chief would be chosen.

I could only shake my head in disbelief as these power brokers threw around the names of the people, they were considering to push to fill Kinsella's job. Some of the choices were not even police officers. They had no law enforcement experience and, if appointed, would take the department down the same road as the man they were replacing. It was hard for me to believe that hiring a man that had never walked a beat or made an arrest, was even being considered.

At one point I could not help myself and asked, "So you guys are going to decide who the next police chief will be? Am I hearing you right?" They glared at me with surprised looks on their faces. I could imagine what they were thinking. Doesn't Vito realize how powerful we are? Doesn't he know that we run the city?

I asked about the Dolan articles and all the issues they raised. Their response was that Dolan was a flash in the pan. His stories would soon be forgotten and things would go on as before. One of the men said, "We're going to pick someone that is beneficial to all of us. We keep track of favors; we know who owes us and who we owe."

Another of the men pulled a small notebook out of his jacket pocket. Flipping it open, he said in support of his buddy, "It's all right here. I owe this guy one favor and this other guy owes me two. It's really pretty simple."

I could not believe the balls these guys had. They were talking to me like I was a student in a class they were teaching about nepotism and corruption. It is hard to describe how I felt as I listened to this crap. I guess it was a combination of anger and disgust. It was one thing to hear the rumors about these things; but to listen to some of the key players talk about it so matter-of-factly blew my mind.

As I sat there taking it all in, their confidence that they would be able to pick the next police chief caused me to wonder about Mayor Clapes. After what seemed like a good start, I had been hearing some rumblings that he was being influenced by the men I was sharing a table with and others like them. And quite frankly, it was hard to see how these guys could carry out their plans without Clapes' cooperation.

What I was hearing and thinking dampened the enthusiasm I had after the Dolan articles ran. The doubts were returning. Maybe the naysayers were right. Maybe these guys were too powerful. Maybe the corruption was too entrenched. Maybe the bad guys *were* going to win.

21

WAS NOT going down without a fight! That is what I decided after thinking things over for a couple of days. I would do everything I could think of to make sure the wheeling and dealing of the power brokers and the activities of the bad apples in the police department were further exposed.

I figured one of the things I could do to stir the pot was to use a technique Joe Ligi had taught me and we had used on the streets many times. It had to do with spreading rumors. In Stamford rumors spread like wildfire—in a matter of hours and sometimes minutes. Drug dealers were in competition with one another and a well-placed rumor that one of them was getting special treatment by the police would almost always generate informants coming forward to bring down their colleague who was allegedly being favored by the cops. And getting the rumor up and running was very simple. If you told your target that what you were going to tell him was strictly confidential and absolutely could not be shared with anyone else, you could rest assured it would start making the rounds as soon as you were out of hearing range.

Politicians and others with political influence also competed with each other. Whomever had the most clout could demand the most from those seeking their help. And the egos of these guys demanded that they be at or near the top of the list of the most powerful influence peddlers. The selection of the new police chief was the current hot item for them and they would pull out all the stops to prove they could get the appointment for the man they backed. I decided to use my own connections with them—both Democrats and Republicans—and through my family, friends, other cops, anybody I knew, to put my plan into play.

I began telling people that I had heard that one of the big shots was supporting a certain person for police chief. I would then give the next people I spoke with a different set of names. And I swore everyone I talked with to secrecy, of course. By the time I was finished I had put about twenty-five different names out there as potential chiefs. Some were current police officers or police commissioners. Others were politicians or City officials. Some sounded like logical choices and others were long shots.

In a day or so I started seeing the results of my rumor mongering. I was contacted by people and told the same story I had started. The Irish were upset that the likely new chief was an Italian. The Italians were angry that an

Irishman was going to be appointed. Why in the hell was a Democrat backing a Republican, they wondered. I personally witnessed arguments between various factions and heard about other altercations. I had wanted to create confusion and turmoil and I was succeeding.

I ran my rumor mill project for about two weeks. In addition to the issue of police chief, I put out some other stuff as well. Things like secret collaboration between Democrats and Republicans to place specially selected people into high level positions that would only benefit specific politicians or businesses; and rigging the process for awarding contracts that would line the pockets of a chosen few.

I laughed to myself as I observed and heard about the jealousies and back stabbing coming into play. Not only was my plan working, I was having a good time doing it besides.

———

While I was doing my thing with rumors, the third article in Anthony Dolan's series came out. This one was titled, "Lax administrative actions, control cited as damaging police efficiency, morale." And in my opinion the stories were getting better and better.

In the very first paragraph Dolan said that outdated police techniques and personnel assignments based on favoritism rather than merit had damaged police morale, according to interviews with a broad range of policemen.

As I read those words, I was encouraged that the reporter was getting input from so many people. Although I would probably never know exactly who or how many, it appeared that a large number of the good, dedicated cops had participated in Dolan's research. There is strength in numbers and Dolan seemingly had no shortage of sources.

The article cited reports of alcohol and drug use and sexual encounters by officers while on duty and the misuse of firearms. I had personally seen officers engage in fast draw contests prior to pre-shift line-up, violating the basics of gun safety. Sometimes the weapons were discharged with bullets striking business and residential buildings in the vicinity of headquarters. And early in my career I had witnessed one officer shoot another as we exited headquarters for a midnight shift. Thankfully the wounded officer survived; but that incident was certainly a glaring example of firearms misuse.

Dolan wrote that the department followed a staffing system that assured personnel shortages on the nighttime shifts. He quoted a ranking officer as stating, "Frequently at night, we have 13 men on duty to cover 110,000 people in a city nearly 40 square miles. How are we supposed to do it? And people wonder why the burglary rate goes up?" I did not know who this ranking officer was, but I could sense his frustration because it was exactly the way I felt. This was not only dangerous; it violated a contract provision that required a minimum of eighteen officers on duty during individual shifts.

The story even pointed out the use of sworn personnel to carry out duties that in other jurisdictions were handled by school crossing guards. That was true. On some occasions there would only be one car available to respond to calls because all the other units were escorting school children across dangerous intersections. An important and necessary job to be sure. But not one that required a uniformed police officer.

And the complaints from officers did not stop at the school crossing assignments. Many of Dolan's sources—including me—had expressed concern over patrol officers being used as delivery boys and chauffeurs for police department and City officials or VIPs.

The lack of updated police procedures and techniques was another area that caused angst and damaged morale. We were probably 20 years behind other departments of our size in that critical area. Our records department was still using manual card indexing rather than the computerized systems used by comparable agencies.

Dolan talked about the department's apparent lack of interest in investigating white collar crime and municipal corruption. And in the one notable white-collar investigation, the 1968 "road oil" scandal, the case was tossed out of court due to faulty affidavits.

The article went on to cite problems caused by the lack of a merit or commendation system, favoritism in making assignments, the lack of discipline and looking the other way when officers were guilty of misconduct, including drinking on the job. Officers reported liquor being kept in the headquarters' water cooler. Police cars were damaged while being operated by intoxicated officers who were never disciplined. And in one case it was alleged that an officer that worked the front desk at headquarters was routinely sent home when his superiors determined he was too intoxicated to handle his job.

I remember that when I was awarded the Combat Cross it was presented to me right at my locker by one of my peers prior to my going on shift. No formal ceremony. No chief or high-ranking officer. No Police Commissioner or other City officials. Just a locker room thing.

But the biggie was the failure of the department to establish an internal affairs unit. The officers Dolan talked with knew that with all the politics and favoritism at play in the department, the powers that be would never go that route and jeopardize their power and control. No, they had to maintain the status quo.

The article did give the department credit for one success, though; the Special Weapons and Tactics squad. However, it quickly pointed out that SWAT was organized primarily at the instigation of rank-and-file officers. And SWAT officers had to violate their own labor contract in order to get the project off the ground because the department refused to compensate them for the extra hours they put in for specialized training. Dolan's sources expressed bitterness that Chief Kinsella arranged extra-contractual pay increases of up to $124 per week to high-ranking officers while declining to pay SWAT members. Mind boggling!

I remember shaking my head as I read. I knew about most of the things in the article and still found them hard to believe when I saw them in print. And the disclosure of some stuff I did not know was stunning to me. *How could all these things have happened? How could the Stamford Police Department have reached this point?*

With emotions ranging from sadness to anger and disbelief, I continued reading. Police cars could frequently be observed near a North Stamford residence late into the midnight shift. The occupant of the home was a female who showed her support for law enforcement by giving out sexual favors. Other on-duty sexual encounters reportedly took place at Cove Island and at a volunteer organization that remained open at night. Regarding police brutality, one source told Dolan, "I can see it happening. You get so frustrated you take a swing at the first guy who talks back to you."

Lax administrative actions, control cited as damaging police efficiency, morale

After finishing the article, I again had mixed feelings about where this would all lead. I did not see how the allegations could be ignored. But I could not shake the doubts I had. One thing was for sure, though. I was even more committed to waging my one-man war, if that was the only way to get justice.

———

While all the drama regarding the corruption in City government and the police department played out, about the only time I was able to relax and enjoy myself was on Sunday afternoons. That was when all my relatives and some family friends would get together at the home of one of my mother's nine sisters and brothers, all of whom resided in Italian neighborhoods in Stamford, or just across the border in Port Chester, New York.

We always ate well at these gatherings, with a fare that included pasta, sausage and meatballs, and hot Italian bread. My job was to go to the closest Italian bakery and pick up the bread fresh out of the oven. The aroma that came from those bakeries and from the wrapped loaves as I took them back to my aunt's or uncle's place was to die for.

After the meal, most of the older adults would start a nickel and dime poker game. I would hang around in the living room and talk with my many cousins and the aunts and uncles that could not get a seat at the poker table. It would be comical to hear the card players argue about who had not put in their ante or failed to put a nickel in the pot when they called a bet. Sometimes their voices got pretty loud and a stranger overhearing them would probably have thought they were bitter enemies rather than brothers and sisters. When these sessions broke up everyone was friends again and there was always a lot of hugging and kissing before we went our separate ways.

On one of these occasions, I got into a conversation with a family friend about the situation in Stamford and the Dolan articles. The guy told me he knew the inside scoop about who the next police chief was going to be. He told me that what he was going to tell me was strictly confidential and made me promise that anything he said would go no further. I vowed that my lips would remain sealed.

Satisfied, he started to talk. For the next several minutes many of the very rumors I had started were repeated back to me. As he mentioned some of the names I had put into circulation, I feigned disbelief and argued that there was no way that person could become the chief. He confidently assured me that this or that group or organization was backing the guy. And then he'd lower his voice conspiratorially and let me know that he and his friends would make sure that particular candidate would not get the appointment.

As he talked, I was struck by the depth of emotions over who the next chief would be and who he'd be beholden to. Almost every major ethnic and political faction in Stamford wanted to have a degree of control over him and the competition was fierce.

I laughed to myself and wanted to let this family friend know that his so-called inside information was all lies planted by me. But I could not.

However, there was another aspect of the situation that was not funny. I found out that word was circulating around the police department that I was Dolan's source. Not necessarily about crooked or corrupt cops. But that I was providing him with information about alcohol and drug use, sex on duty, misuse of firearms, things like that.

I did not like that because a lot of the stuff Dolan wrote I did not know about until I read it in the paper. And I certainly was not the source. But because of my situation with Hogan and Morris, and my excitement over Dolan's series, I became a suspect in the eyes of the 20 or so cops who were implicated in those various activities. I could see it in their demeanor toward me. Some of the guys I used to have decent relationships with even stopped talking to me. One of them asked me outright if I was feeding Dolan. I told him that I had not even been aware of most of the things that Dolan reported were going on in the field or at headquarters.

I had no personal animosity toward any of those officers; and I was not really pleased about taking the rap for something I didn't do. But even though I was not happy about it, I had no choice but to deal with it.

22

OLAN'S NEXT article was titled, "Police brass overlooks suspected crime by rank-and-file members of Department." Oh, brother! What a headline and what a story it ended up being.

The first paragraph was an attention grabber. "The Stamford Police Department has consistently ignored or excused with light penalties, suspected criminal activity by local policemen, an Advocate investigation shows."

That was followed with an acknowledgment that the alleged criminal activity was committed by a small minority of officers and included camera and liquor store thefts, and participation in organized gambling and drug pushing. I was well aware of the gambling and drug stuff. But the camera and liquor store thefts were news to me.

Dolan charged that the department had refused to follow up on leads implicating a policeman in major payoffs from organized gambling interests. Finally, after years of conducting my own investigation and learning the extent of Hogan's involvement in criminal activities, the public was learning what I had known for so long.

The intrepid reporter said that for several years the department ignored frequent warnings about a detective accused of major drug pushing activities. And that an investigation into the matter was suppressed and the officer was allowed to quietly resign. That had to be Duke Morris!

The piece also contained information that I was unaware of, claiming that an officer assigned to the Youth Bureau was guilty of sexual misconduct and indecent exposure. If true, this was not about stopping at a willing woman's home for a quickie during a midnight shift. Depending on the nature of the misconduct, the perpetrator could end up behind bars for a number of years.

Regarding the thefts, Dolan flatly stated the involved officers had committed the crimes and received only minor rebukes. No speculation there. It was a statement of fact. I wondered how the former chief, the commissioners and others in City government, would explain why the culprits weren't fired and criminally prosecuted. The answer was, they probably would not. The entire matter would likely be ignored or denied.

Dolan also pointed out that the officers who had driven City vehicles while drunk, or illegally discharged their weapons, could have been charged, but were not. Yet those very cops would have arrested a civilian for committing the same infraction.

These things were important, but Dolan's sources overwhelmingly felt that the drug and gambling issues were by far the most serious examples of police corruption. The article said that one City and two state officials, had warned the police department about the detective's illegal behavior, but no action had been taken. Incredible!

I asked myself how could the department, knowing that City and state officials were aware of the problem, do nothing? The only answer that made any sense to me was that the enablers within the agency and elsewhere in City government were so entrenched and confident in their ability to do what they pleased and get away with it, that nothing bothered them. The arrogance of these people was stunning.

In the article Dolan said he interviewed the three officials that had given the warning about the crooked detective. They told him that they obtained credible information from police sources and drug users, that the detective in question was the major supplier of illegal drugs in Fairfield County. Some of what they learned could have been attributed to Joe Ligi and me getting the word out. But I was not aware of the cooperation these officials were given by the users. Dolan added that each of the three officials expressed a willingness to testify before an investigative body if called.

Dolan also revealed that drug peddling became so blatant in 1973 that one state official arranged through Governor Thomas Meskill's office a special State Police probe. However, the detective became aware that he was under investigation and temporarily curtailed his illegal activities. The official that arranged the intervention, local attorney and state legislator James Bingham, confirmed the key points about the detective's activities, which he said he had personally investigated and researched.

The next paragraph was about me and Joe Ligi, unnamed of course. It read:

"The Advocate has also learned that Police Department commanders directly suppressed an investigation into the matter on at least one occasion. A patrolman, who obtained incriminating statements from several local addicts about the detective, was abruptly transferred from the rackets squad to a radio car, after, as one source put it, 'getting close enough to blow it wide open.'"

Dolan cited other examples of ignored warnings, the possible use of intimidation tactics against witnesses, and rewarding cops that were willing to look the other way when they observed misconduct by fellow officers.

The article was also critical of the Stamford Police Commission, stating that the Commission frequently took inadequate action, or no action at all, in police brutality and corruption cases. And Dolan noted that members were susceptible to political influence during their investigations. Members were described as lacking in the professional qualifications needed to administer justice and evaluate investigations. He concluded, "And the spirit of compromise which commission members, usually local politicians, bring to such hearings was seen as a dangerous way to deal with criminals, especially those who wear badges."

One veteran officer confided to Dolan that during the 1960s, corruption within the department was so pervasive that he frequently faced considerable pressure from his colleagues to participate in the bribery schemes.

Other policemen told him about a 1970 incident in which patrolman Dominick Possidento was shot and critically wounded by officer Stanley Czupkowski during what police officials described as horseplay. However, when Mr. Possidento recovered from his injuries, he disputed the department's explanation, stating that he had been shot "suddenly and without cause."

Czupkowski revealed that he had been offered a deal in which he would be given a job with the Stamford Fire Department if he quietly resigned from the force. Despite Possidento's serious wounds and the illegal discharge of a firearm, no charges were brought against him.

One of the reporter's sources summed up the corruption situation in the Stamford Police Department nicely when he said, "It's poison. Once somebody gets away with it, it affects everybody. The dishonest cop is wearing the same uniform as the honest cop is wearing, except he breaks the law and gets away with it."

Dolan had written yet another tremendous story and I was very pleased with it. But I was even more excited about what appeared at the end of the article. It said, "The next and final article in this series will discuss local police ties with organized crime figures."

Police brass overlooks suspected crime by rank-and-file members of department

The articles Dolan was producing addressed some very serious issues. But I remember something that took place in 1976 that was very humorous to those of us who found out about it.

Noted attorney Michael "Mickey" Sherman was a prosecutor in Stamford and in 1976 decided he was going to leave the prosecutor's office and go into private practice as a defense attorney. Another prosecutor needed to be appointed to replace him. Word spread around town that organized crime was interested in getting a person friendly to them into that position.

According to the rumor, the mobsters had a particular person in mind. The name that was being circulated surprised people in the know because the guy was genuinely nice and seemingly incapable of doing anything crooked.

Even though the story seemed far out, when Dolan heard about it, he asked for a meeting with chief prosecutor Martin "Marty" Nigro to confirm or dispel the rumor. Nigro agreed and invited the corruption-investigating reporter to meet with him in a room in the courthouse.

When Mickey Sherman got wind of the meeting, he decided to have a little fun. He took a large envelope and stuffed it with cash, leaving some of the bills hanging out. After Nigro and Dolan had been in the room for a few minutes, Sherman burst through the door and as he dropped the envelope in front of Nigro he said, "Here's this week's take." He then pretended to notice Dolan and said sheepishly, "Sorry, Marty, I didn't realize you were busy."

Sherman would later say that as he excused himself and left the room, the expressions on the faces of Nigro and Dolan were priceless.

The rumor about Sherman's replacement was totally false and apparently had been circulated by someone as a practical joke.

I could not wait to get each day's edition of the newspaper in anticipation of Dolan's next story about the police department's ties to organized crime. But even though that article was a few days in coming, there were stories by other reporters regarding problems in other City departments.

One that caught my eye dealt with the sewage treatment plant. The headline stated there was an alleged witch hunt going on in the City's inquiry into the operation of the plant. A public works official contended that the probe by the Board of Representatives was based on capricious information and false charges.

The article was filled with claims and denials, finger pointing and back stabbing. Someone said that the mismanagement at the plant was sinking the city deeper into a potential multi-million-dollar lawsuit. An official responded that the allegations were all crap. How appropriate!

One accuser claimed to have written documentation to support his claims. Another said he would release records damaging to the department unless one of the other persons interviewed retracted a previous statement. Everybody seemed to be looking for justice or seeking cover. The motives and credibility of anyone speaking out immediately came under attack.

But the best part of the article was the paragraph that said that just minutes after opening the proceedings to the public, the Committee voted unanimously to do their work behind closed doors. Spectators had barely had a chance to get comfortable in their seats before they were asked to leave the room. It seemed that transparency was lacking when it came to investigations conducted by any of the City's boards. It was as though the various committees were merely puppets whose strings were being pulled by a master puppeteer.

Another article of interest to me was titled, "Civil Service probers find faults, deficiencies abound." It was a follow up to previous stories about allegations of irregularities in the system that allowed unqualified applicants to be appointed to key positions and encouraged nepotism.

As I read the headline, I thought about what a great time it was to be an investigative reporter in Stamford. Anthony Dolan could not have timed his arrival in town any better. For a sharp, aggressive guy like him, there was no shortage of juicy topics to write about.

Continuing into the article, it said the mayor's "blue ribbon" personnel panel had completed its three-month review of the civil service system and was ready to write its final report. Three months! I and most of the other people in Stamford could have found the problems in three days.

It was anticipated the report would include among the findings that local regulations were at variance with state statutes, qualifications to be appointed to the Personnel Commission differed from state recommendations, the Personnel Department was understaffed, and there were deficiencies in the posting of open positions.

It was believed that the panel had also concluded that in the past, the Personnel Department had deliberately written some job specifications to give an advantage to certain candidates and exclude others. And in addition, no evidence was found that any serious attempt was made to validate the written tests it uses.

Deliberately! There it was. The personnel Department not only could, but had, tailored job qualifications to favor the preferred candidate and exclude the undesirables. The system encouraged nepotism? Yeah, I guess you could say that.

On another day the paper ran an Anthony Dolan story. It was not the one I was waiting for, but it was interesting nonetheless. It was about the state's findings regarding the questionable appointment of former Parks Superintendent Eugene Berube. The headline was, "State brands Berube case 'bizarre' but not criminal."

Dolan said that Donald A. Browne, State's Attorney for Fairfield County, had issued a letter stating that his office "has not been able to determine the actual provable commission of any criminal offense" surrounding the Berube appointment.

Browne's letter indicated he had read a volume of material about the Berube controversy. Browne was quoted as writing, "Without doubt the various investigations, both official and unofficial, clearly disclosed conduct of a bizarre and probably suspicious nature.

"It has satisfied me that there existed within the City of Stamford certain activities normally considered inconsistent with what is anticipated from a prudent, responsible administration of a municipal government.

"My responsibilities consist exclusively in the prosecution of serious felony criminal offenses which occur within the county and obviously do not extend to reprimanding municipal officials for municipal improprieties."

Browne's letter went on to say that while it did not appear that any provable criminal activity took place, "It does appear to me that certain procedures utilized were questionable and of dubious compliance with the spirit of accepted good government. These obviously are matters for the legitimate consideration of the electorate of the City of Stamford."

The attorney also wrote, "It appears to me that some officials were evasive and less than candid and appeared to be interested in stimulating unrelated issues in an apparent attempt to confuse or dilute the investigation from its intended purpose."

Dolan noted that some of the allegations made in the Berube matter involved possible perjury and falsification of records, both criminal offenses, and were not mentioned in the Browne letter. The reporter cited an anonymous criminal justice source who explained, "They're (the state's attorneys) starved for prosecutors and investigators. They probably lack more personnel than any other criminal justice system around. They just don't have the time or the people to look into white collar crime or municipal corruption."

This was yet another head-shaker for me. The ball had been thrown back into the people of Stamford's court. And what did this mean for the chances of getting any action involving the police corruption stuff? Dolan's story was well-written; but the results were a downer.

And things were getting rougher for me on the job. With each passing day more of my fellow cops believed I was the primary source for all of Dolan's articles, even the non-police stories.

———————

Just how bad things were becoming for me at the police department was made clear to me when I reported to the station for an afternoon shift on October 27th. I found a piece of paper taped to my locker that served as a warning. It said, "Carlucci, you're going to get yours." I figured the misspelling of my name was intentional. The rest of the note was mostly name-calling. I will not tell you exactly how the author of the note referred to me. I will just say he accused me of being a rat.

As I was staring at the piece of paper, a friend of mine at a locker behind mine spoke to me. He said he had seen the note and was going to remove it so I would not get upset, but thought better of it and left it there. He said I just needed to understand that most of the cops liked and supported me. I should just accept the note as the work of one of the idiots that were in the minority.

I said I knew I was on the right side. What bothered me was getting the blame for everything Dolan was writing, much of which I was hearing about for the first time. And receiving threatening notes right in police headquarters was over the top.

And then the guy asked me if I had seen the day's newspaper with the final article of Dolan's series in it. I said I had not; but that would be the first item on my agenda when I got out on the street.

I had butterflies in my stomach as I drove to a convenience store to buy the paper. This was the last installment. In my mind it would be the most important one of them all. Please, Dolan, do not let me down now.

23

OLAN DID not let me down. In fact, I think his final article in the series knocked it out of the park. Of all his good work and reporting, I thought this story was his best. The shocking headline was, "Investigation shows seven policemen have close links with organized crime." Not fixing tickets. Not drinking or taking drugs. Not having sex while on duty. Not illegally discharging their service weapons. No, this was *organized crime*. This was the big time.

As I read, I was yet again impressed with Dolan's sourcing. I recognized that some of the information was from me. But it was obvious he had talked with many others. That was encouraging to me because I believed that providing information for this topic would not have been sour grapes.

Cops that felt they had been wronged by the department somehow and were looking for revenge might have done a bit of that in previous articles. But not this one. I felt very strongly that the sources for this piece had provided information because it was the right thing to do and not for personal benefit or to get even.

In the first paragraph Dolan said that the paper's investigation showed that approximately seven policemen, including two sergeants and a lieutenant, were closely linked to a local racketeer with organized crime connections. The racketeer was not named, but was described as a kingpin in Stamford's estimated $30 million a year gambling business and an operative of the Gambino crime family.

Dolan said the guy was a Stamford native who masqueraded as a legitimate businessman interested in charity work; and those seven cops enjoyed a close relationship with him. That relationship included them receiving numerous gratuities from the gambling chief.

I knew who Dolan was talking about and the reporter's description of him was right. He was a made man and of the Gambino family and played the role of wanting to help everyone—a real nice compassionate guy. It reminded me of the way Al Capone became a hero to some of the people in Chicago for running soup kitchens during the depression.

Only a few days earlier when I visited my parents' house, I found they had obtained a fancy kitchen set. I asked my mother about it and she said the son of an elderly woman gave it to her for looking in on his mother and helping her out as needed. As we talked, I learned the appreciative son was none other than the racketeer in Dolan's story. My mother was oblivious to who he was. To her he was just a guy who was good to his mother and very generous.

Not so, according to Dolan. "The racketeer has made a determined effort to cultivate policemen and prominent City politicians in an effort to gain protection for his gambling operation and other illegal activities, according to extensive interviews with local, state and federal law enforcement sources."

One police source that Dolan interviewed alleged he knew of one cop who was making six hundred dollars a week in payoffs from the racketeer and other criminal operatives. And the sentence that followed must have sent chills up some spines. "The Advocate, which has turned over its information on this matter to the federal organized crime strike force in Hartford, recently arranged for a Federal Bureau of Investigation interview with one policeman with this information."

Dolan said that in addition to cases of outright bribery, the relationship between the cops and racketeer was one of dubious legality and was clearly in violation of rules forbidding fraternization with known criminals.

He continued, "At least four of the seven policemen, for example, have taken at least one gambling junket, arranged and financed by the racketeer, to resort areas in Florida, Puerto Rico, New Orleans, La., and Las Vegas, Nev.

"Arrangements for the trips are usually elaborate and the racketeer reportedly enjoys unlimited credit at a Las Vegas casino."

One cop and one politician who had been on the junkets told Dolan, "Everything was first class."

These disclosures about gambling junkets might shock and anger the public, but they were no secret to me and other cops. The guys who went on them used to brag about it right in the locker room in front of everybody. They did not try to hide their relationship with this guy. They were proud of it.

The next paragraph demonstrated the depth of the investigation by Dolan and the newspaper. "On one recent trip whose start at Kennedy airport was observed by Advocate staff members and the FBI, arrangements were handled by the racketeer through an out-of-town travel agency run by relatives of another important organized crime figure in Fairfield County."

I could not help but think that this article was probably the first time the seven dirty cops and the racketeer and his pals would become aware of the scope of the Advocate's efforts and the involvement of the feds. I wondered what impact it would have on them. As I thought of these guys squirming, I am sure a smile crossed my face.

Getting back to the article, Dolan wrote, "The policemen also receive free goods and services at one of the legitimate businesses run by the racketeer and frequented by other well-known gamblers. They often attend parties and other social events together. Recently, the racketeer was a guest at a lavish party thrown by one of the policemen." The host was my former boss, Larry Hogan!

Dolan pointed out that although this socializing was not illegal, it did cause concern among state and federal law enforcement agents. One federal source was quoted as saying, "Anyone around here would turn in his badge the day we found out about it."

State law enforcement sources told Dolan that a State Police undercover agent visited a business run by the racketeer. One of the racketeer's friendly policemen, a sergeant, became suspicious of the agent and ran a license plate check on his vehicle. Stamford Police Department officials questioned the sergeant about the incident after the State Police complained, but no disciplinary action was taken.

The story brought out the concern Joe Ligi and I had expressed about the number of raids we conducted where we came up empty and we believed the targets were being tipped off by members of our department. And it was not just our own investigations that these "friendly" cops compromised. They let the bad guys know when the State Police were active in the city as well. They would tell the crooks to change phone numbers and stop taking betting action until the heat was off.

When I read Dolan's account of a gambler arrested by Stamford police who refused to believe they were locals, I hollered out, that is my case! This was the arrest Ellis Crawford and I made at Joe "Cigar" Nelson's place. The guy kept saying we must be from the state because he was protected by the locals.

Dolan concluded his piece with, "The Advocate investigation clearly shows that the vast majority of policemen are innocent of fraternizing with organized crime figures or of any other improper activities cited in this series. Indeed, interviews show that the average policeman is repulsed by this behavior but is powerless to force department commanders to take action against the minority of policemen who violate criminal statutes or department rules.

"A sense of frustration led many policemen to act as sources for information appearing in this series. These policemen were convinced, however, that the public would unfairly blame an entire police force for the failure of the department's leadership to investigate and discipline errant policemen."

Dolan really nailed it in that last paragraph. He had done his job and done it well. The question now was what the fallout would be.

Investigation shows seven policemen have close links with organized crime

As I was leaving headquarters on the Tuesday afternoon following Dolan's final article, a cop I knew stopped me and said he wanted to talk. He said he had some information for me that I needed to hear in private. We walked over to a secluded corner of the building and I told him to go ahead.

He said he had been contacted by some people from New York City—he did not say who—and that they disliked Larry Hogan immensely for what he had done and was continuing to do in Stamford. These unnamed individuals wanted to know if they could meet with me at a restaurant on South Main Street in Port Chester, New York, just across the state line.

I asked why they wanted this meeting. The guy said they wanted to pick my brain about what I knew about Hogan.

He added, "If you meet with them, they'll make it worth your while if you know what I mean."

What this cop obviously was not aware of was that I knew the identities of the seven cops with ties to organized crime that Dolan had referred to in his article. And he was one of them. He was probably the least important of the bunch, but he was one of them nonetheless. I decided to play along and asked when his friends in New York wanted to get together. He said six o'clock on Thursday. He emphasized that it would be perfectly safe. It would still be daylight and there would be a lot of people in the restaurant at that time of day. This thing had setup written all over it. But I said OKAY, even though I had no intention of being inside that restaurant Thursday evening. However, I was curious and decided to find out who was involved and what they had planned for me.

I used the next day, Wednesday, to check out the meeting site in Port Chester. It was a nice restaurant with parking behind the building and a rear entrance. The paved parking area ended at an upward slope with a chain link fence and thick shrubbery. I found a street a couple of blocks up the hill from the restaurant where I left my car and walked back to the parking lot. I cut into the overgrowth at the chain link fence and made my way to a vantage point from which I would be able to look down and see every car in the lot, with almost no chance of being seen myself. It was perfect.

As I drove to Port Chester on Thursday afternoon, I had second thoughts about what I was doing. I was sure the whole thing was bogus. But to what purpose? Was I on the hit list? I had not told anyone else about the proposed meeting, should I have? Suppose I was not as smart as I thought and was walking into a trap? If I disappeared, would anyone ever know what had happened to me? As my mind worked through the what ifs, I noticed the steering wheel was glistening from the perspiration on my palms; and I felt the uncomfortable wetness in my shirt from armpits drenched in sweat. I continued, but with a lot less confidence than I'd had on Wednesday.

I again parked my car a distance away from the restaurant and was in position on the slope above the parking lot a few minutes before six. Many of my questions were answered almost as soon as I parted the shrubbery and the parking lot came into full view. Not more than thirty yards from me was the back of Lieutenant Larry Hogan's new Pontiac. Hogan was sitting in the car along with another guy I recognized, David "Turk" Avnayim. The Turk was a well-known drug dealer with organized crime ties. They were both slouched down and would have been difficult to spot if not for my elevated position. As confirmation of who Hogan's passenger was, I recognized the Turk's car parked directly in front of Hogan's.

There was no longer any doubt about my suspicions. This had been a setup. If Hogan and Turk had caught me out in that parking lot, they would have killed me right there or taken me somewhere else to do the job. As that realization hit, I felt fear and then anger. I had an urge to come out of hiding and confront them, to get it over with. But I knew this was not the time and that wasn't the way. So, I stayed put.

I kept watch for a few more minutes to see if anyone else I recognized showed up. No one did. I decided it was time to leave and as I started to walk back to the street and to my car an idea struck me. I took my handkerchief out of my pocket and picked up one of the large rocks that littered the ground. With all my might I threw it in the direction of Hogan's car. As luck would have it, I scored a direct hit on Hogan's rear window and it shattered. Before the shards of glass stopped falling, I was long gone, laughing all the way back to my car.

But on my return trip to Stamford the levity faded and the seriousness of the situation set in. Larry Hogan and whoever else wanted me dead, were ready and willing to make that happen. My concerns were no longer just speculation or gut feelings. My life was in real danger and that was now a fact.

Within days of what I thought had been a near death experience in Port Chester, Anthony Dolan's next article appeared. And it was bound to further infuriate Hogan and company. The headline was, "U.S. attorney to investigate charges against City police." The feds were in and that was good news.

The story read, "United States Attorney Peter Dorsey said Thursday his office will investigate allegations of police corruption made this week in an Advocate five-part series on the Stamford Police Department."

In a telephone interview Dorsey told Dolan, "No question about it. We will look into it and, if feasible, we will initiate prosecutions. We're very much interested." Dorsey promised that he would confer with members of his staff about the newspaper stories which alleged cover-ups of police crimes by department commanders, including drug-pushing and gambling payoffs, as well as links between seven

Stamford policemen and operatives of the Carlo Gambino crime family in New York State.

A statement issued by Mayor Clapes was referenced in the article in which he offered to order an investigation if Dolan would provide him with specific information regarding alleged police wrongdoing. "I don't know if this is true or not," Clapes was quoted as saying of Dolan's stories. "However, Dolan's series fell far short of the promise of the headlines. It may be that Dolan declined to specify names due to the libel laws. Nevertheless, if he has specifics and is prepared to make a disclosure to me, and if I am convinced that the situation warrants it, I would tear this City inside out to ferret out the corruption. I will be calling Dolan later today to go over this subject."

I was not happy with the comments from Clapes about Dolan's articles falling short. Other than not identifying his sources by name, I thought the allegations were quite clear. I hoped Clapes did not expect Dolan to reveal the names of his informants.

Dolan further mentioned that a federal grand jury had been looking into the police department's handling of traffic light contracts since June, following a series of Advocate articles on the subject. Mr. Dorsey declined to comment on whether he would order that body to extend its probe into other areas of the department. *The heat was being turned up. Would it reach a boiling point?*

Over the following days my anxiety over my situation grew. While Dolan's articles had been great in exposing the corruption, to some degree they had made my predicament worse. Unfairly or not, to Hogan and most of the police department I was the chief suspect as the reporter's informant. And I still had no one I could trust that I could go to for help. My best shot was probably getting a new police chief who would come into town and clean house. But with the political situation in Stamford what it was, that was probably just wishful thinking. More than likely the new guy would be another insider. The face at the top would change, but everything else would remain the same.

I waited. But my hand was never far from my gun. I was always acutely aware of my surroundings, was very careful of where I went, where I parked and who was near me. If they wanted me, they would have to come at me head on. They were not going to get me by trickery like that Port Chester thing. And if and when they did come, they'd have a fight on their hands.

So, I was staying alive, but not really living. I did not share my feelings with anybody, not even my wife. Something had to happen and soon, though. Something had to break.

And the LORD said to Moses in Midian, "Go back to Egypt, for all the men who were seeking your life are dead."

EXODUS 4:19

24

AFTER CHIEF Kinsella retired, Lieutenant Al Lombardo had been named acting chief. He was a good guy as far as I knew. I did not know him well enough to have complete trust in him, though. And besides, being temporary he was not likely to want to tackle the corruption stuff anyway.

Unfortunately for Lombardo, he suffered an injury a few weeks after being named as acting chief and had to step down. He was replaced by Lieutenant John Considine, for whom I had the utmost respect. However, as with Lombardo, I was sure Considine would not want to jump into the corruption cauldron unless he was appointed to the chief's position on a permanent basis. So, I kept my mouth shut and hoped for a better opportunity.

And then it happened. The word got out that the city was looking at the police chief of Menlo Park, California to fill its chief's vacancy. Mayor Clapes was allegedly going to submit the name of Victor I. Cizanckas [pronounced Cha-zan-kus] to the Board of Representatives for appointment. For me this was very good news in that the city had gone outside the area—all the way across country—to find Kinsella's replacement. But other than being an outsider, what was the potential new chief all about?

I set out to learn whatever I could about Cizanckas. I reached out to two police sources I knew in California that were familiar with Cizanckas. He had been chief in Menlo Park since 1969. My sources described him as a tough ex-Marine; a reformer who did not take crap from anybody. They said he had done some good things in Menlo Park.

The most noteworthy of Menlo Park's accomplishments under Cizanckas was an undercover operation that resulted in the arrests of eight men and one woman for committing more than thirty terrorist-type bombings.

According to a newspaper account of the operation, the nine arrestees were part of a Nazi group. Following their arrests, 30 guns and 75 pounds of black powder were confiscated, along with photos of Adolph Hitler and a copy of Mein Kampf.

When the undercover officer attempted to infiltrate the gang, he had to explain why he was going rogue. He told them that he was upset with the department because the chief was "a Commie pinko." The Nazis seemed to accept that story, but demanded that he prove himself by stealing a police department file and turning it over to the group. Chief Cizanckas created a fake file for the officer to "steal" and give to the gang. That was sufficient for the officer to gain admission to the Nazi club.

I was very impressed with how Cizanckas set up and ran the undercover operation. It demonstrated to me that he had the guts to tackle some very dangerous people. Although I didn't know it then, that very undercover assignment would serve as a model for what I would soon become involved with in Stamford.

And it turned out the story about Cizanckas coming to Stamford was not just rumor. Mayor Clapes did in fact nominate him for the chief's position. An article that appeared in the New York Times on March 6, 1977, made this prediction, "MENLO PARK, CALIF. The Police Department of Stamford is in for a thorough, businesslike modernization if Victor Cizanckas, the police chief of this small suburb south of San Francisco, is approved by Stamford's Board of Representatives as their new police chief."

My faith in Mayor Clapes was restored. He had resisted all the political pressure and sought out a man with a reputation for solving problems. While that was good news to me, the griping and complaining about Clapes' decision started almost immediately. I heard guys who had a lot of juice [pull] moaning that they thought they had a deal with Clapes to get their candidate in. They could not believe he had done what he had done. I had to chuckle as I watched these big shots whine and cry like a bunch of babies.

As good as Cizanckas sounded, there was another article that made me wonder if all the changes under a potential Cizanckas administration would be received positively by the rank and file. It had to do with uniforms. It said, "In 1969, the Chief of Police of the California community of

Menlo Park, in the interest of professionalizing the role of police and improving community relations, embarked on a program whose most apparent feature was a change in the style of police attire. The police of Menlo Park shifted from the typical blue, military style uniform to a civilian green blazer. The results were dramatic, both on the attitudes of the police and the community.

"Stripped of the established symbols of authority, police began to develop new patterns of relating to the community and gradually adopted the role of 'public service officer.' In later years, this shift away from the militaristic model of authority led to the elimination of rank altogether and its replacement by a more horizontal organizational structure."

Green blazers and no rank? I was not sure I liked that type of change. If Cizanckas got the appointment, maybe he would not try to implement that in Stamford.

Despite all the grumbling and name calling, Mayor Clapes did not withdraw his nominee and Cizanckas was in fact appointed to a lifetime term as chief on May 5, 1977. A newspaper story said the lifetime appointment was highly unusual and that the new chief had been given broad investigative and administrative powers to investigate the City's growing reputation for municipal corruption.

The battle to wrest control of the Stamford Police Department and the City itself from the corrupt cops, politicians and power brokers, was about to enter a new stage.

SUNDAY, FEBRUARY 16, 1969   SU 1-2424   SUND

Nine Nazis Captured

In Terror Bombings

Menlo Park Police Chief Victor Cizanckas with guns, ammo, powder, Nazi symbols seized in ring roundup

CHIEF CIZANCKAS OF MENLO PARK CALIFORNIA
WITH A MAJOR ARREST.

CIZANCKAS WOULD BE VITO'S NEW
CHIEF IN STAMFORD CT.

25

I N THE early spring of 1977, I was at a low point in my life. Dolan's series had been great and the news about the new chief was encouraging; but despite that I was down. Maybe I just could not bring myself to believe things were really going to get better. And I was not the only one. Many of my fellow cops said the impact of the newspaper stories would fade away; and when Chief Cizanckas actually took over he'd soon succumb to the pressure the power brokers would apply.

But I think the real reason I was depressed was the realization of how much trouble I was in with Hogan and his pals. Most people never experience knowing that someone wants them dead and is prepared to make that wish a reality. I can tell you that it is not a very comforting feeling. And when you live with it day after day it takes a toll. I had known I was in danger for a long time and had kind of adjusted to that fact. But the Port Chester incident had brought it back into focus for me. And when I thought about it, it almost took my breath away—like getting punched in the stomach.

I had gotten a kick out of smashing the window out of Hogan's car in the parking lot of the restaurant. In hindsight, it had not been very smart, though. Would Hogan think he had been the random victim of a vandal? Or would he put two and two together and come up with me? I was, after all, the guy who was supposed to be at that meeting. Hogan was a crook, but he was not stupid. I was sure he knew it was me who was there and that I knew all about the setup. In his eyes, that would make me an even greater threat. So outwardly I laughed a lot and acted like everything was wonderful. But under that facade, there was no humor.

There was a glimmer of hope on that front, however. My sources told me that the organized crime guys in Fairfield County and New York City were getting fed up with Hogan. He was constantly asking for more payoff money and his demands were wearing thin. I heard that Hogan had been called to a sit down and told to back off. But he had stood his ground and said the mobsters needed him and he was worth every penny they paid him.

I believed those stories because in these kinds of relationships, there is no love. The mobsters are not fond of the cops on their pad. They deal with them out of necessity. It is strictly business and they don't want to get ripped off. And on the other hand, I had no problem believing that Hogan was arrogant enough to defend his monetary demands.

But I thought he was being foolish. The guys he was challenging could only be pushed so far. If it came to the point where they felt he was out of control, he could end up on their hit list instead of the payoff list. They would figure there would be another department official they could corrupt to replace him.

So, as it stood, organized crime hated me and Hogan; Hogan hated me; and I hated Hogan and organized crime. What a pleasant environment!

On top of all this, my marriage was in danger of failing. We were continuing to have financial troubles and not getting along at all. Was I stressed? Yes, to the max. Even when I was playing with the band I kind of went through the gigs in a daze.

On the job I went from preferring to work alone to riding with a partner. Working alone gave me too much time to think and get even more down in the dumps. Having someone with me to talk and joke with took my mind off my problems, at least for eight hours.

———

Even before Cizanckas' appointment was officially approved, Advocate staff reporter Stephen Harrington wrote that police department Captain Kevin Tobin, commander of the uniform division, had requested that the Board of Representatives launch an investigation into the police department due to "persistent and recurring allegations of improprieties within the police force."

In his prepared release Tobin said, "Sufficient doubt has been raised concerning the department and these doubts should be resolved. I personally believe that the Board of Representatives should appoint a competent investigating committee to examine in detail all allegations of wrongdoing within the department and current practices and procedures within the department.

"Such an investigation, conducted in public, in addition to vindicating personnel within the department might also furnish information on practices and procedures which could serve as the basis for necessary reforms."

When asked if he was speaking in an official capacity, Tobin replied that he was "speaking as a cop with 22 years' experience."

I knew Captain Tobin to be a good cop and had a lot of respect for him. But I thought he was wrong regarding the Board of Representatives being the right choice to investigate the police department. This was much too big for them or any Stamford agency. I continued to believe it needed to be done by an outsider like Cizanckas.

———

Chief Victor Cizanckas—who many people were already calling Vic—arrived in Stamford and was sworn in on May 5. I went to a public forum he spoke at to get my first look at my new boss and potential lifeline. He was a very tall man and I listened closely as he talked. He highlighted his experience in police work, his degrees in sociology and police science, and the many articles he had written for law enforcement and other publications, including the New York Times Magazine. I looked around the room and saw many of the politicians and politically connected who had wanted a candidate of their choice to be at that podium rather than this guy. I had heard many of them say exactly that while the position was vacant; and I could read their expressions as the Chief delivered his message.

One of his comments caused my heart to leap with joy and caused the cheeks of many of the power brokers in the crowd to turn red. He said, "I won't fix a case. I won't fix a ticket. And I want you to know that right now."

Upon hearing those words, a top City official sat back in his chair, laughed sarcastically and said aloud, "Man, you'd just better go back to California because you'll never succeed in this town." To me, that was proof my boss was not in anybody's pocket. And it was clear to me he had done his homework in preparation for his new assignment. He knew the situation and who would be in the audience for his arrival speech. He had drawn a line in the sand and I loved it.

I could feel my depression wane as he continued his remarks. When he finished, I wanted to stand up and cheer, but did not dare.

I could not imagine any way the Chief could have gotten off to a better start; but there was more good news to come. Among his first actions at the police department, he called Larry Hogan into his office. According to reliable sources, he told Hogan that he knew he had been bought off and was aware of everything he had been doing. Larry Hogan, with 22 years on the job, was forced to retire on the spot. And after words were exchanged the Chief bodily threw him out the door. Anthony Dolan's screaming headlines and stories had paid dividends and more would follow.

It was amazing. In just a couple of days my doubts and fears about Cizanckas and his intentions were gone. He had come into town with a new broom and the house cleaning had begun. Hogan was the first to go, but he was quickly followed by other firings and demotions, with deserving officers promoted to replace them. And in another dramatic move, the long-sought Internal Affairs Unit was created.

It was an exciting time for me in the police department. Chief Cizanckas was saying the right things and making all the right moves. I had been waiting a long time for somebody I could trust and based on what I had seen and heard, I was convinced that Cizanckas was that guy. I decided that if I received any more threats, nasty notes on my locker or overt action against me like the Port Chester deal, I would request a meeting with him and ask for his help. But unless that time came, I intended to keep my distance from him. If I happened to bump into him around headquarters, we'd exchange a hello and that, was it. As far as I knew he did not know who I was or anything about me.

It was not long before I found out that was not true, though. I was home on my day off when Cizanckas called me. He said he wanted me to come to his office at ten o'clock the next morning and not to be concerned about the afternoon shift I was scheduled to work. I wanted to ask him what this was about, but did not.

After we hung up my mind started racing. What did he want? What had I done? He had been cleaning house. Maybe I would be the next to go. There was no sleep for me that night. I paced and thought. And then paced some more. At long last daylight came. But even as I got cleaned up and had breakfast, I still wondered what fate awaited me.

When I arrived at Cizanckas' office I was ushered right in. It was just the two of us. We made small talk for a few minutes and then he hit me with it. "Vito, I've heard a lot of good things about you just in the few days I've been here. I have an assignment and I think you're the man for the job. I hope you will take it. I'd like you to work undercover organized crime."

PART THREE

The Undercover and Beyond

26

DO NOT know if my feelings were reflected on my face as I sat across the desk from Chief Cizanckas. If they were, he knew I was stunned. Of all the possibilities I had considered for why I had been summoned to this meeting, what I had just been told had never entered my mind. I am not sure how long it took before I responded, but hopefully it was only a couple of seconds. I remember telling him that I had a lot of questions. He said we had plenty of time to talk. I had been taken off my regularly scheduled shift and this meeting was my assignment for the day.

For nearly two hours he explained his plan. As I listened, I realized the scenario was familiar to me. It was very similar to the undercover operation he had run against the Nazi group in Menlo Park and I mentioned that to him. I had been taken aback earlier and now it was his turn. He asked how I had heard about that previous undercover already. I told him that when his name began circulating around Stamford as a replacement for Kinsella I had done some research on him. He laughed and I chuckled along with him. And then it was back to business.

After a lot of discussion between us, it was decided the scenario would be as follows: I would pretend to go rogue, like the undercover officer in Menlo Park. I would resign from the police department under the guise of being a disgruntled cop who was very angry because I had never gotten anywhere when I investigated Larry Hogan. And then this guy from out of state comes in, forces Hogan out and gets all the credit. I did not get a promotion or even honorable mention. So, screw the Stamford Police Department. That was going to be my story and Chief Cizanckas would make sure it got circulated out on the streets.

I would be required to wear a wire and hang out where people who were likely to have information about organized crime could approach me. That could be in restaurants, convenience stores, gas stations or just out on the street. And this was not going to be an entirely local-run operation. The FBI would wire me up each day I worked and monitor me. But once I hit the street I would be primarily on my own. And while I was out there, I would continue to feed the story about how pissed off I was over the Hogan thing.

I liked the plan and thought it could work, but a very important question had to be answered before I made the final commitment. How many other people in the department would know about the operation and who were they?

I was relieved when Cizanckas assured me that he and Lieutenant Considine would be the only people who knew. I trusted both him and Considine, so it was a go. He also promised me that I would be protected against reprisals after the operation concluded and the word got out about what I had been doing.

Cizanckas gave me the name and number of the FBI agent assigned to the Stamford office that I would be working with. He said the agent would call me shortly to set up a time for me to come into his office and meet him.

Every Friday or Saturday I was to call Considine at his home and arrange to go there unseen to pick up my pay-check. But I needed to make an initial visit to Considine's to get a small gun and holster that I could wear around my right ankle.

I surrendered my badge and was given a new one. I could not carry it on me. But I had to be able to get to it quickly should an emergency arise where I had to identify myself to another agency.

There was one more thing, however. Chief Cizanckas said I was to also work on my own time without the wire. He wanted me to be in the bars and restaurants I was comfortable in where I knew gambling went on. If they were running a card game, he wanted me around the table. He said he would personally provide me with the extra money necessary to carry out his orders. And this was just between him and me. No one else was to know about it. Not even Considine or the FBI. And other than my wife, I could not tell anyone anything about my assignment.

He also said that Hogan being ousted from the department was not enough, he needed to be indicted and prosecuted. And that would be accomplished through this assignment along with getting every other corrupt cop out of the department and into jail, if warranted.

I was excited because I had been dreaming about Hogan being indicted for a long time. And if I could help make that happen it would be revenge for me in a way—revenge for all the crap I had taken and for what he planned for me in Port Chester. I asked the Chief if he was sure the plan would work. He said, "It certainly will, Vito. By the time this is over you'll be known as a rogue cop extraordinaire."

We had been talking about some serious stuff. But in a moment of levity, I asked him if he was going to make the cops in Stamford wear green blazers. He laughed and said no, green blazers would not work in Stamford. I think we each recognized that the other had done his homework. I knew a lot about him and he knew a lot about me.

Before our meeting broke up, he pointed out that this was going to be much different from the usual undercover, in that I'd be using my own real identity and working in my home town where I was well known. And he promised me that if I did a good job on this assignment, I would have a job in the Detective Bureau on the day shift for as long as he remained with the department. And in police work, that was about as good as it got.

As I drove home, I realized that word of my resignation would spread throughout the department like a wildfire and Chief Cizanckas would be fanning the flames. Within a couple of hours every officer would know I was an ex-cop and then it would hit the streets. I imagined that a few of my colleagues would be glad. But most would be surprised and sorry to have me gone. And I could not even tell my closest friend on the force, Joe Ligi, what was really going on.

When I got back to my house my wife could sense my nervousness. I only told her that I had been assigned to work plain clothes for a while and that I would be working all different hours. I told her about the false resignation and that she could not tell anyone I was still working for the police department. She said she understood and agreed to guard my secret.

Later on, I spoke with the FBI agent I'd be working with. For the purposes of this book, I'll call him Harvey Fenster. He invited me over to his office which was located on East Main Street, a block from my father's barber shop. We agreed to meet at one o'clock the next afternoon and have lunch in their cafeteria. He took my order for a burger and fries and said he would have them ready for me when I got there.

I left home for the meeting around 12:30 the following afternoon. But as I was driving it dawned on me that the FBI office was in a heavily trafficked area and everybody in Stamford—both the good and the bad—knew they were there. If anybody spotted me around that building it could blow the whole thing. I decided to park my car on a small side street across from the office building called Clark's Hill Avenue. It was only a few yards from my father's business and if anybody saw me in the general area, they could think I was visiting him.

But that would not explain why I would be going into the FBI building. So, from Clark's Hill I cut through backyards to East Main and hid in some bushes until there were no cars coming in either direction, and then ran across the street and got inside. I looked out through the darkly tinted windows and did not see anything that caused concern—no vehicles or faces that I recognized. So far, so good.

I took the elevator up and met Harvey Fenster. He greeted me warmly and I took an immediate liking to him. He asked me if I was ready to do the undercover and I said I was. He said, "This is going to be a big one, Colucci. This is going to change many, many things in this City." I said good, let's get started.

Even with some lingering doubts about how much protection I would actually get if this thing blew up in my face or when it ended in success, I was about to start living the dream—my dream of bringing down Larry Hogan.

———

The day after my meeting with the FBI, Dolan struck again. The new story was about Chief Cizanckas and showed he was going after corruption like a man possessed. It was titled, "Browne eased Berube charges, Chief Cizanackas calls it a travesty."

Dolan began his piece with, "State's Attorney Donald Browne approved a plea-bargaining deal that resulted in reduced charges and a $250 fine against Parks Supervisor Eugene Berube, even though Mr. Berube was accused of breaking and entering an apartment, roughing up and repeatedly threatening to kill its occupants, pointing a gun at one man's head and, as the victim went to his knees and pleaded for his life, firing a shot that missed him by inches."

According to a police report about the incident, Berube and another man broke into the apartment and accused the three people inside of having burglarized Berube's home several days earlier. Statements taken by the police indicated that when one of the occupants threatened to call the police, Berube threatened to kill them with comments such as, "put a bullet through your head" and "throw the bodies in Cove Pond."

Browne defended his decision to reduce the felony charges to a misdemeanor. However, when Chief Cizanackas was asked for a comment, he called that decision a travesty of justice. He said Browne's claim that Berube's actions were taken in an effort to recover allegedly stolen property was, "an invitation to local citizens to take the law into their own hands."

Thinking about this now, it was very similar to what OJ Simpson did years later in Las Vegas that landed him in state prison.

Back to the article. Cizanackas added, "I talked to Mr. Browne and he has assured me that future cases of this magnitude will be the subject of discussion with the police chief."

I was amazed yet again. Here was Chief Cizanackas, on the job only a few weeks and he was taking on anybody and everybody. I had hoped Kinsella's replacement would be an outsider with experience and guts. In that regard there could not have been a better man for the job than Victor Cizanackas.

27

I T WAS the first day of my undercover career. It is hard for me to describe my feelings as I drove to the FBI office to get wired. I would not have to go there every day I worked; we could pick other places to meet. But for my debut I had to go to their office.

As I was walking out the door of the FBI office, I said to one of the agents "how do I look" (hoping a wire would not be visible), the agent replied "you look fine." In my nervousness to break the ice, I said "I went to Caldor yesterday and bought a new Timex watch for $29.99" as I proudly showed the agent what it looked like, his response back to me was "cops wear Timex, the Mob wears Rolex". Needless to say, the watch didn't go over well.

My job was to infiltrate two organized crime groups, the Gambino and Genovese families. And I had to do it right in my home town while using my own name. I still wondered if it would work. I would have to become an actor. And a good enough one to be able to convince some very smart and dangerous people that a decorated cop had become so angry with his department that he quit his job and was willing to do business with the other side. Could I, do it? Would I be able to get the bad guys to trust me? I certainly hope so. But one thing was certain. I would have to play my role as though my life depended on it. Because it did.

I used the same method to get into the FBI building as I did for the initial meeting; parking on the side street and cutting through yards. I had already decided that in the future I would borrow a friend's car when I had to be at the FBI office. But on this day, I drove my own vehicle.

Harvey Fenster gave me a full tour of the office. There were several agents around. Most were in suits and ties, but others were dressed casually like me. Some wore their hair long and had moustaches or beards. Fenster warned me that secrecy was paramount. Not only for me, but for the agents as well. He said I would be in that office many times during the course of my assignment and probably in their Bridgeport office as well. Some of the agents I saw there I might very well see again on the streets in their undercover roles. If that happened, I could not do anything to indicate I knew or recognized them. I could only communicate with them on the street if the agent initiated the contact.

After the tour we went into a back room where another agent was waiting. I took my shirt off and they wired me up. I was fortunate not to have had the amount of body hair then that I have now or getting that wire off day in and day out could have been a rather painful experience. But in those days my body was as smooth as a baby's rear end.

It was entirely my call where I would go and how long I would work. I could work two hours in a day or ten, Fenster did not care. I told him there was a diner that I knew where gambling went on and several organized crime guys hung out at. I said I wanted to start there to let it be known that I was around and see what kind of reaction I got.

We left the office and Fenster and his partner followed me toward the diner. We stopped under a highway overpass as we neared the restaurant. Fenster said they would wait at that location. He asked me to do a mic test just before I got to the diner. If they heard me okay, they would flash their lights. Before I drove away Fenster said to me, "Now don't be nervous. This is going to be right up your alley. You're going to do a great job."

With renewed confidence I headed down the street. Just before pulling into the diner, I did a voice test and saw the headlights of the FBI car flash. I parked my car, got out and took a deep breath. And then I started inside. I will never forget that as I reached the door I said aloud, "Help me Jesus." I do not know why I said it. I was not in the habit of calling on God at that point in my life, it just came out.

As I walked in, I saw a couple of people I recognized and the owner. The owner—who I will call Louie—and I knew each other from when I stopped in his place to eat while on patrol. I knew he was a bookmaker, ran poker games and dabbled in other illegal gambling activities.

I took a seat at the counter and Louie was over to me in a flash. "Hey, Vito. It's all over town that you quit the police department," he said. "What the hell happened?" Before I could answer another one of the guys I knew came over. I had to quickly position myself to face him so he would not slap me on the back or rest his arm there and feel the wire.

After the other guy sat down next to me, I said I had had enough of being a cop in Stamford. The new chief had come in like a big-assed bird with his lifetime appointment. He made a few waves by getting rid of Hogan and some others. But he just wanted to grab a little glory for himself based on the work I had done. I predicted that in a couple of months he would fall into line with the politicians and be as worthless as Kinsella had been.

"That guy sounds like a real piece of garbage," Louie said. And then he started on Hogan. He was a piece of garbage, too. I asked what he meant.

"You gotta be kiddin' me," Louie said. "He keeps askin' for money and more money. He ain't never satisfied." *Great stuff, I thought.*

"And guess what?" Louie continued. "A couple of months ago before he was thrown off the department, Hogan came into my diner one day and he says he heard my card games were doin' well, that I'm runnin' games three or four times a week. I asked him how he knew and he just smiled and said, 'Word gets around.' Then he says I must be makin' good money and he wants a cut of it. He tells me I gotta pay him six hundred bucks a week." Louie's getting mad as he talks and his face is turning red.

"I tried to laugh it off, figurin' he was kiddin' me. He laughed too, and then he got real serious. He looks me right in the eye and says, 'You're gonna give me six hundred a

week or you aren't gonna run any poker games. Got it?'
Louie's face was now almost purple.

"I got mad and told that bastard he wasn't gonna get a
penny from me. Not a damn penny! And then I told him
to get out of my place. When he got to the door he turned
around and smiled at me and said. 'Take care. I'll see you
again.' The way he said it sent a chill down my spine; but I
ran the card games anyway."

Louie explained that on the very next night he ran a game
two uniformed cops showed up and said they had received
several complaints of excessive noise and to tone it down.
The next game night more cops showed up alleging they
had received parking complaints. After that it was alleged
complaints by the wives of the card players that strippers
were performing in the building. The person who supposedly received all these complaints and assigned officers to
investigate them was Lieutenant Larry Hogan. Within a
couple of weeks, the players left Louie's poker games for
less stressful venues. Louie had kept his promise not to pay
Hogan a cent. But true to his own word, Hogan had put
Louie out of business.

Louie added that Hogan's greed and increased power was
annoying the organized crime operatives as well. "I'm tellin'
you, Vito, Hogan's gonna get popped one of these days. If
he keeps it up, they are gonna pop him."

Louie's anger then gave way to hurt and disbelief. "Can
you believe the nerve of this guy?" he went on, seemingly
on the verge of tears. "I went to school with him. We played
ball together. And then he pulls that on me! He's no good,
Vito. He's just no good."

I left the diner and advised the agents to follow me to a secluded city park located a short distance away. We entered the men's room and locked the door behind us. I said I did not want to do anything more that day. I was pumped up over how well things had gone and felt it was a good note to stop on. Harvey Fenster said that was fine and removed the wire. He said I had gotten some very good information from Louie and he was more than satisfied with the first day's results. It was agreed we'd do it again the next day at noon. Harvey promised to call Chief Cizanckas and brief him on the day's events.

From my perspective, it had been a productive day for information, even though it had been relatively easy because Louie had been in the mood to vent. And it had also been a boost for my confidence in working with the FBI. They were really great. I could set my own hours and locations and I would always have backup nearby if things went bad. We had even worked out an arrangement where I would communicate the difficulty of the situation I was in by saying things such as, "Are you threatening me?" "Are you going to pull a gun on me?" Or, "Is that a knife you're reaching for?" The agents would evaluate the severity of the situation based on my words and respond accordingly.

On the way home I picked up a copy of the newspaper and there was Anthony Dolan again. This time he was reporting on an investigation he had done of shoddy practices at a nursing home. My reaction was, this guy is not going to leave anything on the table. Private or City, anything he found that was not right was going to get put out there. And a second article proved just that. In that one

Dolan was back into City employees with connections to organized crime. Only this time it was a fireman, not a cop.

Dolan said his review of Stamford Fire Department records had uncovered a "booming arson industry" in the city; and that a fireman with links to organized crime was not properly investigating the burnings. *An arson industry in addition to everything else? How much more stuff was out there?*

I remember thinking there should be a sign at the city limits reading, "Stamford, We Do It All Here." If you have got a building you need to get out from under and have the connections, it can be made to go up in flames and be determined by fire investigators to have been an accident. If you want to make a little book or run an illegal poker game, and you are willing to share some of your earnings with the local cops, you will have a home in Stamford. Yes sir, Stamford was a mobster-friendly City.

And a subsequent article by Dolan a couple of days later looked back at the police corruption story and Larry Hogan. It said that not too long ago there had been a high-level meeting between Mob big shots and their bookies. The bosses, including at least one Gambino capo, arrived at the get together by chauffeured limousines. The subject of that session was what to do about Hogan and the ever increasing pay he wanted for his services. Were the bookies willing to kick in more money to Hogan? Or should the situation be resolved by killing him?

Dolan reported that in a close vote, attendees grudgingly agreed that although they did not like it, Hogan was still worth the money. But that could change the next time he upped the ante.

What was it Louie had told me? "I'm tellin' you, Vito, Hogan's gonna get popped one of these days. If he keeps it up, they are gonna pop him." Louie may or may not have been at that sit down himself. But if not, it was almost a certainty that he had talked with somebody who had been there.

Dolan brought up another blast from my past, Duke Morris. He said that Morris had pushed drugs for years under the protection of his superiors. During that time, he had been a key witness for state prosecutors in numerous drug trials. When allegations against Morris were brought to the attention of the State Attorney, that office declined to launch a grand jury investigation.

It could be expected that Dolan's articles would not endear him to the drug dealers, bookies and mobsters, or to some civil servants and politicians. But several local businessmen were not happy either. They formed a group and wrote a letter to the newspaper complaining that the seemingly endless stories cast the city in a bad light and created a difficult environment in which to encourage new businesses to invest there.

Anthony Dolan was developing an increasing number of very powerful enemies on both sides of the law.

28

As THE days passed, I grew more comfortable in my undercover role. I went to restaurants, bars and stores where I knew gambling action was going on. And I even spent time on the streets where the low-end bookies did their thing. Other times I would go the other way and stop in at the boat clubs where the big shot gangsters hung out. And I was getting good information. Harvey Fenster was happy and I understood that Chief Cizanckas was happy.

If there was a problem, it was confidence. I was getting too much of it. I had to keep reminding myself how to sit, stand and talk. It would only take one inadvertent touch by somebody to feel the wire and it would be all over with. Although everything was going great so far, I knew that could change in an instant.

One day I got invited to a high stakes card game run by a guy named Antonio. I did not think this would be a good place to wear the wire, so I decided to do it as part of my private assignment for Chief Cizanckas.

For those of you who have never played in an illegal poker game, the operator makes his money by cutting the pot. That means that every so often during each hand, he or one of his helpers reaches into the pot and takes a couple of dollars out for the house. The operator has no interest in who wins or loses. It is all about keeping the game moving and playing a lot of hands. In addition to providing a place to play, the operator also supplies beer, soda and lunch meat to make sandwiches.

When I walked into the room, I got some strange looks from three or four of the players. One of them, a wise-mouthed street gangster, said, "What the hell's he doin' here?"

"He's okay," Antonio said. "He's not on the police department no more."

"What do ya mean he ain't on the police department no more?

"Ah, you know, he left. They let Hogan walk away and Vito didn't like it, so he got out."

The guy with the big mouth looked at me and laughed. "They're never gonna get that guy. He's too locked into all of us," he said. "If you got some money and you ain't a cop, sit down and play."

As the game went on, I was winning pretty steady. I got thinking that if I could play in these games on a regular basis there was potential to make some extra money. Chief Cizanckas was staking me and he never mentioned what I should do with any winnings. As far as I knew I could keep them.

By the end of that first night, I was one of the boys and became a regular at the games. I was picking up some good information, but the beginner's luck I had enjoyed was soon gone. I was not only losing my stake from Cizanckas, I was going into my own pocket as well. The only other downside was that without the wire I had to trust what I heard to memory. To help myself out I started carrying a blank piece of paper in my wallet. Every once in a while, I'd go to the men's room to write myself some notes; and that really helped a lot.

The games ran six nights a week. And because I could set my own schedule, if I was on a losing streak and short of money, I could skip a few days until I replenished my bankroll.

Sometimes I would go to a game after playing a wedding or at a party with the band and still be wearing my velour jacket and tie. On one of those nights a guy who was a regular player seemed to fall in love with my jacket and came over to me saying he wanted to feel the material. The trouble was, this was a guy who had never warmed up to me. And he made comments from time to time like, "Hey, be careful what you say in front of Colucci. Once a cop, always a cop." And as he rubbed his hands across my shoulders and back, I was pretty sure he was more interested in what I might be wearing underneath than he was in the material of my jacket. If I had been wired that night, he would have discovered it for sure. Even though I was clean, I was glad when he had had enough and returned to his seat.

Overall, I enjoyed these extra hours I put in for Chief Cizanckas. They were productive and he was pleased with the results. He never asked how I did financially in the games and I never told him about how much I was losing.

———

There came a day when Harvey Fenster told me that rather than work the undercover, he needed me to go to the FBI office in Bridgeport for a few days. He explained that one of the secretaries there, an older Polish woman, was transcribing my tapes and she was having a difficult time understanding some of the words and phrases she was hearing. He wanted me to spend some time with her to help her out.

The secretary's name was Blanche Gadzinka [not her real name]. She was in her late sixties and was very tiny; I doubt if she was over five feet tall. And she spoke broken English. Harvey had been right; she could not understand what was being said on the tapes in many cases. I knew right away that I would much rather be out in the field than working with Blanche. But it was a job that had to be done.

At lunch on the second day an agent asked me how things were going with Blanche. I said it was pretty slow with a lot of repetition and that she referred to me and the other guys on those tapes as Eye-talians. Pronouncing it as a hyphenated word with a heavy emphasis on the I. A Polish agent who was there asked me if I knew what Gadzinka meant in Polish. I did not. He said it translated roughly to "little reptile." Everyone thought that was pretty funny.

The next day in the office Blanche said to me, "Vito, you've got to explain to me some of these things your cohorts say all the time." I said sure.

She had a tape she was working on and played it until she came to the word Ziti. She said, "All I hear these guys talk about is Ziti. Why didn't you bring more Ziti? You didn't give me enough Ziti! Where's the Ziti?"

Blanche thought Ziti might be a code word for drugs or something else of a sinister nature. I could not help but laugh when I thought about it because I could see where it could be confusing to someone that didn't know the whole story.

I explained to her that she was right, Ziti was being used as a code. The main voice on the tape she was listening to was that of a made man from the Bronx named Tommasello Alfaroni [not his real name], whose nickname was "Ziti." I had been introduced to Alfaroni by some of the Stamford gangsters who told him I could be trusted. He believed that he could fool anybody listening to his conversations by substituting the word Ziti for money. In Alfaroni's jargon, a box of Ziti equaled $1,000. So, if he told someone to bring him three boxes of Ziti, it meant he wanted $3,000.

Blanche still did not get it. "If he's talking about money, why doesn't he just say money?"

I tried again. "Blanche, this is an undercover operation. The guy talking is a crook. He does not want to say things that might incriminate him so he uses Ziti instead of money."

And that is pretty much how the whole assignment with Blanche went. It seemed like every couple of minutes she wanted me to explain the meaning of something to her. What does "whack" mean? What does this or that mean? Why does everyone want to whack everybody else?

I can say in all honesty that those days working with Blanche were the most frustrating for me of the entire operation. Wearing the wire may have been more dangerous, but it was a lot easier on me than sitting in that office. When I left Bridgeport, I hoped I would never be sent back there on that same assignment again.

———

Harvey Fenster had warned me that I might encounter undercover agents on the street during my assignment. And if I did, I was not to acknowledge them or interfere. That actually happened one day when I was riding in a car talking with a guy who was a big-time bookie in Fairfield County. We were driving into downtown Stamford where the bookie was going to drop off some money to one of his bosses.

We hit a traffic snag in the center of town where about ten police cars were parked with their lights flashing and traffic was being diverted. It was obvious that some type of altercation was taking place in the street ahead. We stopped temporarily near the scene of the action and I could see the cops dragging a guy around and tossing him up against a parked car. I recognized him as one of the undercover agents I had seen in the FBI office in Bridgeport. He was working an assignment at a seedy joint called The Stagecoach Bar and Grill, known as a place where drug dealers hung out and did their business.

It turned out that the agent had gotten into a dispute with one of the dealers. They got into a fight on the street in front of the bar and the dealer was armed with a knife. The agent got the knife away from him and then gave the guy a pretty good beating. When the cops showed up, they had no way of knowing who the agent was and treated him pretty roughly. As he leaned up against the parked car, he looked in my direction and our eyes met. I sensed he recognized me and that he did not want me to get involved. I could not have even if I had wanted to because of who I was with.

The cops took him away. I assumed that when he got to headquarters and could make a call, the FBI would straighten things out for him. It was bad enough to almost get knifed without ending up in jail on top of it.

As my assignment went on, I was learning a lot about the scope of criminal operations in Stamford. One of my favorite topics, though, was when the people I was recording on the wire or talking with on my private work for the Chief, talked about Larry Hogan. For me, that was personal and I would get a little extra charge when they would talk about who he was protecting and how much money he was making. How powerful he was is illustrated by the fact that he remained on the Mob payroll even after he was off the force. He not only continued to get paid, he asked for more.

You see, during his time wearing a badge Hogan had developed tremendous influence with cops, politicians, and others in positions of power. He knew a lot about everybody; including many of their dirty little secrets. So even after he turned in his shield, he maintained his influence and connections. About the only thing that had changed is that if someone needed action on a police-related matter, rather than handling it directly, Hogan would contact one of his cronies still on the job and tell him what needed to be done. For non-police issues, Hogan could handle them himself without a middle man.

I also found out that the illegal gambling problem was even worse than I had thought. It was not just going on inside the bars, restaurants and stores. The organized crime guys were so brazen you could see them standing in front of an Italian restaurant in their territory taking action right there on the street. And on streets where territories bordered, you might see a wise guy standing outside a restaurant on the north side of the street, and another wise guy affiliated with a different crime family standing outside a restaurant on the south side. On many occasions I personally watched as a car would pull up and the driver would hand the wise guy money to cover a bet, or receive payment for a winning wager he had made. It was no wonder that some publications—especially those in New York City— were referring to Stamford as one of the most corrupt cities in the United States.

The very fact that these things went on so openly made me even more determined to see my assignment through and bring this stuff to a halt. More than once I thought about the amazing stories Dolan would be able to write when the undercover was over and indictments started coming down.

———

Sometimes when I stopped at my parents' house my mother would show me various items she received from the organized crime kingpin for watching his mother. They ranged from pictures for her wall, to lamps and furniture. In addition to being from this guy, the gifts had something else in common: they were all top quality. He did not give out anything that was chintzy. I did not like what he was doing, especially when my mother said he always told her to make sure she told me how good he was to her. But I could not say too much about it to her. The last thing I wanted to do was to somehow get her involved in what was going on. No, I did not like it; but I did not make an issue out of it.

Another thing that bothered me somewhat was when I bumped into any of my former colleagues that I had been friends with. They knew I had had a bad experience with the department and believed the story that had been circulated as the reason for my resignation. They would ask me what I was doing and I would say that I was still playing with the band and keeping my head above water. In those cases, I was only bothered because I had to lie to them.

I felt really bad one day, though, when four cops I'd had a good relationship with came into a restaurant I was in. Unfortunately, I was at a table schmoozing with three known organized crime guys. The cops sat a table not far away and glanced in my direction. When they first spotted me, I saw expressions of surprise and then smiles. But the smiles disappeared when they realized who I was sitting with.

I excused myself from my table saying I wanted to say hello to my former associates. When I got to their table it was awkward to say the least. One of the cops said, "So what did you do? You went over to the other side?"

I said kind of lamely, "No, nothing like that. I just happen to know those guys and stopped to talk with them."

"Come on, Vito. We all know what they are. They're the same guy's Hogan was protecting. They wanted you dead just like Hogan did and now you're sitting together. Can't you keep any better company than them?" the same cop said.

I did not say any more and went back to my table. But that night I thought about it a lot. It was tough for me to accept that officers who used to like me now held me in contempt. In that regard, I would be glad when the assignment ended and the truth could be told.

———

The next time I went to Lieutenant Considine's house to pick up my check, he took me outside onto his lawn to talk. He said he had received word from one of his informants that a guy had told some organized crime bosses that if they wanted me killed, he'd do the job for them. Considine gave me the guy's name and said some officers he trusted had been keeping an eye on him.

My mind went into high gear as I tried to get my head around what I had just been told. I recognized my potential executioner's name. He was a low-level bookie who owned a couple of car washes in Fairfield County. He was not known as someone who used violence. The only motive I could think of for him volunteering to kill me was that he wanted to impress the mobsters. Maybe he figured that would open the door to him for bigger things.

But why did he think they would be interested in having me dead? A few years or even a few weeks ago, maybe. But why now when I was becoming one of them? The obvious answer was that I had not been accepted by all the bosses. Maybe some of them thought the same way as that one guy at the poker game who said, "Once a cop, always a cop." And maybe to them my regular presence in and around their joints was making them nervous.

And then Considine told me something that made me angry. He said the would-be hit man had a heart attack and died the previous day. I would not have to worry about him. Worry about him! I had not even been told about him!

I asked Considine why no one had bothered to tell me about this potential threat on my life. It seemed like the kind of information the victim-to-be should have. He seemed to be at a loss for words. His answer was a weak, "Well, we had been watching him."

I had always had the greatest respect for Considine. But to me, that explanation did not pass the smell test and I told him so. I said it was a pretty rotten way for him to treat me and told him I couldn't work like that. Between my assignment and the problems in my personal life I was stressed to the max and I had to have the confidence that while I was out on the limb, he wasn't going to be behind me with a saw. I had to be kept informed of what was going on, especially when a death threat was made.

After my tirade he apologized again and again. He promised there would be no further incidents of me being left in the dark. I apologized as well for the way I had talked to him and my lack of respect. We ended up shaking hands and I left.

But I was unnerved, no doubt about it. My confidence in Considine had taken a big hit and I was not as sure of where I stood with my new organized crime friends as I had been. It appeared that at least some of them were still skeptical of me. What would have happened if this guy had not died, I wondered. Then maybe I would have.

29

BETWEEN WORKING the undercover operations and trying to keep my own family together, I had not had much time for my father. So, one afternoon after finishing my FBI shift, I decided to stop at his barber shop. He finished his customer and when the shop was empty, he said, "So, you quit the police department, huh?" I could tell by his voice and the hurt in his eyes that he was disappointed in me.

My father cut the hair of a lot of current and former cops and had done so for many years. He also worked as a special officer and was very pro-law enforcement. So, it should not have surprised me that he'd heard about my resignation; but it did.

I kind of froze while I tried to think of the right thing to say. I finally came up with an expanded version of my undercover story. I was frustrated with the job and the Hogan thing and felt I had to get out. I also told him I felt that leaving the department would give me a chance to devote more time to my passion for music and maybe make it my new career.

He shook his head sadly as he listened. First my cop friends in the restaurant showed their contempt for me and now I had broken my own father's heart. That moment was probably the closest I came to violating my orders and telling him the whole story. I wanted so much for him to know that I was not a quitter. That despite what he had already heard or would hear, I hadn't really turned into a bad guy. I wanted so much to give him a hug and say, "Don't worry, Dad, it's all an act. I'm still on the job." I wanted to, but I could not.

We talked for a few minutes more about other things and then I left. It was a sad, sad day for me. My only consolation was that someday he and everyone else would know the truth.

———

As I infiltrated Stamford organized crime, I had the opportunity to do some sports wagering. I ran the idea by Chief Cizanckas and he liked it, so I decided to do the betting as part of my private work for him. The Chief had to start funneling extra money to me to finance my poker playing and now the sports action. I did not know then where he got that money and still do not know to this day. But I did not really care as long as he didn't ask for it back.

To any gambler reading this you would probably figure the setup I had was a dream come true. After all, I was betting with someone else's money that I did not have to pay back and I got to pocket anything I won. It does not get any better than that, right? And surely between the poker and sports betting there would have to be some wins now and then.

But the reality was that I was in over my head in the poker games trying to compete against guys that always seemed to know what I was thinking and what cards I was holding. It was far different than playing with a bunch of friends and I was definitely outclassed. And as far as the sports stuff, I could not pick my nose, as the saying goes. Every week the Chief's money followed by my own went into the coffers of the gangsters. Doing the right thing was turning out to be a very expensive proposition for me.

That aside, I was learning a lot about the bad guys and the information was flowing. And I was learning about Chief Cizanckas as well. I liked him and trusted him to keep me alive. But I came to realize that he had his own issues. Primarily, he did not seem to trust very many people. He was okay with me and Lieutenant Considine, but that seemed to be as far as it went. He apparently was not even comfortable with the FBI, making me vow not to share with them that I was doing a private assignment for him. While I fully appreciated the need for discretion, Cizanckas seemed obsessed with secrecy.

Having to work with the FBI and then in secret for the Chief meant that I was almost never at home. Joanne could not have been blamed if she thought I had a girlfriend again. To ease the pressure I was under, I decided to cut back on the amount of time I spent wearing the wire. That assignment was going very well and I figured I could get by working short shifts—four hours or so—for the feds and still produce plenty of information. The only drawback on that part of my assignment was that Harvey Fenster continued to send me to Bridgeport every couple of weeks to spend a day or two with Blanche Gadzinka. I had to identify every voice on the tapes for her and answer lots of other questions. Those were trying times for me. But the "little reptile" was really a very nice lady and I did not let my frustration get the best of me.

I did get pretty annoyed one day when I was in Bridgeport, though. And it was not because of Blanche. I was talking with four agents, three of whom were Irish. They were not part of my assignment; but they had heard about it and congratulated me on the work I was doing. And then one of the Irishmen, apparently without thinking, said, "It looks like it won't be long and we'll be able to get these greaseball wops off the street."

Suddenly you could have heard a pin drop in the room and I could feel my cheeks burning. The Irishman and I locked eyes for an instant and I am sure he could tell that I was not happy with him. The agent apologized several times and I told him it was no big deal and to forget about it.

But during the drive back home I thought about my father and grandfather and all they had gone through when he and so many others arrived in America from Italy. Yes, the American Mafia was run by Italian Americans and it was a bad thing. But to denigrate all of us because of that was wrong. Just plain wrong.

I really liked Harvey Fenster and enjoyed working with him. But he was a young agent and not particularly experienced in wire operations. Unlike the technology of today where wires can be placed in a variety of locations, back then there were not many options. I did not like having the unit on my back so I started experimenting with different positions. My preference was to have it on my chest. It could still pick up all the voices and I felt it would be less likely to be detected by an accidental touch. Fenster was okay with the change and I was much more comfortable.

Chief Cizanckas and I usually met twice a week. He would pick the place and almost always it was a deli or restaurant located out of town. His knowledge of the area after being in town for such a short time was very impressive.

During these meetings we would discuss the status of the undercover and he'd give me my gambling money. Depending on the amount of privacy we had in the dining area, we would sometimes go into the rest room, lock the door behind us and talk. In some cases, these were unisex jobs with just a toilet and no urinal. After what I had seen working at the train station, I always felt a little funny about that. What would other patrons think when they saw two men come out of a one-unit bathroom?

He always told me that when the assignment was over, I'd make everyone look like heroes, including him. And as long as Hogan, his organized crime clients and the other dirty cops went down, that was okay with me.

———

Anthony Dolan was back in action again on August 25th. The story alleged that City projects supervised by the Public Works Department operations officer frequently involved conflicts of interest, questionable equipment rentals and unauthorized improvements to private property.

Dolan said that his examination of hundreds of City invoices relating to 10 projects over a seven-year period, showed that two local contractors accounted for more than a half million dollars in equipment rentals for snow removal, garbage disposal and drainage jobs.

Dolan also found that in addition to the rentals and improvement to private property, a pattern of purchasing irregularities occurred on the projects, including overpayments—later confirmed in one case by a city auditing firm's report—and numerous violations of City bid procedures.

According to the reporter, the projects came under the general supervision of the operations officer for the department, whose name appeared most frequently as the requesting officer on purchase orders requesting materials and equipment for the projects.

Dolan reminded his readers that although some of the projects had been the subject of Advocate investigative articles in the past and had stirred controversy, the pattern of irregularities had never been fully identified by the several official investigations which were conducted by the Board of Representatives and other agencies as a result of those earlier disclosures.

———

In mid-December of '77 while working the Cizanckas portion of my assignment, I came up with a rather disturbing piece of information. In fact, it literally had me shaking in my shoes. During one of my poker sessions another player looked at me and asked if I had heard about a recently retired cop from Norwalk who had just been found murdered. I said I had not. The guy said the dead man was former sergeant Charles Dugan. He explained that on December 15, Dugan's car was towed from a no parking zone in Manhattan to the police garage. When the car's trunk was opened Dugan's body was found inside. He had been shot once in the head.

I asked him if anyone had been arrested. He said, "No. But your old boss Larry Hogan was in on it. I hate Hogan's guts, so if you want to give the authorities an anonymous tip, feel free."

I wanted to know where he had gotten his information. A lot of guys knew about it, he said. Tony, Joe, Jimmy and Tommy—all street guys with no last names—had heard Hogan was involved in the former cop's death.

Even though this information seemed to be third or fourth handed, I was definitely interested. Assuming it was true, it further confirmed my thoughts about what Hogan had intended for me in Port Chester. And it made me think that if I was not at the top of Hogan's hit list, I was probably in the top four along with Cizanckas, Joe Ligi and Anthony Dolan.

I pumped my source for a possible motive. He said it was his understanding that Hogan and Dugan had a business relationship that involved Hogan loan sharking with Dugan directing customers to him. Apparently, some of the people that Dugan sent to Hogan for loans were not making their payments. Dugan supposedly paid the ultimate price for failing to better screen his referrals.

I was not sure where to take this information. But since I had learned about it while working for Chief Cizanckas, I decided he was the man it should go to. The very next day I told him about what I had heard. He said he would look into it. I asked if he planned on telling the FBI or the State Police. He said no, he would handle it himself. I was instructed to forget about it, but to keep my ears open should any new information come up.

I followed the Chief's orders pretty much and did not go out of my way to pursue the matter. But I did do a little research on Dugan. From what I could find out he had an okay record with the department in Norwalk. How or why, he got hooked up with Hogan, if he actually did, remained a mystery to me.

Whether the Dugan story was true or not, I started carrying at least one gun, and sometimes two or three, with me always. And I became even more cognizant of my surroundings. When in a bar or restaurant I made sure to sit or stand with my back against the wall. When I was walking on the street my eyes were constantly in motion, watching for anything that did not look right. And when driving I used my mirrors to keep track of what cars were behind me and for how long.

I took extra security measures around my house, too. I installed additional outdoor lights and made sure I had a dog that barked nice and loud when it heard noises outside. Before going to bed at night I made at least one and sometimes two trips around the property. And I always checked my car for any sign of tampering. It was not a great way to live, but the key word was "live." And I was determined to keep Joanne, the kids and me, all alive.

But it was not just us I had to worry about. There were my parents, too. I had thoughts of people entering my father's barber shop after his last customer of the day left and doing him harm. Or the made man who gave my mother gifts sending me a message by hurting her. It was driving me nuts.

So, I took yet another precaution. I started saying prayers. I asked God to protect me and my family. I asked Him to keep all of us all from any harm. I was not really into God then. But if He really existed, I wanted Him on my side.

30

ONE MORNING when I picked up the paper, I saw a Dolan article that jogged my memory. The headline was, "Area men linked to gambling ring sentenced today in federal court." The investigation that took place in 1974 and 1975 and led to the charges being filed was conducted by the FBI and attorneys from the U. S. Department of Justice's Northeast Organized Crime Strike Force.

Although this was a federal case, I remembered it because I had provided information to FBI agents during their investigation. There was a total of eight defendants and I had given the feds some background on three of them. After the five men and three women were arrested in 1976, the story dropped out of the news and I forgot about it.

Dolan wrote that after extensive plea bargaining, three of the defendants received sentences that involved both brief prison time and probation, while five others were sentenced to only probation. The hearing lasted three hours and was attended by State Senator William Strada, Junior. Mr. Strada told Dolan he was there to show support for one of the defendants whose mother worked in his law office.

Dolan ended the piece with, "The gambling syndicate run by the defendants is now considered defunct by local and federal law enforcement. However, the syndicate's previous operations are now believed to have been taken over by a Bridgeport racketeer with ties to the Vito Genovese crime family in New York. Stamford's largest gambling syndicate, however, is still believed to be run by a Shippan [a section of Stamford] businessman with links to the Carlo Gambino crime family and influence with certain policemen and politicians." This was the same man my mother worked for and who hated me. What a tangled mess!

As I reflected on that last paragraph, I was reminded that so far during my undercover assignment I had infiltrated both of those organized crime families.

Although I thought the sentences imposed could have been harsher, I was glad to see that all eight people had entered guilty pleas and would have the convictions on their records. Hopefully the feds had sent a message to the illegal gambling operators that they were serious about putting them out of business. Even if the locals could be bought off, the feds could not.

As the saying goes, sometimes the hits just keep coming and coming. "City building, commerce boom brings code violations, bribery," Dolan's headline read. Is there anything in this town that is not corrupt, I wondered.

According to Dolan, Stamford's growth as the commercial center of Fairfield County, stimulated by an influx of multinational corporations, had produced numerous violations of state and local building codes. And in at least one instance the violations involved bribing a high-level City official. The bribe was discovered during a year-long investigation by the newspaper and was confirmed by an FBI investigation and the government's use of an electronic eavesdropping device. Specific details of the bribe were being withheld from the article at the request of federal authorities who were expected to submit their evidence to a grand jury.

I stopped reading for a moment and asked myself, how does this guy do it? He investigated this bribery thing for a year, while doing all the other corruption investigations and his non-investigative reporting at the same time. I had to chuckle as I concluded that his days must have had more than twenty-four hours in them. What an amazing guy Dolan was.

Returning to the story, Dolan threw out this gem that probably caused distress in certain quarters. "In addition to several other cases of alleged bribery, which sources have also asked the Advocate to make available to the U. S. Attorney's office and the FBI, the recent investigation shows irregularities in construction projects by local developers and contractors. Much of the current federal investigation is reportedly focused on buildings by local developers."

"The Advocate investigation shows that several buildings that do not conform to various provisions in the building codes were constructed by local developers and real estate dealers with whom the City's Building and Zoning Enforcement Officer, James Sotire, took vacation trips, in some cases to Florida and Europe.

"In an interview this week, Sotire confirmed that the trips took place but denied any impropriety. He said that the three developers involved have been his friends since childhood and maintained that seeing them socially was not a conflict of interest. He also said his signature on their building permits was largely a formality, while the real approval for the builders' plans was given by plan examiners in his department."

Later in the article Dolan wrote, "The investigators are probing disclosures made during The Advocate's probe of building code compliance here as well as previous controversy that has surrounded much of the corporate building in Stamford in recent years.

"The most recent controversy occurred following a recent Advocate investigation that raised questions about the Xerox Corp.'s constructional headquarters on High Ridge Rd.

"After the firm's bid to locate its headquarters in Greenwich was turned down following strident local protests, the firm began construction of the building here in 1976 with a permit that had expired the year before."

Dolan said that although Xerox obtained a new permit and paid several thousand dollars in additional building fees, questions remained. He cited that Xerox signed a contract with a New York construction firm for a reported $14.6

million while the City building permit listed a construction cost of $11 million."

As Dolan stated in his piece, this was a boom era for Stamford. In fact, the city was ranked third behind New York and Chicago as home to the most Fortune 500 companies. And if they were so inclined, I guess big companies with lots of money could find people in power who would help them cut a corner here or there.

While doing my private work for Chief Cizanckas I began to develop information from a source I considered highly reliable, as well as from other police sources, about Larry Hogan and the Charles Dugan murder. According to them, the Stamford cops and the FBI were having trouble linking Hogan to the killing. They had developed a possible motive, but their case was not strong enough for an indictment.

According to my sources it had been learned that Dugan was a heavy drinker who tended to brag when he was intoxicated; he had become Hogan's associate in some real estate ventures; and that he had actually been shot not once, but twice behind the ear with .22 caliber bullets.

Investigators also found out that Hogan had gone into loan sharking after he left the police department and that he had given Dugan some money to loan to the proprietor of a Norwalk restaurant. The restaurant owner subsequently told Hogan that Dugan was collecting more money from her to apply to the loans than he was turning over to Hogan.

The working theory was that Hogan became worried that if pressed about the money, Dugan might decide to become an informant for the FBI. The best option was to get rid of the cheating Dugan permanently rather than simply using threats to try to keep him in line. Hogan may well have been justified in his suspicions about Dugan's loyalty. One of my sources told me that Dugan had in fact agreed to cooperate with the feds. And when Dugan's body was found, the address of the FBI office was in his pocket.

The biggest surprise to me, though, was when my source disclosed that my old friend Duke Morris was considered as having been the actual shooter. It was thought that Hogan may have recruited him to do the hit and detectives in New York had questioned Morris about the murder. But their evidence was only circumstantial and insufficient for an arrest. And I learned that Morris' drug distribution network had been even larger than I thought. It had encompassed not only Stamford, but Waterbury and Bridgeport, too. And his tentacles reached as far south as Maryland. Some of this information was actually contained in documents on file in the office of the Superior Court in Bridgeport.

An event that happened later illustrates the nerve of Hogan. Incredibly, not long after Dugan's murder he filed a civil suit against the John Hancock Insurance Company and Dugan's estate. In his filing Hogan alleged that he had in fact been the beneficiary on two of Dugan's life insurance policies and he wanted to collect the money. And that civil action resulted in much more information about his relationship with Dugan coming out.

When the case went to trial, Hogan testified that he had loaned Dugan $30,000 in two $15,000 installments in April and August of 1977. Dugan took out two $15,000 life insurance policies with Hogan as the beneficiary, to cover the loans should something happen to him. Hogan said that Dugan gave him one of the insurance policies outright and told him that the other could be found in his office if necessary.

Under oath, Hogan explained that he obtained the money as a loan from the bank to invest in restaurant and real estate ventures, and that Dugan then loaned the money to the owner of a financially troubled singles' bar. This loan money was allegedly given to the tavern owner in two installments and repayment schedules were drawn up. Dugan supposedly told Hogan that the payment agreement on one of the loans was being adhered to; but that the payments on the second loan were irregular. However, Hogan said that during conversation with the borrower she implied that she was making regular payments on both loans and that Dugan was keeping the payments on the second loan for himself. Hogan said that at the time of his death, Dugan had repaid $6,700 of the debt.

The lawyer representing Dugan's estate had a much different version of events. He said that Dugan had taken out a bank loan in the amount of $42,000 shortly before his death. As security for that loan Dugan had to re-mortgage his home. After receiving the loan money Dugan gave a portion of it to Hogan during a meeting at the Regency Restaurant, located in the Shippan section of Stamford. The owner of the restaurant was reputedly the top organized crime figure in Fairfield County.

When the attorney for Dugan's estate cross-examined Hogan, he asked him whether he and Dugan had been engaged in loan sharking activities; about his relationship with the alleged organized crime kingpin who owned the Regency Restaurant, and other possible illegal activity. Hogan denied he was anything but a retired cop trying to get what was rightfully his. But after leaving the stand he dropped his lawsuit and there was no need for any further testimony.

I thought the information against Hogan in regard to Dugan was very damaging and I was dismayed that it was deemed to be insufficient to charge him in Dugan's murder.

As I drove back home after talking with my sources about the status of the Dugan murder investigation, I thought about my time working in Hogan's squad. As the commander of the elite Narcotics Unit, he would frequently leave the office during the day to talk with school children about the evils of illegal drugs. That is right, the man who was providing protection for drug dealers and profiting from drug distribution was lecturing Stamford's kids about the dangers of those same substances. And all the while he was making sure drugs were available to everyone throughout Fairfield County, including school children. I could not help feeling disgust as I thought about the arrogance of the man.

———

The poker games continued to be one of my best venues for gathering information. During one of the games an organized crime guy brought up the name of Joe Tamburri and asked me if I knew him. I did know of the guy. He was a big tough man who had at one time been a Stamford cop. He was thought to have Mob connections and it was believed he acted as a collector and enforcer for his organized crime friends. I kept my answer to simply that I had seen Tamburri around a couple of times.

The guy then said that Larry Hogan used Tamburri to deliver shakedown demands and threats to his victims. If a visit from Tamburri did not do the trick, Hogan would call on the target personally and read him the riot act. Sometimes Hogan made these follow-up visits during his regular duty hours to emphasize the power he had.

That was interesting, but unfortunately, I knew that Joe Tamburri would never be able to testify against Hogan because he had been shot to death by his girlfriend. They had apparently gotten into a heated argument one night and she blew him away.

On another occasion I was told that Hogan had bought into a bar in Stamford called the Depot Café, which was located on Elm Street. The Depot used to be known as a working man's joint. But after Hogan became an owner, it began to attract the undesirables. Mobsters, drug dealers, robbers and ex-cons, became the regular clientele and the blue-collar guys found other watering holes.

One day I was walking to my car which was parked near the Depot Café when I heard a familiar voice call my name. I turned around and saw Hogan a few yards away. I asked him what he wanted. He looked around to make sure no one was within earshot and then he said, "You think you're a pretty tough guy, don't you? You throw rocks and you broke the window out of my car. But hear me good, Colucci. Your days are numbered. I've got plenty of time to do what I'm gonna do to you, to you and all the others that are trying to get me. I'll get you all before you get me, Colucci, and don't you forget it."

I said, "Well, you do whatever your little brain tells you to do." And then I laughed at him. He cursed at me and then got into his car and drove away.

I started thinking of Hogan as a malignant tumor. Any place he got a foothold in ended up being corrupted and destroyed. The man had no morals, no conscience and not a trace of concern for anyone else. He was all that mattered. You cannot ignore a cancer and hope it goes away; it has to be removed or obliterated. Larry Hogan had to be dealt with the same way.

———

A few days after bumping into Hogan I saw another face I had not seen in a while. I was driving home in the afternoon after completing my day's work for the FBI when a car passed me going in the opposite direction. As I glanced at it, I recognized the driver. It was none other than Arvil Chapman. He noticed me at the same time, beeped his horn and waved. I motioned for him to pull over and then turned my car around and pulled up behind him. We decided to go to a nearby park to talk.

Arvil said he was through with drugs. He had been keeping a low profile and trying to stay clean. I told him I was glad for him and mentioned that we had never finished the work that he, Joe Ligi and I had started. I asked if he had any new information or if there was anything he wanted to tell me that he had not told me before.

Arvil said he did have some stuff that I had never heard. I grabbed my notebook and told him to go ahead. He went back to his days of working for Duke Morris and how Morris was a main man in the drug business. That part was old news. And then he got into exactly how ruthless Morris was regarding running his drug empire. He had his own distributors bringing in tons of money for him. And he also was being paid street tax by independent dealers who needed his blessing and protection to operate in his territory. This brought in additional thousands of dollars.

Arvil poked holes in the air with the tip of his cigarette as he told how Morris controlled his kingdom through fear and intimidation. He said Morris struck such terror into his rivals or into his own people who had gone astray, that they would throw away their weapons and drugs and run away if Morris entered the same bar they were in.

Arvil wanted me to know that for a while he was Morris' right-hand man. He said he made at least two trips a week to Harlem to buy heroin and cocaine. When he got back to Morris' apartment they had cut and bagged the drugs. And then Morris would pay him in heroin for his personal use.

Arvil then started talking about Hogan. "You know," he said, "back then people didn't know a lot about Hogan. He was an overseer and stayed in the background. When Morris introduced me to Hogan in the early 1970s that is what he called him, 'the overseer of our operation.' Morris pointed at Hogan and said to me, 'As long as you're doing drugs for us you'll be okay. Because he's the man charged with curbing the drug trafficking in the city.' Then both of them laughed like hyennas."

In addition to earning his drugs from Morris and Hogan, Arvil said that during one period of time he acted as the pimp for two sisters who wanted to earn some money as prostitutes. When Hogan found out about it, he demanded payments of five hundred dollars every so often as protection money. Arvil said Hogan would collect the payoff money wherever Hogan happened to spot him. It was usually out on the street and in public view. But Hogan never let the presence of witnesses get in the way of making money.

Arvil then asked me if I remembered when Hogan used to send guys from the Narcotics Unit to New Haven for training. Arvil was right. Hogan would send a couple of guys at a time to attend the Search and Seizure School taught by State's Attorney Arnold Markle. I said I remembered.

Arvil laughed uproariously and said, "You guys thought Hogan wanted the best trained squad of cops in Stamford, but you were wrong. He wanted the least number of narcotics cops out on the street. That is why he made sure to always have part of the squad in New Haven. Out of sight, out of mind."

———

One December afternoon when I got home from work, Joanne announced that she'd become a born-again Christian. She explained that one night while I was out, she had watched the Billy Graham Crusade on television. She said on that very night she made the commitment to accept Jesus Christ as her Lord and Savior and to turn her life around.

I put on my happy face and told her that if she felt this was the right thing to do, I was happy for her. But inside I was not so sure this was actually a good thing. Some of the stuff she had said was over my head. And what did "turn my life around" really mean?

Joanne continued that she had found a church, Grace Evangelical Church on Courtland Avenue, and she was going to start attending there that coming Sunday with our daughter Valarie. I asked her if Valarie really wanted to get involved in this church thing and she said yes. And then she said she would like me to come along with them. I said thanks, but no thanks. I was not the least bit interested in her new-found religion or this Grace Evangelical Church. She said OKAY, but the invitation would remain open should I ever change my mind.

After that conversation I had to leave the house to run an errand. As I went out to the car, I felt a sadness because I was afraid that Joanne getting involved with the church might ruin the few fun things we had left in our marriage. I hoped this would just be a phase she was going through and that she would tire of it rather quickly.

Later that same evening I went out to play poker at one of my usual haunts. When I got there, I knocked on the door. It opened slightly and the guy who ran the game said, "No more poker for you, Colucci. You're done. Now get the hell out of here and don't ever come back!"

Something had obviously gone wrong. I did not know what; but the writing was on the wall. December would not only mark the end of the year. It would also see the abrupt termination of my undercover assignment.

31

THE WEATHER on the Monday following my being denied access to the poker game was nasty. There was rain, rain and more rain. I braved the elements in the morning to do my FBI stuff and was at home in the afternoon before starting my nighttime activities for Chief Cizanckas. I remember that I had the stereo on and was listening to "Rainy Days and Mondays" sung by the Carpenters and thinking how appropriate that song was for that day. And then the phone rang.

I picked up the handset and said hello. A deep man's voice on the other end said, "Do yourself a favor and get off the case or something could happen to you." That brief message was followed by a click as the caller disconnected.

I was shaken by the call. In the past I had received written threats left on my locker and under the wiper blade of my car. I had been threatened verbally, too. But never over the phone—a phone in my own house with an unlisted number.

When I calmed down, I did a mental replay of the call. It was a voice I didn't recognize, and in my mind, it had been both a warning and a threat. Get off the case or else. But except for Cizanckas, Considine, Joanne and me, no one was supposed to know there was a case. To everyone else I was an ex-cop with an attitude. First the poker game and now this. Something had definitely happened to cast doubt on my cover story. The first question I wanted answered was, what had leaked out and how did it happen? And following that, what did I need to do about it and how soon?

As I was pacing around the kitchen thinking, our oldest daughter Kimmy—who was by then a teenager— raced into the room and wanted to know if the call had been for her. I told her no. She said she was expecting a call from her boyfriend and to make sure I remembered she was home. I was so preoccupied with what had just happened that I cut her short and she went back to her room.

Free of that distraction, I resumed my pacing. After a few more minutes of that I concluded that the only thing to do was to call Chief Cizanckas and explain what was going on. He was my boss, after all, and needed to be involved in any decision that had an impact on the operation.

I placed a call to his office and told the secretary I needed to speak with him right away. She said that he was in and was on the verge of calling me. While I waited for the Chief to get on the line, I pondered what the secretary had said.

Cizanckas had been about to call me, but why? Did it have something to do with why I was calling him?

When I heard Cizanckas' voice I told him about the phone call I had received. As soon as I finished, he said, "Vito, get in here right away. A similar message was left at the Advocate's office a few minutes ago. Get Colucci off the case or bad things are going to come down."

My mind was so busy trying to figure out what was happening that I had a hard time concentrating on the traffic while driving to headquarters. I asked myself such things as: How bad is it? Do I need to buy more guns? Should I relocate my family?

When I entered the station, the cops milling around looked at me questioningly. They were no doubt curious about why I was heading toward the Chief's office. It was a sure thing that the rumors would be flying within a few minutes.

Cizanckas was waiting for me and took me into his office right away. After shutting the door, he said that my cover had been blown. He did not know how yet, but he had a lot of feelers out trying to get some answers. He said that he was going to meet with the Advocate because they had received their own phone call and planned to run a story about the undercover assignment the next day. Cizanckas complimented me on the work I had done both for him and the FBI. He said the quality and value of my work would be reflected in his statement to the paper.

Regarding how my cover had been blown, he said he was totally puzzled because within the police department, only he, Lieutenant Considine and Lieutenant George Mayer, were aware of the operation.

George Mayer? More breaking news for me. When Cizanckas offered me the assignment he assured me that the only people in the department who would know the real story were him and Considine. Although I had no particular objection to Mayer—who I thought was a great cop and who I trusted completely—being in on the deal, I felt I'd been sandbagged just like when Considine hadn't told me about the death threat against me. I was not happy and told Cizanckas so.

He said that there was no need for me to be upset. Mayer was a dedicated professional lawman and him having knowledge of the undercover carried no risk. I said that was not the point. It was being left in the dark that bothered me. Cizanckas just glossed over the issue and changed the subject.

He said that when I accepted the assignment, he had promised me that if I did a good job he'd put me in the Detective Bureau. I had held up my end of the deal and he was prepared to honor his word. Was I ready to meet my new colleagues?

The Chief walked me to the Detective Bureau and introduced me around. He made an announcement that he was assigning me to the Bureau effective immediately. The faces of the detectives showed their confusion. One of them asked, "Are you saying he's coming back to the department?"

"He never left," Cizanckas said. "He was working undercover and you'll read all about it in tomorrow's paper."

I cannot tell you the relief I felt when Cizanckas uttered those words. I knew that the grapevine would assure that by the next day virtually everyone in the department would know the truth about me. And the civilians would know it as well thanks to the Advocate. My days of feeling uncomfortable in the presence of my own father and other Stamford cops were over. *The real Vito Colucci was coming back with his honor restored.*

After leaving the Detective Bureau we returned to Cizanckas' office. He told me to take the week off and report to work the following Monday. I would be working strictly Monday through Friday with no weekends.

The good news was coming fast and furious and I was starting to feel really upbeat. And then came the downer. Cizanckas said, "Vito, of course you're going to continue to do private undercover work for me, right?"

I could not believe what I'd just heard. My cover had been blown somehow and I had received a direct warning to drop the case. A second warning had been delivered to the newspaper. And this guy is sitting across from me saying he wants me to continue to work his private undercover operation? I did not say he must be kidding; but that is what I was thinking.

Instead, I said, "Chief, nobody is going to talk to me now. I'm going to be persona non grata in all the places I've been hanging in. They aren't going to talk to me and they won't even want me around."

Cizanckas was not about to let it go, though. He liked the information I had been getting for him and was determined to keep it going. He said I could work it from a distance, utilizing snitches rather than hanging around inside the joints myself. The main thing would be that it would remain our secret, just like before. No one else would know, not even Considine or Mayer. And he said if I agreed to continue, he'd make it worth my while. He had already given me the promised assignment to the Bureau with weekends off, so I was not sure what he meant by that.

I told him my head was spinning because of everything that had happened in the past few hours. I said I would like some time to think over his proposal and promised to call him in a day or two and we would discuss it further.

Next on the Chief's agenda was an idea that I found much more appealing. He said that although I was officially off duty for the rest of the week, he would give me free rein to go out on the streets to "jack up" any of the organized crime guys I had issues with. If I wanted to do that, he would assign another officer in plain clothes to accompany me.

My spirits were back up. There were several gangsters who had given me grief during the undercover that I would not mind chatting with under the circumstances the Chief described. I thanked him and said I would be ready to hit the streets on Tuesday.

I had so much on my mind that I did not get much sleep that night. I tossed and turned thinking about who I wanted to see over the next few days and what I would say to them. And the Chief's request that I continue the private work for him was another issue I wrestled with.

Tuesday afternoon I hooked up with the rookie officer Cizanckas had assigned to work with me. He was a nice enough kid and seemed glad for the opportunity to work a plain clothes assignment. But as we drove around looking for the guys on my list, I became increasingly uncomfortable. Did I really want a witness to what I said to these people or how I acted? Probably not. If I was going to "jack them up" as Cizanckas had said, I'd be better off working alone.

I decided to limit who I talked with that day to the low-end street guys. I would use them to help get the word around that I was back on the street carrying a badge and that I'd be calling on their friends and superiors. Let the bigger fish sweat a little wondering if and when it would be their turn, I figured. So, Tuesday went by without incident. I was relatively polite to the street guys I spoke with and kept my emotions under control. The next day was the day I was waiting for.

When I got home that night, I found Dolan's article about the aborted undercover operation on the front page of the paper. The headline was, "Cop loses cover and is off Mob probe; Chief pledges thrust against gambling."

Dolan wrote, "A Stamford patrolman investigating suspected police ties to organized crime was taken off his undercover assignment Tuesday after being threatened by an anonymous caller who contacted the Advocate and the officer himself, Vito Colucci.

"Working under the direction of Police Chief Victor I. Cizanckas and federal authorities—who are probing allegations of police ties to racketeering—Ptl. Colucci submitted a fake resignation several months ago while false rumors were planted about his involvement with local gamblers.

"Ptl. Colucci reportedly developed evidence critical to the corruption investigation during his undercover assignment. Although only three law enforcement officials and one outside source knew of Ptl. Colucci's assignment, his undercover work was exposed Monday when he received a call telling him 'Do yourself a favor and get off the case or something could happen,' according to the chief.

"The call was apparently made only a few minutes after a message was left at the Advocate saying that the police chief should be told to 'get Colucci off the case.'

"Chief Cizanckas, in an announcement that said Ptl. Colucci's identity had been compromised, praised the patrolman for undercover work that 'contributed greatly to the investigation at great personal risk to himself.'"

Cizanckas was also quoted as saying, "The Stamford Police Department will not respond to threats from criminals except to increase our efforts to resolve the case under investigation."

Dolan wrote that Cizanckas was instituting special training that would encourage uniformed personnel to make

Cop loses cover and is off mob probe; Chief pledges thrust against gambling

by ANTHONY R. DOLAN
Advocate Staff Reporter

A Stamford patrolman investigating suspected police ties to organized crime was taken off his undercover assignment Tuesday after being threatened by an anonymous caller who contacted The Advocate and the officer himself, Vito Colucci.

Working under the direction of Police Chief Victor I. Cizanckas and federal authorities — who are probing allegations of police ties to racketeers — Ptl. Colucci submitted a fake resignation

"on view" gambling arrests. Cizanckas also asked that citizens with information on gambling activities share their knowledge with the police.

Cizanckas also told Dolan that, "Ptl. Colucci would be reassigned to the detective bureau where he would complete his investigation."

Dolan ended the article stating that in addition to the police probe, the U.S. attorney's office and a federal grand jury were also investigating. A piece on the editorial page was complimentary of the undercover operation and me as well.

Dolan may not have known I was one of his anonymous callers; but now he at least knew my name.

On Wednesday I was back out on the streets alone. I was not really by myself, though, because I had Mr. Smith and Mr. Wesson with me. I made the rounds of the locations I had been working while undercover, talking to guys who were higher up on the crime ladder. My modus operandi was to park near the place and see if my target was outside on the sidewalk. If so, I would confront him right there. If not, I would go inside and look for him. If there were too many people around, I would go back outside and wait in my car until he came out.

When I got to talk to them the message was the same. I would say, "Have you been looking for me? Are you the one who's going to hurt me or my family? Well, here I am. If you've got something to say or do, here's your chance."

Some of them responded with denials. Others would tell me to leave them alone and then turn and walk away. When they did, I would follow them saying, "No. I'm right here and we can settle this now. If you want to do something to me this is the time. Let's go you yellow-bellied son of a bitch!"

As I was driving through a heavily Italian section of town, I spotted a pretty high-level gangster on the street near the Brass Rail restaurant. I did not like this guy at all and suspected that he might have been behind the threats that the Advocate and I had received. I pulled over and jumped out of my car without putting on my jacket and made a run at him. My .357 was clearly visible in the holster on my hip. I said, "Hey you, hold it right there!"

He was visibly spooked and started backing up while telling me to calm down and not to do anything crazy. I kept moving forward toward him. He retreated until he backed into the wall of a building and I closed in on him. He was still telling me to stay calm. But if anything, I was getting even more agitated. Like I said, I did not like him at all.

When I was right in his face I said, "Don't make anonymous calls on the phone or have your people do it. You want me? Well, you've got me. I'm right here, not on the telephone. Come on, let's do it!"

He just stood there with his mouth shut and fear in his eyes. I went on, "I want you to listen closely, very closely, and tell your friends what I say. I don't know yet who's behind these threats to me and my family, but I'm going to find out. And if you or anybody working for you tries to hurt me or any member of my family, here's what I'm going to do."

Before I tell you the rest of what I said, I need to let you know that they were words I'd never used before and haven't used since. I guess that reflects the frame of mind I was in at that particular moment and I kind of lost it temporarily.

I leaned in even closer to him and said in kind of a hiss, "If anybody ever tries to do anything to me or my loved ones, I will kill you and anybody that is close to you in any kind of way. I don't care if it's your immediate family or your first cousin or fifth cousin. It won't matter to me if it's your cat, your dog or your goldfish. I will kill anything and everything that is close to you."

As I was saying these things, I can remember that my heart was pounding and my temples were throbbing. I had never been that angry before in my life and the guy in front of me was taking the brunt of my rage. And I do not believe it was all bluster. I really think that had something been done to me or those close to me, I would have done a lot of damage to whoever I thought was responsible.

After I finished talking, I glared at him for a few seconds. He never said a word, but from his expression and the way he was shaking I knew I had made my point. As I drove away and my heart rate slowed, I experienced mixed emotions about my tirade. I felt some satisfaction over making the guy tremble. But I did not like the fact that I had lost control of my emotions. I promised myself that would not happen again. And it did not.

I was in headquarters several times during that week and most of the cops I ran into—including three of the four cops I had seen in the restaurant while I was sitting with the gangsters—treated me with respect, slapping me on the back and telling me they were proud of me for the work I'd done and the sacrifices I had made. They said I was a hell of a cop. Even more important, my father was proud of me again, too. And I found out that the Chief had put the word out on the street that if anyone bothered me, they would feel the wrath of the Stamford Police Department. I felt as though the weight of the world had been lifted from my shoulders.

There was a slight problem with my mother, though. The first time I saw her after the story broke in the paper she was quite upset. She was concerned about my safety, of course. But she was also worried that one of the targets of the undercover was "that nice man who gives me all these things." I told her he was not a nice guy and let it go at that.

Also, that week I had to stop at the court house and bumped into a secretary from the prosecutor's office who knew me. As soon as she saw me, she started singing "Undercover Angel" at the top of her lungs. We both laughed and that became the routine whenever we ran into each other.

At the end of my "week off" I went into headquarters to meet with Chief Cizanckas. I told him I was not sure about continuing my private work for him. I said it did not make sense to me and I didn't see how it could work. He disagreed. He figured that me being out there asking questions would let the bad guys know I had

Ptl. Vito Colucci

Vito Colucci ia a good cop and so are most of his colleagues on the Stamford police force. According to Chief Cizanckas, it is a small though influential group of cops that are the bad ones.

They are the ones who, according to a series of articles on the police department in The Advocate, have links to two local gambling syndicates connected with the Genovese and Gambino crime families in New York City.

not gone away and would put additional pressure on them. I argued some more, but he would not take no for an answer. So, I agreed to resume working for him on the side.

The messages that Cizanckas and I sent must have found the right ears, because there were no more threats.

32

THE DESKS in the Detective Bureau were arranged by twos and positioned face-to-face. On my first day assigned to the Bureau I was setting up my desk when the detective who had the desk facing mine walked in. It was Jerry Hogan, brother of my arch enemy Larry Hogan. From the look on his face, he was as stunned about the seating arrangements as I was. I tried to ignore him, but every time I raised my eyes, I found him glaring at me.

This has zero chance of working, I thought to myself. Almost always during my police career I had done what I was told, even when I did not agree with the order. But not this time. Less than two hours into my new position I found myself going to see Chief Cizanckas to complain. He was surprised when I told him about the desk situation.

He told me to stay in his office while he went to have a talk with somebody. The Chief was back in a few minutes and told me to take the rest of the day off and report for the day shift the next day. That is when Hogan's squad would rotate from days to another shift, virtually eliminating Hogan and me seeing each other.

I thanked him and then asked for clarification about my new status. In Dolan's article Cizanckas was quoted as saying I was being promoted to detective. But my badge and pay were still a patrolman's. Was I a detective?

His initial answer was vague and confusing so I repeated the question. After some more back and forth, the bottom line was that I was working as a detective, but was still a patrolman. Sometimes when I had these kinds of conversations with Cizanckas I felt like I was the Costello half of an Abbott and Costello skit.

Before I left his office Cizanckas gave me some more money to fund my extra work. The source of all this money continued to be of concern to me. I only hoped he was not doing anything shady to get the cash and that it would not come back to haunt me later on.

━━━━━━

I knew that the boss of one of the bookie operations—a high-ranking member of the Genovese family— had gone on vacation to the Islands for a couple of weeks and had left town before everything hit the fan about the undercover. I was flush with money from Cizanckas and I figured that for the heck of it I would see if maybe one of the mobster's flunkies would still take my sports action. I spotted one of his young guys on the street. The kid apparently was oblivious to the fact that I was still a cop and took my wager. For the first time since I do not know when, I actually won! We met a couple of days later and the bookie paid me $775. I wanted to get some more action in before the kid's boss got back and I called in bets for the next four days. My bad luck returned, though, and I ended up owing $850.

The big shot got back on the scene and found out what his underling had done. I heard through my sources that he gave the kid a beating for taking my bets after my cover had been blown, paying me off, and then letting me place more bets on the cuff.

And then he had the gall to call me to see if I planned to make good on my debt. Now remember, this guy knew that I had been part of an undercover operation targeting illegal gambling and that I was now working openly as a detective. Despite that, he called me on the phone and wanted payment for illegal bets that had been accepted on his behalf. Duh!

I told him to get lost and that the conversation we were having was being taped. He was not happy about that, cursed me out and then slammed down the phone. He probably would have been even angrier had he known how much good information his bookie had given me each time I called in a bet. He told me who else had gone on the vacation with his boss, who had paid for the trip, who brought their goomahs [also spelled cumad—Italian slang for girlfriend on the side] with them and their names, and other interesting stuff.

Anyway, I could not believe how stupid he was to call me. And when I took the tape to Chief Cizanckas, he was stunned as well. We both found it to be rather humorous.

———

As 1977 drew to an end, one of Dolan's colleagues got a story on the front page with the headline, "Threats on cops, others to be probed, chief says." Reporter Jim Mulvaney wrote that Chief Cizanckas said that he had begun an "intensive investigation" into a rash of threatening telephone calls that had been made to members of the police department's Internal Affairs Division, Board of Representatives and other City agencies involved in investigating municipal corruption.

According to Mulvaney, the most recent call was made to the mother of the police department captain who headed the municipal corruption and internal affairs units, while she was hospitalized recovering from her third heart attack. The caller allegedly told the ailing mother to tell her son to, "Lay off—he is dealing with the wrong people."

Chief Cizanckas stated that the call was so upsetting to the patient that she had to be rushed into the facility's intensive care unit, delaying her release from the hospital by at least a week. He added, "I find such behavior and conduct abhorrent and unacceptable. Whoever is doing this should know that I have a long memory and a lot of patience."

Cizanckas cited a call received by the secretary of Personnel Director Seymour Bernstein, in which the caller said,

"If Mr. Bernstein wants to keep his health," he wouldn't investigate certain people.

Cizanckas further said that his investigation had already uncovered evidence of illegal wiretaps and that several people had been making the threatening phone calls. He claimed that the New York City Police Department and the federal government were providing special training sessions for Stamford detectives and that the NYPD was giving his department "special assistance." In addition, local prosecutors and the U.S. Attorney's office had offered their assistance.

Cizanckas declined to say if special security details had been formed to protect those under threat; but did say "special investigative techniques" were being employed. And he declared that the threats would not deter his officers from doing what needed to be done.

When I finished the story, I sat for a few minutes letting the seriousness of the situation sink in. The crooks were threatening anybody and everybody who was in a position to cause them problems. No one was off limits from receiving these calls. Not even secretaries or elderly women in their hospital beds. The bad guys were apparently willing to do whatever it took to thwart the efforts to lock them up or at least dismantle their empire. But in my mind, they crossed a line when they called the cop's ill mother. That would only serve to infuriate every lawman—local, state or federal—and possibly the public. While some citizens might think that illegal gambling was merely a harmless form of entertainment, they all had mothers and this kind of conduct would not endear the gangsters to them.

On my home front, Joanne and Valarie had begun attending services at the Grace Evangelical Church and seemed to be loving it. I could already see a difference in Joanne. She was kinder and gentler. She never swore much, but now she was not swearing at all.

Valarie was changing, too. She would sit in her room and deliver religious messages onto her tape recorder. Joanne played some of them back to me. As I listened, I thought Valarie sounded like a young preacher. She would say things like, "You need to know Jesus Christ as your Lord and Savior." And, "The only way to Heaven is through Jesus Christ. You need to understand that."

I just smiled and told Joanne I was happy for her and Valarie; and I was. But there were too many other things going on in my life right then and their religion was not a priority for me. Kimmy was more interested in her friends and boyfriends and had absolutely no desire to go to church with her mother and sister. And that was okay, too. I was more than satisfied just knowing that the girls were all happy and did not give it much more thought.

And then one day Joanne told me that she did not want to go to the Bridgeport Jai Alai any more. Jai Alai is a sport that originated in Spain and was fairly new in Connecticut at the time. It really caught on with the locals and was drawing standing room only crowds. There was always a lot of excitement with the fans yelling and screaming as their favorite players made miraculous jumps and sometimes climbed the walls in pursuit of the ball. We always enjoyed ourselves there and I could not understand why she wanted to stop going. Joanne followed that announcement up with the fact that she no longer wanted to go to Atlantic City any more either. She was very nice when she delivered those declarations. But she was also firm.

So, there it was. My wife's new religion had soured her on going anywhere that allowed gambling. I wondered what was left for us, because it appeared she was going to be content to drop anything that was fun and turn into a holy roller.

In early 1978, almost six years after it happened, I began having nightly flashbacks of the 1972 shootout Joe Ligi and I had been involved in with prison escapees Thomas Murphy and Charles Blevins. I would be asleep and suddenly there I was in that parking lot with shots being fired by me and at me. I would wake up covered in sweat. Unable to get back to sleep I would pace the rest of the night. Although Post-Traumatic Stress Disorder had yet to be defined back then, I think that is what I had. I talked it over with Joanne and she asked if I would go to a counselor if she could find one for me. Things were getting pretty bad for me so I said yes.

She located a Christian psychologist through sources at her church and we started seeing him. We would sit and talk and I'd tell him what was happening to me and how I was feeling. He was a great guy, very patient and caring. He explained what was going on and answered any questions I had. After several sessions I was feeling better and thought it would be safe to stop seeing him. Joanne said that she, her mother, and several people from her church would pray for me and that God would see me through.

I told her that I did not want too many people at the church praying for me because I didn't want word to get back to the police department. If they found out what was going on they might think I had a mental problem. Then they could possibly take my gun away, take me off the street and assign me to desk duty. I did not want that to happen. At no time while I was having the flashbacks did I want to harm myself or anyone else. I believed I was perfectly capable of staying on the street and doing my job. So, we kept people with knowledge of my problem to a minimum.

The flashbacks stopped completely and never returned. I did not know how much of my recovery was the result of the praying that was done for me. But I thought maybe there was something to this God thing and it could be utilized from time to time.

———

I continued working in the Detective Bureau handling the full range of investigations—rape, robbery, burglary, and anything else that came along—as well as organized crime stuff and my private work for Chief Cizanckas. On top of that I was playing with the band two or three times a week and trying to spend more time with Joanne and the kids. There did not seem to be enough hours in the day for me to do everything I had to do or wanted to do.

It reached a point where I felt I needed to talk things over with Cizanckas. During our next covert meeting at a secluded park in Norwalk, we discussed the status of my work and that I was still getting some information from low-level organized crime guys—many of whom I had known since high school—about locations that were still taking betting action or running card games.

But I was not happy. Larry Hogan and other guys that wanted to hurt me were still out there. And the people I was able to get information from were putting themselves in danger if their bosses saw them talking to me. The bottom line was that I was getting burned out and just did not want to do it anymore. I told Cizanckas how I felt.

What I did not tell him was that I had seen changes in him that I didn't like and they contributed to my decision that it was time for me to make a change. What I mean by that is Cizanckas had become obsessed with wanting to know everything that was going on and he wanted to be the only one who knew the entire picture. I do not know how many sources he had gathering information for him about different things, but I was sure I was not the only one. And if knowledge is indeed power, Chief Cizanckas was becoming a very powerful man.

He had also developed an affinity for press microphones and cameras. I nicknamed him "the moth," because if there was a camera light anywhere nearby, he was drawn to it.

Anyway, I thought I presented a strong case for why I should quit the private assignment. But Cizanckas pleaded with me to continue and he was a tough man to say no to. As I drove home from that meeting, I was a little disappointed in myself for giving in to him. On the other hand, now that there was not a bookie in town who would take my bets or let me in their card game, all the money Cizanckas gave me went right into my pocket. Between that, the band money and my regular paycheck, I hadn't been in such good shape financially in a long time.

━━━━━

Whenever Cizanckas wanted to talk with me he would call to set up a meeting either in his office at headquarters or at some other place of his choosing. It seemed to me that we could have taken care of most of our business over the phone rather than meeting in person, but he insisted on doing it his way.

One day he summoned me to his office. He smiled at me and said he had news. He said, "I found out how your cover got blown." I told him I was all ears and to go ahead.

He said he had learned from his sources on the street that just prior to me being banned from the poker games and the threatening phone calls to me and the Advocate, there had been a large party at the home of one of the organized crime big shots. It was attended by other high-ranking figures as well as street-level guys and their wives or girlfriends. During conversation my name had come up and how I had left the police department and was spending most of my time hanging out with them.

It happened that the sister of one of the mobsters overheard that conversation. It also happened this woman worked in the department where City paychecks were processed. She asked if they were talking about Vito Colucci and they said yes. She said that I had not left the police department and that a paycheck was issued to me every week.

The wise guys were reportedly stunned at first, and then the light bulb came on. They asked that when the woman went to work the next day, she make absolutely sure she was correct about me receiving regular checks. She did as ordered, and then called her brother to report that she was right; I had received checks from the police department non-stop.

The now furious mobsters met to evaluate the potential damage the information I had obtained could cause to their operations and what other agencies that information might have been shared with. At the same time, they decided to exclude me from participation in any illegal gambling activities, make me feel uncomfortable in establishments under their control, and to deliver threatening phone messages to me and the Advocate. And the mobster who had authorized the phone calls was the same guy I had threatened to kill along with his cat, dog and goldfish. I had been right on that one.

I did not know who Cizanckas had gotten this information from. But I was very thankful that he had.

━━━

I found my time in the Detective Bureau to be very rewarding in the sense of the education I received. George Mayer was then the Bureau commander and he was a genius at putting cases together. I also learned a lot from two excellent detectives. Tommy Rowan and Lee Odle were top notch crime solvers. What they taught me served me well then and all through my subsequent career as a private investigator.

But I had some types of cases that I liked better than others. I was the least interested in burglaries and larcenies and had a problem in really sinking my teeth into them. And sometimes case assignments ran in streaks where I might get several burglary and larceny complaints in a row. When that happened, I had to fight off a sense of boredom until crimes I found more interesting came my way.

And then I began to experience stomach problems and went to a doctor to get checked out. After an examination and some tests, he told me that I might have the start of an ulcer. My father, who lived to be nearly 99, was only hospitalized once in his life and that was due to a severe case of bleeding ulcers. I did not want that to happen to me.

I went straight from the doctor's office to headquarters to see Chief Cizanckas. He was not in so I stopped at the office of one of the captains and announced that I was resigning and this time it was for real.

I turned in my badge and service weapon and signed some paperwork saying that I was leaving of my own free will and that I had not been asked or coerced into resigning. I even explained to the guys in the office that I had just had enough. I said I needed to get rid of the stress of the job and would probably spend more time playing with the band and that I was also considering becoming a bail bondsman.

After I completed the paperwork, I was told that I would receive a final check that would include a lump sum payment of all the money I had contributed toward my retirement over the years. I left headquarters with mixed feelings. I was sad that my police career was over. But I was also excited about what the future might hold.

I returned home and broke the news to Joanne. I think the fact that I made such an important decision without even discussing it with her speaks volumes about my state of mind at that time. I also told her that Chief Cizanckas had not been at headquarters when I resigned and that I had no doubt but that he would call and ask me to reconsider.

As predicted, Cizanckas was on the phone bright and early the next morning and he asked me to come to his office. I agreed, albeit reluctantly. When we met, he was not angry. He just said he wished I had talked with him before submitting my resignation. I told him about my stomach problems and that I needed more peace in my life. But I might as well have been talking to a wall because he either did not understand or did not care. He just looked at me and said, "Here's what we're going to do."

With that we started another of our Abbott and Costello routines. Cizanckas reached into his desk, pulled out a badge and handed it to me. He said I was still a cop. I said no, I was not. I had resigned. He said something to the effect that I was not really a cop, but I was kind of a cop. He told me to put the badge somewhere safe and only show it if absolutely necessary, such as to get out of a scrape with another police agency. I could show the badge, give them his name and number and everything would get straightened out. He said he would continue to bankroll me just like before and I would carry on as his private operative.

I kept going back to the fact that I had resigned my position. I had turned in my equipment and signed the paperwork. Unlike the fake resignation for the undercover assignment, this was the real deal. But to Cizanckas that was a mere technicality. He reached into his pocket and pulled out a couple hundred dollars to get me started.

I wanted so bad to tell him to keep his money, but I could not. As I took it from him, I asked him outright if the money he gave me was all legitimate. He assured me that it was. He said that since I was no longer officially a cop, he could give me even more money. Because for all practical purposes I was now an informant and he was paying me for information.

I said OKAY, I would do what I could when I had the time. And there would be no more of these meetings in his office every time I turned around. I had let him know when I had something for him and then we would make our arrangements.

He accepted that and added some clarification of what he expected from me. Larry Hogan and organized crime were my first priority. After that he wanted information on any unsolved crimes—rape, robbery, burglary, whatever.

We shook hands, he told me that I was a heck of a cop, and then I left. I drove out of the parking lot and turned down an alley where I stopped and stashed my new badge under the spare tire in the trunk. As I pulled away, I knew that I had not given my desire for peace in my life much of a chance. I had resigned from the police department, but not from Cizanckas.

33

URING THE early months of 1978 I was still struggling with my arrangement with Cizanckas. I did not like what I was doing and regretted letting him talk me into it. What made it even worse was my growing feeling that he did not really care about me at all as a person. To him I was just a tool he could use to get him what he wanted: power and glory.

I developed a plan to confirm my thoughts the next time Cizanckas and I met, which took place at a restaurant in Rowayton, Connecticut. We were making small talk when I said, "You know, Chief, it is too bad that phone call that ended the undercover was made to the Advocate and not just to me. Because if the paper hadn't gotten hold of it, you would probably have left me out there, even though my cover had been blown."

Incredibly, he admitted that he would have done exactly that. If that warning had only been delivered to me, he would have been willing to leave me out on the streets, blown cover, death threats, and all. Would I have let him talk me into doing it? Maybe or maybe not. But he would have tried; and that was all I needed to know about my relationship with him. Chief Victor Cizanckas was only looking out for Victor Cizanckas. From that point on I knew I had to be extra careful with him because he was not the least bit concerned about my well-being. Any feelings I had previously had for the man were gone.

———

On Tuesday, April 18, there were three stories on the front page of the Advocate that were of interest to me. The first was titled, "Court probe of City begins." The article quoted two state legislators as saying the Superior Court had agreed to investigate allegations of municipal corruption. Christopher Shays and Thom Serrani, said that after meeting with Judge Irving Levine they were confident that a special prosecutor would be appointed to get to the bottom of the numerous corruption allegations.

The plan called for State's Attorney Donald Browne— who also attended the meeting— to appoint one of his assistants to look into possible official misconduct on a full-time basis and submit a written report to Judge Levine. If probable cause was found a special one-man grand jury would be created and he would have a special prosecutor under his authority.

This sounded good to me. The only potential problem I could see was that if any of the people assigned to the probe were themselves corrupt, the whole thing could go down the tubes.

The next story was written by Dolan with the headline, "Conspiracy laid to Fusaro." It said that attorney and top Democratic politician John Fusaro, along with a Rhode Island lawyer, had been indicted on Monday on charges of conspiracy to defraud the U.S. Government, obstructing justice, and making false statements to IRS agents. Fusaro was accused of conspiring to conceal a $25,000 payment he had received from the Rhode Island attorney. Grand jury investigations were continuing in both Connecticut and Rhode Island.

But the biggest headline of that day was that Anthony Dolan had been awarded the 1978 Pulitzer Prize for his series on municipal corruption. The story said that the announcement was made on the day the twenty-nine-year-old Dolan began his fourth year as an Advocate reporter. It cited his 75 articles about municipal corruption in Stamford, including ties between organized crime and the City's police department. It said those articles resulted in the firing or forced resignations of seven City officials and the launching of eight separate investigations by the FBI, U.S. Postal Service, and other federal agencies. The stories were also credited with creating an aura of reform in Stamford.

Dolan was quoted in the article as saying that, "The award belongs to the employees in City government who sometimes risked their jobs and their careers to tell the truth about what was going on." He went on to say that he was donating the prize money to the family of Don Bolles, an investigative reporter for the Arizona Republic newspaper, who was killed in June 1976 while probing an alleged land deal involving top state politicians and the Mob.

Although I had not foreseen the Pulitzer coming, I was elated for Dolan and felt there was no one more deserving of it than him.

Shortly after the award was announced, a man named Bernard Cohen wrote a letter to the editor that was published in the Advocate. It read, "I believe that we, the people of Stamford, should express our appreciation to Anthony Dolan for the great effort he has made to ferret out and expose corruption." I was glad to see that kind of response from a citizen; and it was one that was echoed by many others over the coming days.

Although the accolades were well deserved, Dolan's hectic work schedule had taken a toll on him. It was disclosed near the end of the year that in November he collapsed, suffering from exhaustion and mononucleosis. Following that episode his arm was seriously injured during an incident at his apartment. While asleep in his bed he was awakened by two loud crashing sounds. With nerves already frayed from months of living under constant threats and harassment, he went to investigate the cause of the noises. He saw a reflection in the door's window and thinking it was an intruder, took a swing at it. His arm shattered the glass and went through. The damage to his arm caused by the glass shards required nearly three and a half hours of surgery to repair. The cause of the crashing sounds was never determined.

Also, by the end of the year, Chief Cizanckas was coming under ferocious political attack for his total inflexibility and his "righteous zeal" in how he ran the police department.

ANTHONY DOLAN

1978 PULITZER PRIZE WINNER FOR HIS
SERIES ON MUNICIPAL CORRUPTION.

———

In the early fall of 1978, I took my mother to a doctor's appointment. She was 66-years-old and had never been to a doctor in her life other than for childbirth. I was in the waiting room when the doctor came out and called me into an empty exam room. He told me that my mother had lung cancer and showed me her x-rays. One lung was completely gone from her many years of smoking over two packs a day, and the other lung was partially gone. I stood in shock as he delivered the news. I had thought this was only going to be a routine visit because she was suffering from a cough and feeling a little weak, like maybe she was coming down with a cold.

When I asked the doctor about treatment, he said there wasn't really anything that could be done to reverse her condition. Treatment would only delay the inevitable. He estimated she had six to nine months to live.

My mother and I left the doctor's office in silence. The doctor had not said if he had told her the results of the x-rays. But I knew her well enough to know that he had. Her demeanor gave it away. Neither of us mentioned what we had just learned. Based on the little bit of conversation we had we could just as well have been returning from a trip to the store rather than the doctor's office. So, on the outside we ignored it. But inside I was devastated.

34

THINGS SLOWED down for me during the first several months of 1979. Although I still did some things for Cizanckas, I was able to spend a lot more time playing in the band and with my family. I even started to take some interest in Joanne's church activities. I still had not committed to getting involved, but I was intrigued by how at peace she seemed to be. Under the surface, though, things were perking and I knew it would be just a matter of time until they started to break. And when they did, the news seemed to be non-stop.

The first thing was an Advocate article on October 17. The title was, "Judges rule in favor of Advocate reporter." It said that in separate decisions, Superior Court judges in Stamford and Bridgeport allowed reporter Anthony Dolan to continue to protect the confidential sources he used in his municipal corruption series. The identities of those individuals had been sought by former State Senator William Strada and a former public works official. Dolan was quoted as saying, "I am very pleased with the decision. This is a step forward for the press."

The judges' rulings said that Dolan would not have to testify at a hearing before the Personnel Appeals Board and that the reporter had a qualified First Amendment privilege against compelled testimony and production of documents.

Another win for the good guys, I thought. Since being awarded the Pulitzer Dolan had been receiving invitations for speaking engagements and other personal appearances. Stories like this would bring him even more attention and open more doors. I hoped some of the offers would be paying gigs, because the word was that Dolan was heavily in debt after nearly five years as a lowly-paid reporter.

But even with other opportunities coming his way, Dolan stayed with the newspaper for several more months and continued to focus on corruption and the Gambino crime family. In one magazine article Dolan was referred to as "The scourge of Stamford." In order to stay with the Advocate and continue his investigative work he turned down job offers from the New York Times and Westinghouse Broadcasting. But in May 1980, somebody made Dolan an "offer he couldn't refuse" and he left Stamford.

Around the same time as the article about Dolan's court victory ran, Chief Cizanckas was back in the news due to an action before the State of Connecticut Labor Department. Titled, "In the Matter of City of Stamford, Stamford Police Department, Mayor Louis A. Clapes and Chief Victor

Cizanckas Against Stamford Police Association Officer Salvatore Ladestro and Police Captain Joseph Ligi."

When I heard about this, I wondered what the heck Cizanckas was up to. I obtained a copy of the paperwork and went through it page by page. I read that in October of 1979 Officer Ladestro filed a complaint with the Connecticut State Board of Labor Relations alleging that Cizanckas had interfered with and coerced Ladestro in regard to his position as a union representative. And on October 29, Captain Ligi filed a complaint stating that Cizanckas was interfering with, restraining and coercing employees in exercising their rights; and also engaging in unlawful surveillance of employees.

This confirmed to me that Cizanckas was not the same man who had arrived in town on his white horse less than three years earlier to save and restore the Stamford Police Department. Through his accomplishments in the police department, that man had helped Mayor Clapes win a second term. But the current version of Cizanckas had received a no-confidence vote from the police union and seemed to be running amok.

The complaints by Ladestro and Ligi alleged that two days after the no-confidence vote, Cizanckas directed the department's Internal Affairs Division to conduct a comprehensive investigation into the matter forthwith. Pursuant to that order, Sergeant Walter Barrett launched an investigation. That probe resulted in a number of findings. But the one that bothered me the most was Cizanckas' allegation that Ladestro and Ligi were jointly responsible for gross dereliction of duty by depriving the citizens of Stamford of needed police services and jeopardizing the safety of other police officers.

I knew that as a union official, Sal Ladestro would sometimes need to conduct union business while on duty. As a captain in the department, Joe Ligi wanted to implement a procedure by which other officers would handle incoming service calls that would have gone to Ladestro during those times. That did not seem to go over well with Cizanckas; and prior to holding a hearing on the matter he assigned Ligi to the training unit where he would have absolutely no responsibility for supervising police personnel. He dealt with Ladestro by assigning him as a "utility desk officer," where he would be closely supervised pending a Police Commission hearing. Those actions resulted in the complaints being filed by Ladestro and Ligi.

After one of the longest hearings in the history of the Board of Labor Relations, that body issued a ruling that ordered the City of Stamford to cease and desist from continuing to implement the current assignments of Ladestro and Ligi and the restrictions that had been placed on Ladestro's on-duty union activities. Both men were to be returned to the duties and schedules they had been on prior to their re-assignments.

I figured Cizanckas would not be in a very good mood after the spanking he'd received from the Board of Labor Relations and I tried to stay away from him. He called me two or three times a day, but I ignored his calls for several days. When I did respond, I stalled him by saying I was tied up with taking my mother for radiation treatments, playing with the band and pursuing getting my bail bond business started, and that I simply didn't have the time to meet with him.

So as 1979 came to a close Cizanckas was becoming more and more unpopular with his police officers and the city politicians.

But for me personally, the biggest event of the year came on Christmas Eve. It was on that night that I attended the candlelight service at the Grace Evangelical Church with Joanne and accepted Jesus Christ as my Lord and the Savior of my life. I have referred to other incidents in this book as "life changing," and they were. But none had the positive impact on me that the events of that night did.

Prior to that night I had last been inside a church when I was about fourteen. That had been at a Catholic service in which there was no music and the priest spoke in Latin. I decided to go with Joanne that night because she assured me there would be lots of music that I would enjoy and the whole experience would be a new awakening for me.

I remember being awed by the way the people attending the service welcomed me. They hugged me when we were introduced and their warmth was real—no phony stuff. When the service was nearly over the pastor gave what he called an "invitation." He said that right then was the time for those who had not done so before to accept Jesus Christ. We could do that and then say a "sinner's prayer," in which we would admit that we were sinners, denounce our sins and acknowledge Jesus Christ as our Lord and Master. As I raised my hand to make that pledge, I felt a peace come over me. It was a feeling I had never experienced before in my life. After that night I became a regular churchgoer along with Joanne and Valarie, and our son Marc began to attend with us, too.

I can honestly say that in the over thirty years that have passed since that night, I have personally seen hard core alcoholics and drug addicts say that prayer and make that commitment who have never taken another drink or illegal drug. For other people the change is not as immediate and it takes longer for the Lord to work on their lives. That was more the case with me. I felt the peace right then, but there was more to be done. My walk with the Lord was a tricky one for many years; but Jesus stayed with me and never took his hand off me.

As 1980 began my mother was becoming very weak. We all knew that she had only a few weeks left. The support Joanne and I received from the church during that very difficult time was overwhelming. People who had never met my mother visited her and prayed with her and for her. When my mother passed away on January 20, I was at peace because she had made the same commitment to Jesus Christ that I had. I knew that she was with Him in Heaven.

In a much different manner, Stamford lost Anthony Dolan in 1980 when he received the one offer, he was unable to turn down: an invitation to join the presidential campaign of Ronald Reagan as a researcher and speechwriter. To the politically conservative Dolan, it was an opportunity too good to pass up. When Dolan announced his decision to leave, he said, "It [joining the Reagan campaign] is a great opportunity, but it is also painful to leave Stamford. This is a great City and people here have been very kind to me." Upon Dolan's departure from the Advocate, senior management vigorously praised him for his skills as a reporter and the professionalism he brought to the newspaper.

After Reagan won the election and took office in 1981, Dolan served as his chief speechwriter until Reagan left office in 1989. He authored Reagan's famous 1987 Berlin Wall speech. Also, while serving in the Reagan administration, Dolan utilized the experience he gained in Stamford to help craft Reagan's initiative against the Mob.

Dolan continued in government service during the presidency of George W. Bush, serving as Senior Advisor in the office of Secretary of State and Special Advisor in the Office of the Secretary of Defense.

Another person who departed the scene in 1980 was David "Turk" Avnayim. He was the drug dealer who had been with Hogan waiting to ambush me at the restaurant in Port Chester. He was found murdered in Redding, Connecticut, on July 24.

———

As time went by, I became increasingly more convinced that Chief Cizanckas had a mental problem. I say that based on the fact that I probably had more direct contact with him than anyone else in the police department. And for the past several months when we talked or met our conversations had been bizarre at best. No matter how much information I brought to him it was never enough. He would tell me repeatedly, "Get me more. Get me more." And I did.

It may surprise you, but getting good information for Cizanckas was not all that difficult. There were enough people on the street—such as independent bookies and drug dealers—that hated Hogan and his mobster associates who were willing to talk to me. They often picked up the word that something was coming down or that made men would be in town for meetings or parties—all the what, where and when stuff. And Cizanckas absolutely loved it. But like I said, no matter how much information I gave him or how good it was, it was never enough.

And to validate my thoughts about Cizanckas' mental condition, over the summer he went to the residence of Mayor Clapes—the man who had hired him—reportedly to arrest him on unspecified charges. A confrontation ensued and Clapes threw Cizanckas out. Although the details behind Cizanckas' visit were never made public, his actions that day were not those of a totally rational man.

By that fall I had had enough of Cizanckas. My bail bond business was up and running and I was making good money from it. Between that and the band I was doing pretty well. I no longer needed his money or had the time to devote to his endless demands for more intelligence data. I decided that when we met again in person, I would pull the plug on him once and for all. He had a strong personality and it would not be easy to sever our relationship. I was not looking forward to it, but it was something I knew I had to do.

However, everything changed for me when I opened the newspaper on November 23. The front-page story was that Stamford Police Chief Victor I Cizanckas had died in his sleep from an apparent heart attack at the age of 43. Although my relationship with him had deteriorated, I was sad that he had died, but mainly I was stunned. As I read and re-read the story, I wondered if the job-related stress Cizanckas had been under recently had caused his demise at such a young age. I recalled how bad he looked the last time I had seen him in person. He was very pale and I thought then that he was sick.

In the days immediately following Cizanckas' death, rumors circulated that he had not died of natural causes, that his organized crime enemies had done him in. I did not buy into that theory, but it did cause a buzz for a while in some quarters.

As 1980 turned into 1981, Cizanckas and Turk Avnayim were gone, but Larry Hogan was still alive and free. That would soon come to an end, though. On July 24, Lawrence A. Hogan was arrested by agents of the Drug Enforcement Administration after being indicted by a federal grand jury for conspiracy to possess with intent to distribute two kilos [4.4 pounds] of heroin. He was also charged with multiple counts of using a telephone to facilitate his intent to possess and distribute heroin. Indicted with Hogan was his associate, Leonard Patricelli.

I cannot tell you the excitement I felt when I heard that news! I'd been waiting for this day for many, many years and it had finally arrived. I felt peace in the sense that justice was being done and I thanked God for that.

As I reflected back on the lives of Cizanckas and Hogan a word came to mind that I felt applied to both men: hubris— extreme pride or arrogance which often indicates a loss of contact with reality and an overestimation of one's own competence or capabilities, especially when the person is in a position of power. It seemed to me that hubris had contributed to Cizanckas' untimely death and would likely lead to a prison sentence for Hogan.

Yes, it was finally over. Or so I thought.

VITO'S FORMER BOSS, LARRY HOGAN
WALKING OUT OF COURT.

VITO DIDN'T KNOW IF THIS DAY WOULD
EVER HAPPEN, BUT IT DID.

35

L ARRY HOGAN went on trial at the federal courthouse in Hartford in April 1982. According to newspaper accounts, DEA Special Agent Nicholas Alleva testified about several conversations he had with Hogan in various Stamford bars while working in an undercover capacity in February and March 1981. Alleva said Hogan told him that he was involved in illegal activities with the late Frank Piccolo, reputedly a capo in the Gambino crime family and the kingpin of Connecticut organized crime. The 58-year-old Piccolo had been shot to death in Bridgeport in September 1981 in an apparent gangland hit.

Agent Alleva told the jurors that during the undercover operation a proposal was made to Hogan in which Hogan would purchase four and a half pounds of heroin from

Alleva for $250,000. Hogan would then distribute the heroin, which had an estimated street value of $1 million.

Although Hogan subsequently backed out of the deal, he and Leonard Patricelli were indicted by a federal grand jury and each faced a maximum prison sentence of 15 years if convicted. However, their attorneys said they would prove their clients were unfairly entrapped by government agents.

After reading the story I felt confident that the prosecution had a strong case. The posturing by the defense attorneys was to be expected and did not cause me any great concern.

On May 7, Larry Hogan took the stand in his own defense. He said that he was angry and ashamed with himself for being tempted to buy heroin from undercover agents, but he vehemently denied that he ever made a "firm deal" to purchase the drugs. Hogan's testimony supported the defense contention that he was on the fence about the deal and the agents tried to convince him to move forward and actually buy the heroin, thereby trying to entrap him.

I thought Hogan's defense was weak and would not work. But I knew him and what kind of man he really was. Would twelve of his peers feel the same way I did?

On May 13, after only four hours of jury deliberations, Larry Hogan and Leonard Patricelli were found guilty of the drug-trafficking-conspiracy charge. Hogan was also convicted on three of the four charges that he used a telephone to facilitate his intent to possess and distribute heroin. I had been waiting for over a decade for justice to be served. And to say this was one of the happiest days of my life would not be an overstatement.

On June 16, Hogan and Patricelli each received sentences of 5 years in prison. I would have preferred something more, but for me the slate was now clean and I could leave Larry Hogan behind me.

But less than two weeks later, on June 30, the first signs of trouble appeared. Hogan's lawyer, premier defense attorney David Golub, filed documents seeking a new trial for his client. According to his filing, Golub alleged that a government informant named Martin "Yogi" Ruggiri, whom neither side called as a witness, had been coerced by the government to cooperate in its investigation. Golub said that had he been aware of the government's tactics he would have called Ruggiri to testify on Hogan's behalf. That motion was denied. But Golub followed-up by filing an appeal citing prosecutorial misconduct.

The case was argued before the United States Court of Appeals, Second Circuit, on February 7, 1983. And then the torture of waiting for the decision began. Had Golub convinced the three-judge panel that government lawyers had been overzealous in their prosecution of his client?

If May 13, 1982, had been one of my happiest days, then June 28, 1983, was one of my saddest. That is the day the Second Circuit announced the convictions against Hogan and Patricelli were reversed and the indictments that led to their arrests in July 1981 were thrown out. Larry Hogan was again a free man.

I obtained a copy of the decision rendered by the court. It read, "On this appeal our principal concern is directed not at the jury trial where the accused were found guilty, but at the earlier events—those that transpired before the grand jury which indicted the appellants. More than in other cases, the minutes of the grand jury proceedings in this case reveal what can happen when the prosecutor is too determined to obtain an indictment. The temptation to cut corners, to ignore the rights of an accused, and to toss fair play to the winds gain ascendancy. Prosecutors presenting cases to grand juries are firmly subject to due process limitations and bound by ethical considerations. While we fully recognize that a court's power to dismiss an indictment following a conviction at trial is rarely exercised, the prosecution so violated these limitations and obligations as to mandate this indictment's dismissal. Here prosecutorial zeal only illuminates anew the insight of the old adage that the ends cannot justify the means."

The judges obviously felt the prosecutor had gone way out of bounds in his grand jury presentation. As I continued to read the decision, I understood their reasoning. The citations below were taken directly from that document:

> Bearing in mind these general obligations, we turn to the specific instances of prosecutorial misconduct which occurred before the grand jury in this case. At one point during the proceedings, a grand juror, apparently troubled by the proposed prosecution, posed the following question to the Assistant United States Attorney (AUSA):
>
> What I do not understand is if this case fell through, in other words, if there was no deal made what is the purpose of us listening to this?
>
> The AUSA's response, in pertinent part, was as follows:
>
> If the deal would have gone forward, we would have had a real hoodlum trying to sell heroin.... I think even though in a general case where somebody backs out

and decides not to do the crime it probably should not
be prosecuted

In a case like this I think is [sic] a matter of equity
it should.

Having characterized Hogan as a real hoodlum, who
should be indicted as "a matter of equity," the AUSA proceeded to present to the grand jury hearsay testimony to the
effect that Connecticut police officials thought that Hogan
had committed crimes wholly irrelevant to the alleged drug
transaction then under federal investigation. Specifically,
the prosecutor introduced testimony that Hogan was a
"suspect" in the apparently unrelated murders of a drug
dealer named David Avnayim and a Norwalk Connecticut policeman named Charles Dugan. The grand jury was
never asked to consider returning indictments for any federal
offenses relating to these two murders.

In addition to the testimony regarding the two murders,
the AUSA suggested that Hogan was guilty of misconduct
while he was a police officer. Making himself an unsworn
witness, the prosecutor informed the grand jury that he
had read various articles in a Stamford newspaper which
accused "a high-ranking officer" of receiving bribes from
gamblers. Then the same AUSA went on to relate that Leo
Tobin, a Stamford police officer, had told him that Stamford
Police Chief Czankis had mentioned to Tobin that Hogan
was "suspected of having been on the take from gambling
establishments."

Further, the prosecutor, faced with explaining Hogan's
refusal to go through with the drug deal, elicited the following testimony. In response to a question posed by the prose-

cutor, Agent Alleva testified that he had no direct knowledge of why Hogan had changed his mind, but that he had "heard why through other agents." The AUSA immediately followed up that question by asking Alleva whether "[t]he speculation is that Yogi told Hogan that this was an undercover deal?" To this Agent Alleva responded affirmatively. The identity of the persons so speculating and the basis for their conclusions were never explored. Moreover, evidence in the DEA's possession in the form of the recording of the May 12 conversation between Hogan and Yogi casts serious doubt on the accuracy of this speculation.

Concerned with the obvious possibility that the grand jury might not indict because no drugs were ever purchased, possessed, or distributed, it was apparently the prosecution's view that it would be helpful to show appellants' predisposition to possess heroin; but much of the evidence it presented in this regard later proved to be false. This seems the only plausible explanation for the AUSA having elicited repeated testimony from Agents Salute and Alleva that in January 1981, prior to the proposed narcotics deal in question, Hogan and Patricelli had been caught in Rye, New York attempting to obtain heroin. Agent Salute categorically denied any DEA role in the Rye incident and Agent Alleva testified that he had thoroughly investigated the incident and that the stop of appellants by the Rye police was in no way caused by the DEA. But the facts in the record indicate just the opposite. Confronted with statements of the Rye police and writings made at the time of the stop, Agent Salute admitted in post-trial proceedings that the DEA had in fact called the Rye police and instigated the detention of Hogan and Patricelli.

Additionally, Agent Salute told the grand jury that he had discussed heroin over the telephone with Patricelli prior to the first meeting with Hogan. This evidence, which tended to show that appellants were arranging a heroin deal even before the first meeting with DEA undercover agents, was later conceded by the government to be untrue. The subject of heroin was not mentioned until the first meeting in February. Similarly, Agent Alleva "mistakenly" testified before the grand jury that he had informed Hogan at the first meeting that Hogan would have to pay $50,000 prior to the heroin delivery. In fact, Hogan was initially offered nearly $2,000,000 worth of heroin for no cash down payment. This offer—one that Hogan admitted had tempted him—differed significantly from the offer Alleva described to the grand jury. At trial Agent Alleva conceded that on this particular point he had made an error. He testified that the $50,000 demand on Hogan was not made at the first meeting, but was in fact made several meetings later. His explanation was that he had "confused" the meetings during his grand jury testimony.

Finally, the DEA agents' false testimony to the grand jury on the issues of predisposition and inducement is most disturbing. Although the government was not required to anticipate a defense of entrapment and introduce evidence of predisposition, having elected to do so it was duty bound not to introduce false and misleading testimony. While the factual misstatements in the agents' testimony may have been inadvertent, as the government now argues, the fact remains that the appellants were prejudiced by the misstatements of important facts and the grand jury's independent role was impaired. Regardless of the government's intent, we believe that the grand jury was probably misled by this presentation.

In summary, the incidents related are flagrant and unconscionable. Taking advantage of his special position of trust, the AUSA impaired the grand jury's integrity as an independent body. Thus, based on the particular facts of this case, we believe that the indictment below must be dismissed.

Because of the determination reached, we need not decide the numerous other issues raised on appeal. The judgments of conviction are reversed and the case remanded to the district court with instructions to dismiss the underlying indictment against appellants.

After I finished reading the numerous reasons the judges cited for their decision, I knew in my heart they had done the right thing. But even though I understood it, I was still bitterly disappointed. Although prosecutors might ask the appeals court to reconsider or even request a review by the United States Supreme Court, I believed those actions would almost certainly fail. I felt I had to come to grips with the fact that Larry Hogan would never be brought to justice. Yes, he had been forced out of the police department. And yes, even with the reversal of his conviction he had still taken a big hit regarding his character and reputation within the community. But to a guy like Hogan those things would not matter. In my mind, and I am sure in his, he had beaten the system.

Over the following months I tried to keep Hogan out of my mind as much as possible. A rumor circulated that he was still being investigated by the Connecticut State Police. But that did not excite me very much. Investigations seemed to bounce off him like bullets off Superman. When it came to the law, Larry Hogan was invincible.

And there was another rumor that Hogan had been diagnosed with liver cancer. Not that long ago I might have gotten some sense of satisfaction from that news. But after finding God I had mellowed. I did not want to see anyone suffer and die. Not even him. Besides, there was no guarantee the story was true. I would not have been surprised to find out Hogan had put the rumor out himself figuring the law would not expend a lot of effort investigating or prosecuting a seriously ill man.

"Ex-cop indicted for 1980 murder." That was the headline in the Advocate on May 12, 1984. Larry Hogan had been indicted for the murder of David "Turk" Avnayim and various drug charges. The article said that according to State's Attorney Walter Flanagan, Hogan and his associates George Bratsenis and Louis Sclafani, had made a deal to purchase cocaine from Avnayim. However, when Avnayim went to Redding to complete the transaction he was murdered by Bratsenis and Sclafani in the presence of Hogan. The three men then took possession of the drugs and attempted to distribute them. If convicted, Hogan faced 57 years in prison on the drug charges and 25 years to life for the murder of Avnayim. And at the same time the feds reindicted him on the charges he had been convicted of in May of 1982.

When asked to comment, Hogan's lawyer, David Golub, said he was upset about the new charges because the information prosecutors relied on came from a witness—Sclafani—who had made a deal to cooperate to try to save his own neck. He added that the federal charges had been thrown out once and would be again. Then, referring to his client's ongoing battle with liver cancer, Golub said his first step would be to try to get Hogan released from jail on bond so that he could continue his medical treatments.

It looked like I had been wrong. Law enforcement officials—both state and federal—apparently were determined that Hogan be held accountable for his crimes. And what he was facing this time made that earlier 5-year sentence look like child's play. I hoped that this time the investigators and prosecutors had conducted themselves in a manner that would leave Hogan no wiggle room and no way out.

Less than three months later that became a moot point, though. Cancer claimed Larry Hogan on August 4, 1984, at the age of 52. I knew there would be no loopholes for him when he faced his Maker. No lawyer and no appeals process, just him and God. I did not know what Hogan's fate would be there, but I hoped that he had cried out to God for forgiveness before he took his last breath.

BONUS CHAPTERS FOR

ROGUE TOWN

REVISED EDITION

THE REAL BRA MURDERER,

WHITING EXPOSED

&

BRIA FAMILY WANTS ANSWERS IN SON'S OVERDOSE

AUTHORS CONTRIBUTING TO
THE NEXT THREE CHAPTERS ARE:

Vito Colucci, Jr., Joe Cochran & Jane Ryder

THE REAL BRA MURDERER

ETWEEN 1967 and 1971, the bodies of five black women were found within a 750-foot section of the Merritt Parkway right-of-way in Stamford, Connecticut—specifically within a quarter-mile radius of the Riverbank-Roxbury Road overpass. All the women had been strangled, four of them with their own brassieres, leading the case to be referred to as "The Parkway Bra Murders."

There was little for police to go on. Though tire marks were found at some of the scenes, that was the only hard evidence, and it was a heavily trafficked area. Other than race the women had little in common: their ages ranged from late teens to early thirties; most but not all were from Stamford (one was from Mount Vernon, New York); four of them had been single; at least one was thought to be a junkie while three were known prostitutes; some had been sexually assaulted but not all; and one was married with four young children.

The first victim to be found—though not the first to be killed—was Donna Roberts, age 22. She had disappeared from Stamford on May 2, 1968, and her body was discovered the next day. Gloria Kahn, 21, was found on September 8 of the same year, 200 feet from where Roberts had been found. The body of 29-year-old Rosell "Sissie" Rush was found in April of the next year, 1969, but she'd been reported missing on August 4 of 1967, and forensic examination determined she had in fact been the first to be killed. The fourth victim, 19-year-old Gail Thompson, died and was discovered on the same day: July 10, 1971. Alma Henry, 34, the only married victim, was found on August 22 of 1971 by two motorists when they pulled over to switch drivers.

By the summer of 1971, police had made little progress, and still weren't even certain all the murders had been committed by a single perpetrator. As Connecticut state police field investigator Captain Joseph Ciecierski told reporters, "If we had something to go on, we wouldn't have tolerated these killings since 1968."

But the black community felt there was more to the case's lack of momentum than an absence of clues, and that if the victims had been white, law enforcement would have taken a more aggressive approach to the investigation. A New York Times article by Linda Greenhouse from August 29, 1971 stated that "The killing seemed to have evoked interest but little fear and no panic among the residents of the predominantly white city of 108,000." Greenhouse also quoted the supervisor of the Stamford Housing Authority as saying "If it were a Boston strangler, everybody would be scared, but don't you see it's not that type of killing."

In following up on an anonymous call that had been made to a local clergyman in April 1969, investigators— now a full-time task force made up of both state and local police—questioned a man named Benjamin (Ben) Miller.

Ben Miller was a white postal worker and (possibly self-ordained) minister who often preached on street corners, specially targeting black women. He had a history of mental illness and had been hospitalized as early as 1953, and the task force quickly labeled him a person of interest, questioning him several times and at great length over the next few weeks.

According to police, Miller denied committing the murders but said he'd had sex with Gail Thompson. Though Thompson's autopsy report had revealed no recent sexual intercourse, police said other statements Miller made accurately described information that had not been made public. For instance, the detectives showed Miller a photograph of Thompson's body and asked what he thought was around her neck. Miller replied (correctly) that he thought it was a handkerchief, even though the press and public had been told Thompson was strangled with a brassiere. Miller was given a polygraph test, but the results were inconclusive.

During an interrogation on February 16, 1972, the detectives suggested Miller speak with a psychiatrist, confusingly also named Miller but no relation to the postal worker. Ben Miller declined to meet with Dr. Miller, but said he would talk to Dr. Shirley Williams, a psychiatrist he'd previously seen when he was hospitalized at Norwalk Hospital. After meeting with Dr. Williams and another psychiatrist, Ben

Miller was involuntarily committed to Fairfield Hills hospital, where he was diagnosed with chronic undifferentiated schizophrenia. According to hospital records, Miller was delusional, fanatically religious, and exhibited "low self-esteem, flat affect, thought disorders, poor judgment and insight."

While confined at Fairfield Hills, Miller was interviewed several times by Dr. Robert Miller, the psychiatrist Ben Miller had declined to see when it was suggested by police. As a result of these sessions, Dr. Miller (with whom the investigators had previously consulted about Ben Miller) told the task force the he believed Ben Miller had committed the murders, and recommended that they continue to investigate him.

On February 29, Dr. Miller called the detectives, saying Ben Miller wanted to talk to them. When they arrived, they advised Miller of his rights, and on a pad he wrote that he had killed seven women. Police said he described Thompson's murder in detail and talked about three others in more general terms. He not only signed typed versions of these statements, but accompanied detectives to the Riverbank-Roxbury Road overpass area, reenacted Thompson's murder, and showed them where the bodies had been found.

Two days later, Miller signed a detailed statement admitting he'd murdered Alma Henry and on March 10, another admitting to the murder of Donna Roberts. He again led detectives to the spots where their bodies had been discovered, and signed police statements describing these trips, attesting to their accuracy.

Miller was arrested on March 17, 1972, and on May 15, he was indicted for the murders of Sissie Rush, Donna Roberts, Gloria Kahn, Gail Thompson, and Alma Henry.

Public defender Herbert J. Bundock was appointed Miller's lawyer. In preparing Miller's defense, Bundock interviewed not only Miller himself, but Miller's father ("Miller Sr.") and Dr. Williams, and reviewed Miller's psychiatric records. Miller Sr. told Bundock that Miller had telephoned Miller Sr. in February and said he had signed a confession but that he was sick and would have signed anything.

Ben Miller also told Bundock that despite his frequent protestations of innocence, during the interrogation the investigators had repeatedly tried to get him to confess to the murders. Miller claimed he was not only afraid of being beaten and that his wife would find out about his adultery, but that detectives had told him that if he didn't confess, he would lose his job and his family would suffer. Miller said that the police asked him leading questions and he gave them the answers he thought they wanted to hear, and as for taking them to the crime scenes, Miller said they'd shown him photographs of the murder scenes many times, so when they drove him to the area and asked if it was the right place, he'd said "I think so" to be cooperative.

Ben Miller said Dr. Robert Miller had also tried to get him to confess during the many interviews they had while Ben Miller was confined at Fairfield Hills and had even shown him a statement he could sign saying he wasn't guilty by reason of insanity, but Ben Miller said his response had been that the doctor was trying to get him to confess to something he didn't do. According to Ben Miller, he had only confessed because Dr. Robert Miller and another doctor at Fairfield Hills had broken him down, and that additionally he was under the influence of medication at the time of the confession.

Bundock didn't interview Dr. Robert Miller or anyone else on the staff of Fairfield Hills, but he did have Ben Miller evaluated by a court-appointed psychiatrist. The psychiatrist's report stated that although it was clear Miller "is and has been chronically psychotic and delusional and totally incapable of discerning right from wrong," and that "[t]he force of his insanity drove him into the midst of the daily life of the people he is accused of having murdered," the psychiatrist had "no certain idea" whether Miller had actually committed the murders.

In January of 1973, Bundock came to an agreement with Joseph T. Gormley, Jr., the state's attorney in charge of the prosecution: if Miller would plead insanity, the state would drop two of the charges and encourage the court to accept the plea. After a one-day trial conducted before a three-judge panel of the Connecticut Superior Court for Fairfield County, Benjamin Miller was found not guilty by reason of insanity, and after a hearing in March to determine whether he was a danger to himself or others, was committed to the custody of the commissioner of mental health for a maximum of 25 years. He was confined to Whiting Forensic Hospital in Middletown, Connecticut, outside of Hartford.

In 1982 Miller filed a writ of habeas corpus with the state court, primarily alleging that Bundock's failure to pursue certain lines of inquiry violated his right to effective assistance of counsel, and that the state had failed to disclose evidence to the defense team that connected another man to at least four of the five murdered women.

That man's name was Robert Lupinacci.

Lupinacci, a white man of Italian descent, was arrested just a few weeks after Miller in 1972 for attempting to strangle a black prostitute in the same area where the other victims had been killed. At the time, Stamford police officer Joseph Ligi—who later became chief of police in Winsted, Connecticut—had tried to get the task force detectives to reassess the case, but they felt they had their man in Ben Miller and didn't pursue Lupinacci.

After Ben Miller's arrest, Miller Sr. had also sent Bundock a packet of clippings and ideas for investigation by the defense team, including articles that described Lupinacci's arrest. But Bundock was convinced by Miller's confessions, or at least convinced the court would find the confessions irrefutable, so he didn't pursue Luppinaci or any other alternative theories or persons.

Other evidence indicating Robert Lupinacci as a person of interest was also later found in the state's file, which was not disclosed to the defense at the time of Ben Miller's trial, including these facts:

- Lupinacci was known to patronize black prostitutes and was considered by those who knew him to be a "sex nut"
- He often used disparaging language with regard to black people
- His car had been seen near the murder scenes several times
- In 1968, he'd been seen by employees at the Hotel Hazelton, where Gloria Kahn lived

- He'd also been seen cruising Stamford the night Kahn was killed
- In 1971, Lupinacci worked in the motel where Gail Thompson lived, and Thompson was last seen in a car that looked like Lupinaci's
- Hairs consistent with those from a black female had been found in the trunk of Lupinacci's car
- Also in Lupinacci's trunk was a deck of pornographic playing cards, which he was known to sell, but this particular deck was missing the queen of hearts— and such a card had been found near Gail Thompson's body
- Alma Henry was last seen alive on Grey Rock Place in Stamford, and Lupinacci belonged to a club which was then located on Grey Rock Place
- A local police officer had reported that Lupinacci had asked about stakeouts during the investigations of the deaths of Thompson and Henry, and had commented that not all of the victims had been strangled with brassieres—a fact police had not made public.

Because of the similarity between the crimes of which Miller was accused and the act in which Lupinacci was caught, the detectives who investigated Lupinacci turned over complete reports of the information gathered to Gormley, the state's attorney in charge of prosecuting Miller at the time of Lupinacci's arrest, while Miller was being held for trial. In June 1972, as part of his defense investigation and legal due diligence, Bundock had moved for the state to produce all its evidence for the defense to review. Gormley, although he agreed the defense could have free access to the state's file on Miller, never formally responded to Bundock's request, and never turned over any of its information on Lupinacci to Miller's defense team.

The state court which heard these arguments denied Miller's habeas corpus petition, saying they doubted whether any of the Lupinacci evidence would have been admissible at Miller's trial and that it therefore wouldn't have affected the outcome. They also rejected Miller's claim that his defense had been ineffective, saying Bundock had had enough information to make an informed recommendation regarding the plea bargain, and that the public information available to Bundock had been enough to provide him with the Lupinacci evidence he claimed the prosecutor had suppressed. Miller remained in psychiatric custody.

But in 1988, the U.S. Court of Appeals reversed the decision and decreed that Miller have a new trial. This time, the court held that "when the undisclosed facts possessed by the prosecution are added to the fact that Lupinacci was arrested in the act of attempting to strangle a black prostitute in the very area where the other victims had been found strangled, we conclude that the withheld information is sufficient to undermine confidence in the outcome of both Miller's decision to forgo any challenge to the State's assertion that he was the murderer and the decision of a rational fact finder as to whether the identity of Miller as the murderer was established beyond a reasonable doubt."

On May 8, 1989, a judge ruled that retrying Miller for the murders would constitute double jeopardy, and dismissed the case. 17 years after his arrest, Benjamin Miller was released.

Sadly, Miller's mental and emotional state after his years of incarceration left him unable to live on his own or adapt to life outside an institution, and he voluntarily recommitted to a mental institution. He died in 2010 at the age of 80.

After the first edition of *Rogue Town* was released, I was contacted by Jeff Lupinacci, Robert Lupinacci's son. He'd read the book, and with everything he knew about his father and the Bra Murders, and because of my time with the Stamford PD, he wondered if I knew why Robert hadn't been arrested. Jeff believed then and continues to believe that Robert Lupinacci—whom he prefers not be called his father, since the younger Lupinacci doesn't feel he ever filled that role—committed those and other murders.

For instance, in 2018, Robert Lupinacci was investigated for the murder of 36-year-old Carrie Lee Mock, who was killed on July 19, 1980. Jeff provided a DNA sample to detectives as part of that investigation, and later recognized a cold case file photograph of a woman missing since 1981 as someone who'd been with Robert at an IHOP in Stamford, the last time Jeff ever saw Lupinacci senior, in late 1980 or early 1981.

According to Jeff, Lupinacci senior was an abusive, unstable, frequently violent, alcoholic racist, traits which only became more pronounced after his stint in prison for the assault (negotiated down from attempted murder) of the prostitute that got him arrested around the same time as Ben Miller. The elder Lupinacci eventually retired to Norwalk, Connecticut, where he regularly attended criminal trials and spoke to reporters about how the police didn't know what they were doing.

In writing this chapter I relied on personal interviews with Jeff Lupinacci—written up in Jeff's own words and presented beginning on the next page, unedited except to correct some typos and protect the privacy of Jeff and others—as well as other personal and confidential correspondence and my own knowledge of the case, but filled in gaps in the narrative (and my memory) with public records and news articles from the time. Those additional sources are listed below.

https://www.law.umich.edu/special/exoneration/Pages/casedetail.aspx?caseid=4080

https://www.nytimes.com/1972/03/18/archives/a-minister-is-seized-in-5-connecticut-stranglings.html

https://www.nytimes.com/1971/08/29/archives/police-seek-clue-to-stamford-murders.html

Reproduction of Benjamin Miller's final appeal court document at https://murderpedia.org/male.M/m/miller-benjamin.htm

MY LIFE WITH ROBERT F. LUPINACCI

L IFE WITH Robert F. Lupinacci was not a normal life. The family lived under constant fear as to his temperament and volatility at any particular time.

I was the youngest of three children. The oldest died (of brain cancer) at age 6, when I was 2. So I don't really have any memories of her. But her loss pushed Robert further into his crazy behaviors.

He was never faithful to my mother and went out alone often during the week and on weekends. When I was young, I would ask, "Where are you going? Can I come too?" But the answer was "To talk to a man about a horse." Early on I actually thought *Are we getting a horse?* But I soon figured out it was an avoidance tactic. We lived on the Westside of Stamford and would have had no place to keep a horse anyway.

I went to school at Stevens School (which later became the Yearwood Center) from K – 2nd grade. It was a rough part of town, and I got beat up at school the week after Martin Luther King, Jr. was assassinated. The racially diverse makeup of the Westside changed a great deal from the time my Grandparents owned the house we lived in and had a large garden there. The Westside had the projects at this time built right next to our house. Although there was a fence between our house and the projects, folks climbed it to take a shortcut across our yard (which was a parking lot). That did not sit well with Robert, and he would chase them and throw things at them, which gained him the neighborhood nickname Mean Man. When I started school, I was immediately known as Mean Man's Son, which caused trouble for me from the start.

I remember an incident when Robert was drunk and upset with my mother. He pulled out a revolver and put it right between her eyes and told her that he was going to kill her. She started to back up and fell onto the bed, and he kept moving up on top of her and the gun stayed on her face. She saw that I was looking and scared. She was crying and yelling "Not in front of Jeffrey!" Then I was sent to my room until the event was over, and we could not talk about it.

In later years I heard about all the women who would call or show up looking for him at our house, and found out that once when he was treated for a venereal disease, he suggested she too get tested. The infidelity was not a new thing. My mother caught him with the nurse that was caring for my dying sister.

Robert was a member of the Turner-Lieder-Tafel, as the German Club was known. We were not German, but they had a bar downtown and he would drink there. Often when he had to watch me, we would go to the German Club: he would drink, and I played pool and ate chips. The German Club broke ground on a Long Ridge Road location and we began to go there for parties with oom-pah bands, food, folk dancing and of course alcohol. It was Robert's typical behavior to get drunk and then dance with a cocky expression on this face; he thought he was talented and considered himself God's gift to all. Occasionally he would come home from a night of drinking with a split lip or black eye, and we knew not to ask about it.

The summer before I started 3rd grade, we moved to the Turn of River area, and went to Willard School for 3rd – 5th grades. I was involved with music and Scouting at school. Robert would attend performances and attempted to present himself as a good parent in public, but he was getting worse with alcohol and his behavior at home. His physical abuse was frequent. For instance, every time a report card came home, he'd place me in a chair and give me a slap in the face for every unacceptable grade. After this my mother would ice my face before I was allowed out of the house.

The summer between 5th and 6th grades is when Robert was arrested for attempted murder (later negotiated down to assault) of a black female. She was allegedly a prostitute. He was found guilty and went away to prison for a couple years. Every weekend, my mother would drive me two hours to the prison for a visit. I remember a specific trip when I saw a girl from my school also in the visitor room. I freaked out and jumped below my chair, trying to hide. But my mother said that she was there for the same reason I was, and not to be embarrassed. I think I was more ashamed of him putting me in that situation. Before he left for prison, I was made to help him box up a significant number of rifles, shotguns, and handguns. He moved them to his sister's house to hide them from the police, rather than surrender them.

Robert's family was usually the main group we would visit for holidays. During his time in prison they would check in on us, but stayed away. My uncles were all in business together and had successful careers, but they never included Robert in their dealing. It was obvious that he was just a responsibility that they had to deal with, even a liability.

When I was in junior high there were kids who knew about Robert and would occasionally call me out about it in front of a crowd. I went through some tough times with fights, theft, drugs, and drinking too. I thought that was what was "normal."

Prison for Robert was, like for so many, a school on how to do better crimes, and figure out loopholes around the police he thought were so ignorant. He came to the visitation room with black eyes more than once. He started to wear a coke spoon around his neck; I can only assume it was a habit that he could access behind bars. During his time in prison (and subsequent parole) he was court ordered to not drink, but the thought of alcohol never left him. When he was paroled he brought home some personal possessions from prison, and the artwork was all different alcohol bottles and labels.

Everything Robert did was to excess. If one was good, ten was better. That rule was not just for drinking, but also guns, knives, raising dogs, raising fish, tools, antiques … anything and everything. He would become obsessed with everything. We had a dog that he wanted to show, but it was underweight, so he force fed the dog, who would get sick, and back and forth until he finally killed the dog in front of me with ether he stole from the hospital where he worked. Another dog would only produce one puppy in her litters, so he had her injected with hormones that produced eight pups, but killed her during delivery.

This was also an example of how everything was not his fault. Everyone and everything else was stupid, and he would show them.

By the end of 1976 his parole was over and he immediately began (openly) drinking again. His downward spiral was fast. He would go out drinking for a couple of days at a time, steal things from job, come home after being beaten up.

By the summer of 1978 my mother finally left him. Why didn't she do it before, you may ask? She told me she wanted me to see that she tried everything to save the family, and didn't want me to blame her. My response was, "What took you so long?"

At the end of 1978, the court ordered him out of our house so my mother and I could get back in and I could go to school. A protection from abuse order [PFA] was in place and he could not drive on our street, nor be within a certain number of feet from my mother. He called me to ask me to go bowling and have pizza with him. I thought maybe this was your typical divorced parent activity so I agreed to go, and said I would come to his apartment. But he said he would pick me up. I reminded him that the PFA stated he couldn't be on our street. I should have known better. He told me that he would go on any G.D. street he wanted and nobody told him what to do, and if I wanted to see him that's the way it would be. I replied that if he wanted to see me, to call me and let me know where to meet him. That was the last thing we ever said to each other.

In late 1980 or early 1981 (it was cold outside), I saw Robert eating at the IHOP on Summer Street in Stamford. I had been to a movie and went there after to eat. He did not speak to me, but I knew he saw me by his smirking face. He was with a woman who may have been Carol Gates, a nurse missing from 8-11-1981. This was the last time I ever saw him.

I got a call from his sister Emma in 2000. She wanted to ask me to reach out to Robert and let bygones be bygones. I asked if he was sick, or why she called: she said she was terminally ill and was trying to make an effort on her brother's behalf. I let her know that as easy as it was for her to find my phone number, he could do the same, and that he was the adult while I was the child in the relationship so it was up to him.

After he retired, to Norwalk, there was an article in the local newspaper, where he spoke to a reporter covering some trial. Robert was a regular in the gallery and spoke about how the police didn't know what they were doing.

Years later I saw his obituary. He died on February 14, 2013. I wish I knew the person they described in that obituary, but it was definitely not Robert—at least not the Robert that I knew. I reached out to his widow to see what he died from, so I knew what my personal medical history included. She told me he had Wernicke-Korsakoff Syndrome (aka "wet brain"), and in his later years he drank himself into a coma on more than one occasion, was paranoid and scared of everything, lost his wits, and was incontinent. She passed later that year.

There were articles in the Stamford Advocate that detailed why Robert should have been arrested for the Bra Murders that happed in the 1970's. I wondered why this never happened even though the man originally arrested for the crimes was later released.

I read *Rogue Town* about corruption in Stamford, which is when I reached out to you. I wonder if you had any knowledge about how Robert was dismissed as a suspect, based on your time with the Stamford PD? I also wonder if my uncle (who was in city government) got things suppressed?

A brief history of my life is that I graduated Central Connecticut State University, and have been working in the telecommunications industry for nearly 40 years, with the last ten years focused on 911 communications. I have been married and divorced, with two children. I am now remarried to a wonderful woman, and we have two granddaughters.

**Jeff Lupinacci,
as told to Vito Colucci,
spring 2023**

ROBERT LUPINACCI, 1968

ROBERT LUPINACCI, 1970

ROBERT LUPINACCI, HUNTING TRIP, 1970

ROBERT LUPINACCI, 2006

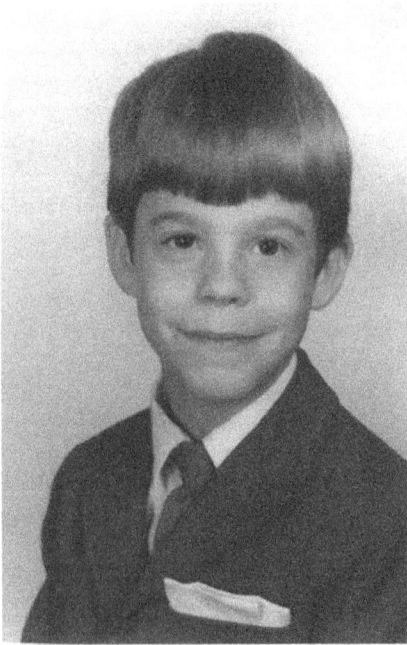

JEFF LUPINACCI, 1966   JEFF LUPINACCI, 2022

WHITING EXPOSED

WHITING FORENSIC Hospital, a facility that's part of Connecticut's Department of Mental Health and Addiction Services (DMHAS) and the maximum-security psychiatric hospital where Ben Miller spent so many years, has recently become rather infamous, at least in Connecticut.

In 1995, a man named William (Bill) Shehadi was committed to Whiting after being found not guilty by reason of insanity in the death of his father in Greenwich. According to his brother Albert (Al) Shehadi, Bill had a long, sad history of mental illness and had been in and out of inpatient treatment for years when he was placed in an apartment. A nonprofit worker would visit three times a day to make sure he took his medication, but otherwise he was left on his own. Al Shehadi said, "Here was this troubled man with a history of psychiatric instability who was left alone for the other 22.5 hours of the day with a TV set and his thoughts." Al Shehadi says he's still unclear about exactly what happened, but one day when his parents visited Bill something happened in the stairwell and Bill—described as "a large, heavy man"—landed on top of his 89-year-old father near the bottom of the stairs, injuring the elderly man badly enough that he died a little more than two weeks later. Bill Shehadi was committed for a mandatory ten years.

Fast forward to 2017, when Al, who was and remains his brother's executor, was notified that Bill was being moved to a new unit of the hospital, due to the discovery of abuse by workers where he was. In a later interview, Al said, "They had started out thinking it was one incident, and every time they reviewed another day of video they found more stuff, and then it was a three-alarm fire."

According to Al Shehadi's testimony before a public hearing of the Public Health Committee on November 13, 2017:

> There have been rumors of abuse and neglect for years. My brother was held in physical restraint for the better part of three years, largely tied to a bed. His medical records include letters he wrote to Whiting staff alleging abuse. One letter from 10 years ago that I recently received a copy of says: "Today I was put in seclusion. I was threatened, humiliated and abused." That was far from the only letter.

The abuse of William Shehadi dated back to 2006, and wasn't limited to him alone. In 2007, Connecticut Valley Hospital, also part of the DMHAS system, was investigated by the U.S. Department of Justice for gross inadequacies in its conditions and practices. As a result of that investigation, Connecticut Valley Hospital became subject to a federal consent decree, a legally binding agreement with the DOJ meant to ensure DMHAS would do a better job of caring for its patients. It obviously wasn't enough.

The Praise Band I was in played at Whiting a couple of times after being invited by the pastor, who felt the music would be therapeutic for the patients. As a result I received the following letter from a patient/inmate at Whiting who asked to remain anonymous.

> Whiting Forensic Institute, the State's maximum security institute for the criminally insane, had both uniformed Agency Police officers and Forensic Treatment Specialists who staffed each unit. Inmates were also referred to as "patients" because this facility was under the control of the Commissioner of Mental Health, not the Department of Corrections. The staff-to-inmate ratio at Whiting was different than at a correctional facility in order to maintain control over the type of offender housed here—many with significant mental disorders.
>
> Unlike the correctional officer in regular jails and prisons, the W.F.I. Agency Police are a division of State Police, with full powers of arrest, and were the uniformed officers (guards) of the Institute who were responsible for the overall security of the facility which included prisoner/patient transport outside of the facility for court appearances, hospital or outside doctor

visits, processing inmates in and out, processing visitors in and out and overseeing the security in the visiting room.

Inmates were strip-searched upon arrival and after being moved to their respective units, were "de-loused" and cleaned up in the shower while being watched by the staff. Unlike the traditional correctional facility, no items for personal grooming were allowed. Nail clippers and disposable razors were kept by the staff and inmates were monitored while using these items which had to be turned back in to the staff after each use.

The personal belongings and living spaces of inmates were monitored and randomly checked each shift. Entire unit "shakedowns" were conducted by Agency Police and included full body strip searches (strip down naked, bend over, spread your cheeks, cough, turn and lift-up the "nut sack," etc.) and every article of clothing, reading material and bedding thoroughly searched.

It was much more difficult for an inmate to have contraband at Whiting because of mental instability. At correctional facilities such as county jails and state prisons, inmates could make purchases from the commissary which included food items, personal care items, etc. This was not allowed at Whiting. Also, anti-psychotic drugs and other "meds" for control were dispensed each day which kept many of the inmate-patients in a drugged state.

Sexual abuse among inmates is a reality in all penal institutions and Whiting was no exception. However, it was easier for staff to abuse inmate-patients at Whiting because of their mental status. Groping and fondling were common by one staff member in particular who denied being homosexual. He later died of AIDS. Accusations against staff for sexual misconduct were easily dismissed because inmate-patients with mental disorders often had delusions which were not reality. Daily life at Whiting was filled with conversations and behavior that was the product of these delusional minds, so it was difficult to determine what reality was.

Inmate-patient Ben Miller's conversations focused on religious issues, specifically a desire to preach to the "Soap Stars." He never spoke of or referenced the crime he was accused of. He seemed to be focused on what he believed was his "ministry." The unit staff and guards had no respect for the personal faith of inmates. Ben Miller and other inmates like him were said to have a "religious preoccupation." At times it was dangerous for the inmate (like Ben) who felt compelled to share his faith with other inmates. One cop-killer inmate promised to "slit the throat" of any man who "preached the gospel" to him. Another inmate ripped up a Bible while screaming "this is what I think of your God!" Because one inmate was praying another started hissing like a snake and made a striking motion with his hand, which had very long finger nails, and said "I'm going to rip your eyes out."

Inmate-patients often talked to themselves or appeared to be answering someone back when no one else was talking to them. It was common to see bizarre behavior or violent outbursts and be attacked for no apparent reason.

One inmate-patient was seen with a white substance under his nose after leaving the shower room. When asked what it was he explained that he had been getting high snorting Baby powder. He went on to explain that he was hoping to be transferred back to a Department of Corrections' facility so he could get real drugs.

Each unit had a central bathroom and shower room. Some inmates simply relieved themselves in their clothing. The stalls were beyond dirty, a combination of dried fecal matter and urine coated the toilets while the panels of the stall were stained in white drips from frequent masturbation sessions. The shower room was a haven of sodomy and sexual activity was rampant. Some inmates continually preyed upon others.

The chow hall was a place where inmates often vomited as medication and food didn't mix well for some of them. One inmate was eating a bowl of stew, threw up in his bowl, and then kept on eating it. The food itself was enough to make you sick, the lowest grade and artificial as much as possible, such as powdered eggs.

Female staff members teased the inmates with sexual gestures and behavior in order to set them up. Any improper comments resulted in a negative write-up on the inmate. Staff members would threaten inmates and provoke them to say something back to them so they could write them up. If an inmate did not offer any kind of resistance to the abuse then they would get a positive write-up. One female guard would pat the inmates down after every activity and run her hands up into the groin in a motion to stimulate the inmates. Any response would result in severe punishment by the staff.

One staff member actually said his pen was mightier than the sword and that they can do a great deal of harm by what they wrote in the inmate-patient charts.

There were no limits to the abuse of power and sexual assaults on the inmate-patients. A mental illness diagnosis is the perfect cover for such abuse.

Clearly it would take more than one investigation and a federal consent decree to change things at Whiting.

When he became aware of the abuses and how long they'd been going on, Albert Shehadi filed a lawsuit against the State of Connecticut, as well as DMHAS, its commissioner, and eleven Whiting employees and administrators. The Shehadis' lawyer, Antonio Ponvert III, had also represented the family of an inmate who had died under restraint while in DMHAS custody in 2006—another tragic indication of the ongoing problems in a system meant to provide safe containment and treatment for the mentally ill. "Our goal in bringing these lawsuits was to hold abusers and State officials accountable for the torture of a profoundly vulnerable human being who depended upon them for treatment and care," Ponvert said later.

A task force was created to investigate the reports of abuse, and according to testifying patients, who were identified only by first name in order to protect them against reprisals, the atmosphere was one of punishment rather than healing or even basic care. One said "This place seems to be treated more like a prison than it is actually a hospital." And according to Paul Acker, a member of the task force and a senior policy advisor for Advocacy Unlimited, "We've heard people, time and time again, say they don't feel safe there."

One of the most disturbing aspects of the case was that video cameras were constantly in use at Whiting, for the purpose of providing an inarguable record to protect both patients and staff. Yet knowing they were being recorded did nothing to inhibit the abusers, who were repeatedly caught on tape, suggesting they had no concerns about accountability. In addition to the testimony of patients and staff— many of whom were truly dedicated and did their best to work around and mitigate the systemic problems—the task force reviewed countless hours of these tapes, and in the Shehadis' civil suit, Ponvert stated that cameras recorded more than 50 incidents of abuse against William Shehadi alone. According to various sources, the abuse included:

- A nurse gyrating his groin in Bill Shehadi's face
- Throwing food at him
- Forcing him to wear a diaper on his head
- Pouring liquid onto his head as he lay in bed, then using a mop to "mop" it up, while other staff members stood by
- Entering his room in the middle of the night and flipping him onto the floor, then flipping his mattress on top of him

In Al Shehadi's testimony, he referred to the scale of the abuse on the videotapes as "incomprehensible," saying:

Beyond almost daily acts of similar abuse, the videos convey an atmosphere of constant menace. It wasn't just staff kicking my brother. It was the long periods in between kicks with staff resting their feet and legs on his bed, next to his head and body, their feet constantly tapping, stretching, moving. As if to remind him they could kick again whenever they wanted. It wasn't just staff pushing him down on his bed or kicking him off his bed, it was the staff circling around his bed again and again, leaning over and staring at him. It was the feeling of cats playing with a cornered mouse that was most disturbing....

The warrants are based on videos preserved by DHMAS that cover the 24 day period from February 27th to March 22nd. There are roughly 50 incidents of abuse described in the warrants during those 24 days. There was at least one incident on 21 of those 24 days. There were two or more incidents on 14 days. Five or more incidents on four days. The granddaddy of all days was March 11th, with separate incidents caught on video at 1:04, 5:57, 8:14 and 8:19 AM, and 7:02, 7:36 and 9:05 PM. As for staff, in addition to the ten who have been criminally charged so far, another 22 are named in the warrants as witnesses. The Department of Public Health and CMS report this summer, based on the same videos, put the number of staff involved in or aware of the abuse at more than 40.

The investigation led to the arrests of 10 Whiting staff members and the dismissal of more than 35 employees, including Whiting Chief of Patient Care Services Renata Kozak, whose employment was terminated for her role in the abuse. Shehadi was awarded $9 million by the State of Connecticut—the largest payout to an individual by the state in Connecticut's history—as well as a $100,000 settlement reached with a former top Whiting official, and additional undisclosed settlements with other individuals named in the federal lawsuit. The money will be placed in a trust fund for William Shehadi's care until the end of his life, at which time his brother plans to donate the remainder to help fund creative nonprofit organizations that provide housing and treatment for people with severe mental illnesses. One of his goals, he said, is to show the State of Connecticut that if they had provided an appropriate level of care to his brother when he was younger, not only would their father most likely have died of natural causes and Bill been saved decades of suffering, but it all would have cost the state a lot less money.

Unfortunately, despite the investigation, the lawsuit, the firings, and the no-doubt good intentions of many within the system, I'm informed by reputable sources that things aren't changing as much or as quickly as Al Shehadi and other patients and patient advocates would have hoped.

BRIA FAMILY WANTS ANSWERS IN SON'S OVERDOSE

P OLICE OFFICIALS in towns within Fairfield County have said that the Greenwich Police Department have "marched to a different drummer in the past".

They have unsolved murders such as 13 year-old Matthew Margolies in 1984. Carrie Lee Mock was strangled and stabbed in 1981. Mary Macari Capozza (whom I went to school with), was found in the Kensico Reservoir in North Castle NY. The cause of death was ruled to be asphyxiation by drowning and the investigation was changed by the

Medical Examiner from accidental to a homicide. Lastly, the mess they made with the Martha Moxley homicide involving Michael Skakel.

In 2004 John Bria, III, had a party at his parent's home where he had his own lower-level apartment. By the end of the night, he laid dead in his bed from an overdose from the drugs that party attendees brought to the home.

Four friends came to that party and they brought cocaine, Prozac and various prescription medications. They have all admitted to the police that they brought these items. Each one stating what they brought. Greenwich Police, after their short investigation, said they would not press any charges against any of the subjects that attended the party.

Many of the officer's work side-jobs for high-net-worth individuals in Greenwich. One of the "partygoers" parents was a Hollywood producer. They subsequently closed the case by saying nobody forced John Bria, III to take the drugs.

The Bria family and myself then hired Dr. Michael Baden (physician and board-certified forensic pathologist known for his work investigating high-profile deaths) to review John's case forensically. Also hired were outside narcotics and organized crime investigators, computer forensic individuals, talented writers from newspapers and magazines and everyone who would have the professional ability to provide support in our quest to find the truth to get "justice for Johnny".

Subsequently, Greenwich Police knew this private investigation on behalf of the Bria family was not going to go away until justice prevailed. Numerous articles in the local newspapers and magazines had headlines reading "Death in Greenwich Raises Questions," "Case Not Closed" and "Parents want Answers in Son's Death".

Finally due to the pressure in 2008, Greenwich Police arrested two of the teens that were in attendance and charged them with possession.

Below, is a letter from "Johnny's" father, John Bria, II detailing further what transpired from start to finish.

I want to add that I'm thankful the new regime within the Greenwich Police Department has improved significantly over the years.

TO READ THE CHAPTER IN ITS ENTIRETY
STAY TUNED FOR ROGUE TOWN II.

Death in Greenwich raises questions

John J. Bria III, 19, joined a fitness club and hired a personal trainer while studying music production in Florida. Friends and family described him as health conscious.

The young man grew up in the Byram section of Greenwich, on the New York border.

This part of Greenwich is much like any town: Houses are close together, families know each other and they work at real jobs. Byram is not a high-income area — unlike other parts of Greenwich that help make Connecticut the top per capita income state in the nation. Some of Bria's friends were from Byram and others were from that larger universe where parents run big chunks of the country, from Wall Street to Hollywood.

Bria earned an associate's degree. He sent out resumes while working for his father's landscaping business. He had an internship at a recording studio. Prospects looked bright.

It all changed forever beginning Jan. 15, 2004. Bria was not known to be a major drug abuser. But, in the next 24 hours, plenty of drugs — including Prozac, cocaine, marijuana and Clonezepam, an anti-seizure medication — were brought to the Bria house.

One of Bria's friends, Savannah Lamotte, would tell police about their activities that evening: "Maria and Jason picked me up around 9 p.m. ... We went to Shell and got some cigarettes, and then we went

somewhere to shoot some heroin. We then went to get some cocaine. ... We went back to Shell and got some other stuff, and we went to shoot up some more heroin somewhere. Then we went to John's house. When we got to John's house, Katie, Megan and John were all there."

Katie Hanscom, Megan Caron and Jason Cunningham were high school friends of Bria. Maria Scinto, also in the group, is from nearby Port Chester, N.Y.

Cunningham would tell police that during the day, Bria "was feeling really high from the pills that Megan had given him."

Dead for several hours

As the night wore on, most of the group left. Cunningham stayed behind, calling his mother about 4 a.m. She arrived to pick him up about 8:30 a.m. Bria had been dead for several hours by that time. Jason told Bria's father that his son was still sleeping.

"John was always a late sleeper, so I didn't think anything of it," the father told me.

John Bria Jr. had arisen about 6 a.m. to work on files in his home office. He took a nap later that morning and arose mid-day. After taking a shower, he tried to call his son on the intercom. He went downstairs and saw his son's door wide open.

John Bria III was lying on the bed on his left side with his head on the pillow. He was fully clothed. There was a small silver pipe on his pillow next to his head. There were no ashes on the pillow.

It looked like the room had been set up, according to police. Credit cards were left conspicuously on

ANDY THIBAULT

a nightstand, on an armrest, on an amplifier. Several ashtrays were empty or wiped clean.

An autopsy revealed heroin and cocaine in Bria's body. The medical examiner who conducted it resigned in disgrace after taking a bribe in another case. His findings have been challenged. Later lab tests found codeine in Bria's body. More lab results are expected.

The Bria estate has sued the partygoers and Cunningham's mother for, among other things, failing to notify anyone that young Bria had overdosed.

The family is also pressing Greenwich police to re-open the investigation.

Police found a sealed cellophane wrapper containing 19 Prozac pills and six Clonezepam in the Bria bedroom, along with eight glyceine bags containing drug residue. In some cases these facts could generate arrests on charges from drug possession and sale up to homicide.

By Lennie Grimaldi

Case Not Closed

Who's to blame for what happened one night in a Greenwich basement?

Stamford private detective Vito Colucci Jr. likes long odds and high-profile cases.

On the morning of Jan. 16, 2004, John Bria Jr. thought his 19-year-old son was sleeping late after reconnecting the night before with five high school pals. When 3 p.m. rolled around and John III still had not emerged from his basement apartment in the family's Greenwich home, his father walked downstairs into his son's bedroom.

What he saw made him lose it.

"John was on the bed and I screamed," Bria says. "I jumped on top of him. He was ice cold." There was a three-inch smoking pipe on the pillow next to John's face. Bria made a panicky call to 911. "I had to press against my stomach to make the words come out."

By the time emergency crews arrived, it was far too late. John Bria III, the young audio engineer, had already been dead for nearly 12 hours from a drug overdose.

For the nearly two years since that morning, John and Peggy Bria's lives have been consumed with finding out what happened to their son. What they know is that on the evening of Jan. 15, 2004, six friends from high school had partied well into the morning hours. According to police reports, the friends partook of cocaine, heroin and marijuana, and prescription pills such as Prozac and the powerful anti-seizure drug Clonazepam.

The Bria parents knew their son had smoked marijuana but the police reports came as a shock. Whether by desire, by dare or by accident, John had consumed way too much of too many substances.

Jason Cunningham, a longtime friend and college classmate of young John's at Full Sail Real World Education in Florida, told Greenwich police that he and John had snorted lines of a powdered substance that night. But he added that John had gotten a head start on the proceedings. "John told me he was feeling really high from the pills" that Megan Caron, another friend, had shared with him, Cunningham told police. (Megan Caron is the daughter of director Glenn Gordon Caron, creator of the "Moonlighting" TV series and "Medium," a current hit about a psychic who sees and hears the dead.) Cunningham told police he thought John was so high he didn't tell him about other pills he'd brought with him.

Still, Cunningham wasn't concerned enough to call an ambulance. He remained in the Bria family's basement until his mother arrived to pick him up around 8 a.m. Before he left, Cunningham told Mr. Bria that John was sleeping. The investigation later determined, however, that he had already been dead for roughly four hours.

In the days following John's death, Greenwich police treated the incident as a criminal investigation. They interviewed several partygoers who admitted excessive drug consumption. Then weeks passed and, according to the senior Bria, Greenwich police stopped talking to him. They characterized the case as an accidental overdose. The cops were unwavering: no arrests despite the many illegal drugs brought into the house by John's friends.

Five months after his son's death, Bria felt shut out and lost. He had no police report, no photographs of the scene and no knowledge of forensics. Police had not even fingerprinted the scene, despite calling it a criminal investigation. He called lawyers for help.

"When you walk into a lawyer's office with a story like this," says Bria, "you realize as time goes on that very few people have the balls to meet the police head on and make demands."

Frustrated and searching for clues, Bria turned to Vito Colucci Jr., a Stamford-based private investigator with a penchant for high-profile cases. Colucci urged Bria to demand the police report: "You have the right to have it; go get it." It took five weeks for police to turn over documents that revealed multiple admissions by John's friends that they had brought drugs into his house and a series of circumstantial events that Bria claims show the death could have been prevented.

Colucci's probe, with assistance from Bria, raises a number of questions about what happened that night. Both Colucci and Bria question the credibility of the Greenwich police and the state's attorney's office for refusing to issue arrests, even for simple possession, despite the overwhelming evidence of drugs.

"Here we had a group of Greenwich kids who went to high school together," says Colucci. "One person says, 'I'll bring the cocaine'; another says, 'I'll bring the heroin', the daughter of a big Hollywood producer brings in the prescription pills. The bottom line is someone ends up dead. The right thing to do is call 911. Maybe they could save his life. The Bria family didn't let it go. This isn't going away. Greenwich police is in a jam on this one."

In hiring Vito Colucci, Bria made a well-considered choice. A former Stamford cop decorated for bravery, Colucci had opened his own private-investigation firm in 1990 and used his law-enforcement know-how, verbal agility and ambition to get to the top of his profession, not only in Fairfield County but far beyond.

Crime

from the basement.

Bria offered Donna Cunningham coffee, but she declined, he says, because Jason had a prior commitment. Later that morning, according to a Greenwich police report, Donna Cunningham found her son on their bathroom floor with a cellophane package of prescription pills. Bria and Colucci maintain Donna Cunningham knows more about the events of Jan. 15 than she's willing to share.

"Jason Cunningham's friend is overdosing, he calls his mom at 4 a.m. 'Mom, what do I do?' Do you think the Cunninghams are going to call the police department when their son has a drug history?" Colucci asks.

For his part, Bria laments a conversation he says he had with Jason Cunningham two days before his son's death.

"It's not a secret that you have a problem with drugs," he recalls telling Jason. "If any-

> John Bria may have been
> so disoriented from
> the toxicity of cocaine,
> heroin and Prozac that by
> the time Cunningham
> says they sniffed the
> Clonazepam, he lacked the
> capacity to take it in.

At present, however, the private investigator and John Bria continue to poke for clues that they hope will explain what occurred in Bria's basement that night in January 2004. They have assembled legal and forensics specialists to recreate the scene.

"We're conducting interviews, talking to witnesses," Colucci says. "Sometimes people would rather talk to a private detective than a police officer. I don't have to read them their rights. I don't have to tell them to sign anything."

Every day, Bria thinks about his son and the hours before he found him dead. He was asleep in his upstairs bedroom on the night of the party. Messages found on his son's computer show explicit chatter about drug use among the partygoers that night. One of young John's last acts, at approximately 2:15 a.m., turns up in an electronic exchange with Megan Caron, who had left the party earlier while Jason Cunningham stayed.

"You still fuced [sic] up?" John wrote.

"Yup," Megan responded.

"Cool."

Megan ended the instant message with a parting happy face.

Six hours later Donna Cunningham knocked on the Brias' front door to pick up her son.

"John's still sleeping," Bria recalls Jason Cunningham telling him as he came up

thing bad ever happens in my house, it will destroy my reputation and family."

Bria says Jason Cunningham reassured him that he would show restraint. But on the night in question, as Jason Cunningham later related to police, restraint was nowhere to be found.

"Megan poured five white pills into her hand . . . poured them into my hand, and I took four of the pills at once, and I cut up the last one. I broke it down to two lines. I didn't sniff them then, but saved them for later. I called my mom around 4 a.m., and right around that time [John Bria and I] sniffed the lines. It was the last drug that we did before we fell asleep."

Despite Cunningham's assertions that Caron had supplied Clonazepam (Maria Scinto, another partygoer at the Brias' that night, also told police that Caron told her she was bringing Prozac and Clonazepam), Bria's cause of death was certified as acute heroin and cocaine toxicity. Prozac was also

found in his blood. John Bria may have been so disoriented from the toxicity of cocaine, heroin and Prozac that by the time Cunningham says they "sniffed" the Clonazepam, he lacked the capacity to take it in.

The Brias hope Greenwich police will someday reopen the tangled case. Greenwich Police Chief James Walters says there could be some interest in doing so. At the same time, he emphasizes that the decision not to issue arrest warrants was made not by police but by a state prosecutor.

"If there's additional information, we would take it and review it to see if anything can be done," Walters says. "We did discuss this case with the state. A determination was made by the state's attorney's office that an arrest should not be made." James Bernardi, the state prosecutor who made the decision, says "sufficient facts to support a conviction" were not present. He adds that "we always keep an open mind" to the possibility of arrests in the future.

Meanwhile, John and Peggy Bria (the couple were divorced before their son's death) slapped wrongful death lawsuits five months ago on all five participants at the party, as well as Donna Cunningham, for the negligent death of their son, asserting his friends provided "one or more of the following: cocaine, heroin, Prozac, marijuana, or oxycodone" and conspired to rearrange evidence in his bedroom in an effort to hide what happened.

Defendants in the case have ceded comment to their lawyers. "John Bria's death is unfortunate," says Megan Caron's attorney, Gene Riccio. "I can understand, as a parent, why his parents are on this search for answers. However, it is not fair to start pointing fingers at Megan Caron. She's not the person responsible for it." Stephen Walko, the Greenwich attorney representing Donna Cunningham, had no comment for this story.

"My son needs vindication," says John Bria. "We need to find out the truth regarding every detail of what happened in his bedroom that night, from the time the first person walked in until the last person walked out."

Vito Colucci Jr. is determined to get that for his client.

"Greenwich police gave the Brias the typical police lines: 'It's a tragedy, it's horrible, but we're not making arrests.' At the very minimum, I'd have to arrest these people for possession and sale of narcotics. We're going to place people under oath through depositions and ask them to tell us what they saw. We will learn the truth." ∎

Greenwich police arrest 2 linked to 2004 drug overdose

Sep 10, 2008, 9:54pm • Updated on Sep 10, 2008

By: **News 12 Staff**

From: "John Bria" ·
To: "Colucci Investigations"
Sent: Tuesday, September 13, 2005 5:42 PM
Subject: Here's what I sent to lennie Grimaldi

Lennie,

This is how we met Vito Colucci, and the role he played in the private investigation into our son's death. Of course I can't condense all of the noteworthy tributary events over the past 1 1/2 years into one email, but at least you will have the general feeling of where it started, and where we are now.

The events surrounding John's passing didn't become suspicious until we received the first toxicology report from the medical examiner. The results were mis-aligned to a large degree with what we were told, that he died from taking prescription medications, and there was cocaine present, and Prozac, but no heroin. At that point it had just been two months into our living hell. The investigators were surprised and I feel somewhat stifled by the results. They said, "we know for sure he was taking pills that night" That's when the case officially ended, abruptly it seemed.

Where do parents turn, when the police shut you down after repeated attempts to gain more information and insight into a tragic event like this? We had no idea. No police report, no photo's, no idea of what evidence existed...nothing! We only knew John was gone forever, and that was all anyone wanted us to know.

We were still dealing with the severe trauma, acute grief, and all of the emotional fallout of loosing our son. We both had months of therapy, and me to help deal with finding my son laying there dead, something I'll never recover from. My therapist gave me names of lawyers, and private investigators. We called a few lawyers first. But when you walk into a lawyers office with a story like this, complicated and surreal you realize as time goes on that very few people have the balls to meet the police head on and make demands. After all, the police the governing party who's job it is to protect the community, identify criminal activity, and hold those responsible for breaking the law.

The lawyer approach didn't work, the timing wasn't right. It was July of 2004, 5 months had passed and then we decided to look at the list of private investigators. This guy with the Italian last name who works in Stamford who came highly recommended was the only basis for our decision. We didn't know any of these people, Vito or anything about him. He was Italian, and that was good enough for us.

I'll never forget the first time we walked into his office. He had Kris Steele there with him. A 6'6", 350 lb. guy built of of solid muscle. I could smell the spaghetti sauce in the background. I knew we were in the right place. He investigated it objectively. He critiqued everything, with an open mind. He wanted to see the crime scene. At that point, and for a few weeks thereafter he was still evaluating the situation. We didn't know what he was thinking or where this was going.

Then things started to surface, like the Dr. Katsnelson debocle,

9/13/2005

367

And of course the low batting average of the local authorities, who have never solved a homicide here.

I believe, that is when that certain smell, and taste of the case became evident. The inner workings of what happened 6 months prior had all of the scripting of an HBO movie, Vito said once. He was right.

He sat me down one day and said, I want you to go to the police and demand the police report. I didn't think I had the strength, or the legal right. He said get in there and do it, your the father, you have every right to have it. It took five weeks to get the report, as it had to go through a so called approval process and internal channels first.

After we got the (redacted) police report, we realized that the kids that were with my son that night brought the drugs into my home, they actually admitted it.

Then came the photos- Vito said go in there and demand the photos! All of them. He said don't touch or look at them. Keep them sealed, and immediately bring them to me. I did. At that point I felt the police knew something was up, Even though we had the right to have that information, we did it in a very slick way, without the FOI procedures.

After the police photos came, we realized that objects in the room were suspiciously placed in the their locations.

Vito was instrumental in connecting us with excellent lawyers, Dr. Baden who reviewed John's case forensically, outside narcotics and organized crime investigators, computer forensic people, talented writers, and everyone who would have the professional ability to provide support in our quest to find the truth, and get "justice for Johnny".

He got to know our son, and had a grasp on what type of family we had, and how we raised or kids. We got more than we asked for, an uncle my son never got to meet.

We love Vito Collucci.

EPILOGUE

AFTER LEAVING the Stamford Police Department I ran my
bail bond business for a few years; and then my wife
Joanne took it over from me when I became licensed
as a private investigator. In that capacity for the past 36
years, I have been involved in several cases that made the
national headlines.

They include doing work for defendant Michael Skakel
in the Martha Moxley murder case, the disappearance of
honeymooner George Smith from a Royal Caribbean cruise
ship, plaintiff Charla Nash—the woman attacked and seriously injured by a friend's chimpanzee in February 2009,
and for NBA star Jayson Williams following his arrest in
the shooting death of his driver, among others.

Following the Skakel trial I began to get calls from television and radio news show producers asking me to be on their programs as an analyst. As of this writing I have done over 600 such appearances. The venues include the Fox News Channel, 48 Hours, MSNBC, CNN and CNN Headline News, with hosts such as Bill O'Reilly, Larry King, Nancy Grace, Joy Behar and Star Jones. In 2011 and 2012, I was in the 14-part series Blood Work on the A&E Television Network. I also had my own nationwide radio show called Crime Time with Vito Colucci, PI. It aired Sunday nights on the Business Talk Radio and Lifestyle Talk Radio Networks. I have been truly blessed and I owe it all to Jesus Christ.

Joanne and I have continued to devote our lives to Him. Both of us have been Elders in our church and we have taught marriage groups. That is right, the once—and nearly twice—divorced Vito Colucci has offered guidance to married couples. Only God can take a person with my history and put him in a position to counsel others. I also participated musically in the Praise and Worship Ministries at the churches we have attended and have sometimes been a Praise Leader.

On a personal level, Joanne and I have been together for 49 years and our marriage has grown steadily stronger. Our children are all doing well and we are grandparents and great-grandparents.

In closing I feel compelled to again issue a warning. Although I believe the vast, vast majority of police officers are honest and dedicated professionals, there are exceptions. What happened in Stamford has and continues to happen elsewhere. So, keep your eyes open.

Anthony Dolan, Joe Ligi and I, may no longer be out there investigating and reporting, but there are others like us across the country who are. And I thank the Lord for them.

**God Bless!
Vito Colucci, Jr.**

Private investigator becomes TV regular

THE **dish**
with susie

Out there ...
Former Stamford police detective turned private investigator, **Vito Colucci** of Colucci Investigations, had his share of TV time this week.

Colucci made appearances on CNN's "Larry King Show," MSNBC's "Scarborough Country," Court TV's "Catherine Crier Live" and Fox News Channel's "Heartland With John Kasich."

Out there ... Stamford resident and private investigator **Vito Colucci** was in the spotlight this week on the Fox News Channel.

Colucci filmed several shows out of the station's studios in Stamford, New Haven and New York, appearing on "DaySide" with **Linda Vester**, "Heartland" with **John Kasich**, and with anchor **Bridgette Quinn**.

Colucci will also serve as one of the highlighted speakers at the World Investigators Conference in Las Vegas in September joining notables including **Judge Andrew Napolitano**, senior judicial analyst, Fox News Channel; **John Walsh** of "America's Most Wanted;" **Bill Kurtis** of "American Justice and Cold Case Files," **Dr. Henry Lee**, forensic expert, Court TV's "Forensic Files" and "Trace Evidence: The Case Files;" Ver-

VITO AND HIS DAD VITO SR. AT HIS
95TH BIRTHDAY PARTY.

VITO SR. PASSED AWAY IN 2010, A FEW
MONTHS SHORT OF HIS 99TH BIRTHDAY.

A PHOTO OF VITO AND HIS WIFE JOANNE. FORTY-NINE
YEARS TOGETHER & ENJOYING THE GOOD TIMES.

2011 VITO & HENRY HILL SPEAKING AT A
DINNER TOGETHER IN NEW YORK STATE.

WHO WOULD HAVE THOUGHT THAT I WOULD
BECOME FRIENDS WITH HENRY HILL?

VITO SPEAKING ON MSNBC ABOUT HENRY
HILL AFTER HENRY'S PASSING IN 2012.

HENRY WROTE A BLURB FOR THIS BOOK

PSALM 91

Whoever dwells in the shelter of the Most High
will rest in the shadow of the Almighty.

I will say of the LORD, "He is my refuge and my fortress,
my God, in whom I trust."

Surely, he will save you
from the fowler's snare
and from the deadly pestilence.

He will cover you with his feathers,
and under his wings you will find refuge;
his faithfulness will be your shield and rampart.

You will not fear the terror of night,
nor the arrow that flies by day,
nor the pestilence that stalks in the darkness,
nor the plague that destroys at midday.

A thousand may fall at your side,
ten thousand at your right hand,
but it will not come near you.

You will only observe with your eyes
and see the punishment of the wicked.

If you say, "The LORD is my refuge,"
and you make the Most High your dwelling,
no harm will overtake you,
no disaster will come near your tent.

For he will command his angels concerning you
to guard you in all your ways;
they will lift you up in their hands,
so that you will not strike your foot against a stone.

You will tread on the lion and the cobra;
you will trample the great lion and the serpent.

"Because he loves me," says the LORD, "I will rescue him;
I will protect him, for he acknowledges my name.

He will call on me, and I will answer him;
I will be with him in trouble,
I will deliver him and honor him.

With long life I will satisfy him
and show him my salvation."

9 7 9 8 9 8 7 8 4 7 7 0 1 *